Six Sigma for Growth
Driving Profitable
Top-Line Results

Six Sigma for Growth
Driving Profitable
Top-Line Results

Edward Abramowich
www.sixsigmagrowth.com

John Wiley & Sons (Asia) Pte Ltd.

Published in 2005 by John Wiley & Sons (Asia) Pte Ltd
2 Clementi Loop, #02-01, Singapore 129809

Other Wiley Editorial Offices

John Wiley & Sons, Inc., 111 River Street, Hoboken, NJ 07030, USA
John Wiley & Sons Ltd, The Atrium Southern gate, Chichester PO19 8SQ, England
John Wiley & Sons (Canada) Ltd, 22 Worcester Road, Rexdale, Ontario M9W 1L1, Canada
John Wiley & Sons Australia Ltd, 33 Park Road (PO Box 1226), Milton, Queensland 4064, Australia
Wiley-VCH, Pappelallee 3, 69469 Weinheim, Germany

Library of Congress Cataloging-in-Publication Data
ISBN: 0-470-82133-7

Typeset in 12/14 points, ITC Berkeley Oldstyle by Cepha Imaging Pvt, Ltd
Printed in Singapore by Saik Wah Press
10 9 8 7 6 5 4 3 2 1

To my wife Felicity and daughter Elle, whose love and support made this possible

Contents

About the Author

Edward Abramowich has more than a decade of experience driving major strategic change and profit improvements through Six Sigma and Lean Enterprise in leading multinational companies. He has worked with Allied Signal (Honeywell), Johnson Controls, Johnson & Johnson, General Electric, and major aerospace and high technology companies. He was a senior member of the strategy practice of IBM Business Consulting Services (PWC Consulting). Currently Edward is leading a Six Sigma initiative at Sun Microsystems aimed at business growth.

Edward specializes in applying Six Sigma methods to drive top line growth through solution selling, sales force effectiveness, channel optimization and inter-organizational growth projects.

Acknowledgments

I am indebted to Dr. Mina K. Gabriel of Honeywell's Six Sigma Plus Growth program for his support and invaluable input into this book. Sean Curran and Kwok-Wai Lem from Honeywell also provided valuable feedback, for which I am grateful. I would also like to thank Dr. Johann-Peter Friedmann and David Marra from A.T. Kearney for their contributions to the methodologies presented in this book, Antony Snelleman from General Electric Commercial Finance for his advice and support, Subhash Bajaj for his useful comments on DMAIC, Russell Brown for his input on Six Sigma and strategy and Leo Gough for helping to work the manuscript into shape.

Preface

Six Sigma is one of the most successful management initiatives of recent times and is now well established in a wide variety of industries. Companies that adopt Six Sigma send a strong message to their customers and shareholders that they are committed to delivering the highest quality products and services at competitive prices.

Many Six Sigma initiatives are focused mainly on process *efficiency*: lowering costs, improving quality, and streamlining business processes. Efficiency, however, is not synonymous with growth. The reality is that no matter how efficient your production, how high your quality, and how cheap your products, if customers do not buy, your business is in trouble!

This book presents a new approach that several leading Six Sigma companies are using to drive business growth. It offers a vision of how to identify and profitably solve customers' problems—helping *them* become successful—and introduces a Six Sigma for Growth tool set based on enhanced Six Sigma and Design for Six Sigma methods. The aim is to set out a framework for applying Six Sigma methodologies to make the biggest difference, namely to drive growth directly.

The doyen of quality, W. Edwards Deming, noted long ago that meeting customer's expectations and building customer loyalty is not sufficient to sustain growth. For example, the nineteenth-century manufacturers of horse-drawn buggies were efficient producers with happy and loyal customers, but they failed to foresee or respond to the coming of the automobile.

Efficiency alone cannot help a business adapt to a changing environment. Efforts must be made to focus on the *effectiveness* of the products and services offered to the marketplace. To be effective, we must supply customers with the products they need now, but we must also create new, innovative offerings.

Recently, many leading Six Sigma organizations have developed Six Sigma initiatives aimed at generating business growth. Customized Six Sigma methods are now common for sales, marketing, and business development; others are focused on creating solutions to customer problems. This shift in the focus of Six Sigma initiatives from *efficiency* to *effectiveness* marks a fundamental change in approach and is vital to sustain continued growth and shareholder value.

The approach outlined in this book enables companies to focus their Six Sigma initiatives on growth by expanding their scope from continuous improvement to include the development and exploitation of growth opportunities. It applies the structured Six Sigma methodology to understanding customers and their problems in depth, so that companies can work continuously to offer products and services that their customers value.

Edward Abramowich
October 2004

Introduction

Six Sigma needs to be more than metrics and improvements to existing processes. To maintain customer relationships, a company must create a culture in which innovation occurs continuously within the company's services and products.
                        —Forrest W. Breyfogle III[1]

The approach outlined in this book is new. It is aimed at helping companies focus their Six Sigma initiatives on profitable growth. In this respect, it is intended for seasoned practitioners and provides them with a new perspective on Six Sigma. It is designed to add to existing programs and assumes that the reader has a basic knowledge of Six Sigma methods. The latest approaches in Six Sigma are examined by giving an overview of best practices and highlighting some important tools. Because many of the approaches outlined in this book are new, the emphasis is on explaining the motivation and reasoning behind the approaches, rather than on providing an exhaustive review of all tools. Instead, a few select tools that are particularly relevant to growth are discussed.

Several simplified case studies help the reader understand how Six Sigma for Growth methods are applied. These elaborate on specific concepts and solutions, and are not intended to be replicable: case studies that are sufficiently detailed for this purpose will be presented in a subsequent book. This book provides a framework for how companies can use Six Sigma to identify growth opportunities and to develop them from initial concept to commercial success. Building on the conventional approach, the book introduces important additions to the Six Sigma framework as well as highlighting the best practices and the pitfalls observed in many companies that have deployed Six Sigma.

As with conventional Six Sigma, Six Sigma for Growth applies a wide range of tools and methodologies in a systematic fashion. The approach presented is as close as possible to a step-by-step method for driving business growth. It is unlikely, however, that there is any single recipe that will work for all situations, so readers are encouraged to appreciate the concepts behind the tools and to adapt them appropriately for their specific needs.

The book is in two parts: "The New Focus on Growth" and "The Growth Tool Set." "The New Focus on Growth" discusses Six Sigma's expansion from cost cutting to driving business growth. "The Growth Tool Set" outlines the tools that enable Six Sigma practitioners to identify growth opportunities and turn them into commercial successes. The tools provide a means both to achieve growth by improving on existing products and services and to design successful solution-selling programs (developing new offerings for customers).

Chapter 1 discusses the ways in which many leading organizations are using Six Sigma as a means to drive top-line growth. It outlines Six Sigma's evolution from a problem-solving tool, applied mainly to manufacturing processes, to becoming a general driver for growth. Overviews of companies such as General Electric and Honeywell's approach are examined, as well as other leading practices, including solution selling, which some companies base on Six Sigma methods, and Six Sigma's role in sales, marketing, and channel management.

For readers who have encountered only a few Six Sigma applications, Chapter 2 presents an overview of Six Sigma fundamentals. This includes the basic Six Sigma process improvement approach and introduces leading notions of quality. It distinguishes between the Six Sigma tool set and its strategic aspects, and describes new (Six Sigma) tools such as Lean, Design for Six Sigma, and Total Productive Maintenance (TPM).

Chapter 3 outlines the Six Sigma for Growth approach, making important additions to the traditional Six Sigma framework. One such addition is the Discovery Phase, which is primarily concerned with searching for growth opportunities and prioritizing them. The result of the Discovery Phase is a growth project that then goes on to use a more conventional Six Sigma approach.

Chapter 4 details the Discovery Phase. This is broken into three steps, the *search* for opportunities, *assessing* those opportunities, and then *targeting* a select few. These steps generate growth projects that are led by Six Sigma teams, often collaboratively with customers. A new addition to Six Sigma project planning, the Growth Plan, is introduced.

Chapter 5 introduces D²MAIC, which generates revenues by examining existing products and services in order to find how to enhance them further in order to add value for customers. This approach builds upon the traditional Six Sigma steps of *Discovery, Define, Measure, Analyze, Improve and Control* (D²MAIC). Market penetration, margin enhancement, and gaining customer wallet share are common focus areas.

Chapter 6 discusses the tools used to develop new value-added offerings or solutions for customers. This builds upon the traditional Design for Six Sigma steps of *Discovery, Define, Measure, Analyze, Design,* and *Validate* (D²MADV). Important additions to the tool set are introduced, including understanding the customer's total value equation and wallet share, value maps, and replicating new offerings to other customers.

Chapter 7 details some of the Six Sigma for Growth tool set. This includes new additions such as Market Indicator Analysis, Value Comparison Curves and Mapping Customer Core and Peripheral Activities.

The Appendix is a Six Sigma readiness assessment, which is used to gauge whether customers or suppliers are ready for collaborative Six Sigma initiatives. The readiness assessment mitigates the risks associated with joint projects or collaborative Six Sigma initiatives with customers or suppliers.

The approach and methods presented in this book are evolving. Feedback and participation in developing Six Sigma methods for growth are welcome and readers are encouraged to participate in discussions and share their experiences in applying Six Sigma to drive growth at *www.sixsigmagrowth.com*.

PART I

The New Focus on Growth

CHAPTER 1

From Cost Cutting to Driving Growth

Absence of defects does not necessarily build business, does not keep the plant open. Something more is required.

— W. Edwards Deming[1]

Six Sigma started in Motorola in the 1980s. It was developed in response to the onslaught from Japanese firms that had gained significant market share in the United States and elsewhere by providing products of superior quality at lower prices. At the time, Six Sigma offered Motorola a simple way to track quality by comparing product performance to customer requirements. By 1988, the Six Sigma methodology had been fully embraced by Motorola and had also been adopted by Asea Brown Bovari (ABB), Raytheon, Computer Dynamics Inc. (CDI), and Kodak. In 1993, Larry Bossidy of AlliedSignal added a new dimension to Six Sigma by creating a management structure around it and creating full-time positions for practitioners, usually referred to as Black Belts.

Since then, Six Sigma has been adopted by many of the world's most successful companies, including giants such as General Electric, DuPont, and Sony. In its 1998 annual report, General Electric attributed more than $1.2 billion in cost reductions and revenue gains from its Six Sigma initiative. Such dramatic improvements from General Electric and a host of other Six Sigma success stories have led to its enthusiastic adoption by large-cap corporations.

Unlike many management fads, Six Sigma has demonstrated its ability to deliver significant bottom-line savings and is expected to continue to do so for many years to come. AlliedSignal first applied Six Sigma primarily to quality improvement, focusing on operational efficiency. AlliedSignal was able to deliver a huge 6% gain in manufacturing productivity and a record 13% profit margin that, at the time, made it the darling of Wall Street. Since then, the application of Six Sigma has expanded to other business functions, and its benefits have been amply demonstrated. Six Sigma's expansion to other business areas and GE's extraordinary 1998 gains were the catalyst for a massive popularization of the Six Sigma methodology.

Although Six Sigma is a recent innovation, it builds upon many long-established improvement tools and methods. For example, the pioneering work of Walter Shewhart in the use of control charts began in the 1930s and forms the basis of modern statistical process-control techniques. In the 1950s, W. Edwards Deming was teaching companies about systems thinking and how improvements in quality lead to an enhanced competitive position. Deming established management's understanding that quality cannot be delegated and that management must lead the transformation process.

Six Sigma has organized many of these well-known tools into a systematic improvement methodology and has combined it with newer management techniques. It sets itself apart from previous methodologies and tool sets by:

- Focusing on customers

- Using proven tools

- Delivering results that matter to the business

- Integrating process improvement into the business

The combination of an effective process-improvement methodology and a strategic management structure has made Six Sigma such a success.

As is to be expected of any good improvement methodology, Six Sigma has been evolving to meet the needs of companies and the marketplace. Today, Six Sigma deployments can vary significantly, both in terms of structure and technicality, depending on the specific needs of a company. Many companies such as Honeywell now include Lean Enterprise, Design for Six Sigma and Total Productive Maintenance (TPM) or a combination of each within their Six Sigma frameworks.

DuPont developed a hybrid approach—combining both DMAIC (Define, Measure, Analyze, Improve, and Control) and Design for Six Sigma—to Six Sigma called Design for Growth. The focus is revenue-generating areas in the business, such as new product development, service improvement, new market development, and selling and branding effectiveness.

The expansion of the Six Sigma tool set has been evolutionary in nature, as approaches were developed to meet the challenges of the marketplace. For example, as the rate of market change increases, the pressure for companies to design and develop reliable products and services is rapidly becoming greater than ever before. The original focus of Six Sigma on reducing defects in production was unable to meet these challenges. This led organizations to introduce Design For Six Sigma methods (DFSS). By improving the effective design of products, companies can achieve quantum improvements in quality, cost, and performance with relatively low development costs. As well as improving the quality and cost of products, DFSS plays a very important strategic role for companies. Today, it is often the first companies to launch a product to the market that reap the greatest rewards. Time to market is a competitive weapon, and an effective DFSS program aids companies in ultimately reducing their product development times.

The Six Sigma tool set is changing yet again; this time, it is responding to the challenges organizations are facing to grow their businesses in the face of intense market competition. To understand how Six Sigma is changing, we need to look at companies that are leading the change and who have refocused Six Sigma to meet these challenges.

THE NEXT BIG CHANGE IN SIX SIGMA

Companies such as Motorola, Kodak, AlliedSignal (now Honeywell), and Asea Brown Bovari (ABB) have well-established Six Sigma programs that have delivered huge savings over many years. These programs continue to generate savings and improvements in quality; nevertheless, many such companies have been facing declining revenues and loss of market share. Honeywell's share price dropped to such a level that it was the target of an attempted takeover bid by General Electric. Numerous other Six Sigma organizations have experienced similar declines and been forced to close facilities and downsize.

How can organizations with established Six Sigma programs have fallen victim to such losses? How can companies that focus on defect reduction and customer satisfaction be losing so many customers? These questions have been the catalyst for major changes in the Six Sigma world, pioneered by companies such as Honeywell and General Electric. The changes are refocusing traditional Six Sigma initiatives from problem solving to delivering increased revenue, margin, and market share.

Recently, criticisms of traditional Six Sigma's "rigidity" and "failure to innovate" have been on the increase. Lucent Technologies, under pressure to develop new products, has decided not to adopt Six Sigma, while Michael Hammer, founder of Hammer and Co., a management education firm, was reported as saying, "Six Sigma will get you to parity, but not ahead of your competition .... It's for fixing problems, not for innovation." Reuters, in a recent article entitled "Six Sigma is no longer enough," noted that IBM used Six Sigma to improve efficiency while its competitors gained ground with new products.[2] Wall Street investors are now seeking firms that are achieving top-line growth fueled by new products.

Some major companies are looking to Six Sigma to deliver profitable growth and are modifying the classical tool set in order to achieve it. The focus now is on becoming truly customer-centric and developing new offerings that customers value. This has manifested itself in several ways, including the development of customized Six Sigma training programs for customer-facing groups such as sales and marketing. These approaches integrate sales and marketing tools into the classical Six Sigma tool set. Other organizations have created Six Sigma approaches to new growth initiatives such as solution selling aimed at developing customized offerings that solve customer problems. These efforts are a high priority for companies such as Honeywell, General Electric, and a host of others, who are using Six Sigma to engage with customers, identify and diagnose problems, and create profitable solutions.

In these organizations, Six Sigma is evolving to meet the challenges of the marketplace. The focus is now on growth. This change builds upon the traditional bottom-line focus that has made Six Sigma such a success and expands it to profitable top-line growth through direct customer engagements and solving customer problems profitably (see Figure 1.1).

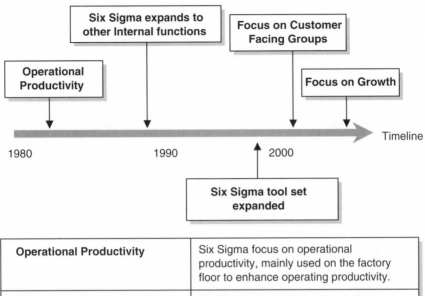

Figure 1.1   Six Sigma's Evolution from Cost Cutting to Business
Growth

Operational Productivity	Six Sigma focus on operational productivity, mainly used on the factory floor to enhance operating productivity.
Six Sigma expands to other Internal functions	Six Sigma expanded from manufacturing to other functions such as procurement, engineering and administration. Focus on internal process improvement and cost reductions.
Six Sigma tool set expanded	Six Sigma tool set includes Lean Manufacturing used to reduce waste, production cycle times, and Design for Six Sigma targets design processes.
Focus on Customer-Facing Groups	Focus on groups such as sales, marketing, service & credit. Sales force and marketing effectiveness and analysis of customer touch points.
Focus on Growth	Six Sigma moves outside the organization to the customer. Focus on revenue generation. New programs such as GE's At the Customer, For the Customer, Honeywell's Green Belt Growth and numerous "solution selling" approaches developed.

QUALITY IS NOT JUST DEFECT REDUCTION

Before we explore the details of the new Six Sigma approaches being adopted by companies today, it is useful to discuss some core ideas of Six Sigma, especially the notions of quality and meeting customer requirements.

The great pioneers of quality, such as W. Edwards Deming, emphasized the importance of considering customers' current *and* future needs. Since then, many improvement initiatives seem to have overlooked this stricture by focusing exclusively on customers' current needs. They have assumed that business growth is achieved by cutting costs and providing customers with products that are free of defects. That is, if you provide cheaper product and services with fewer defects, customers will purchase more and more, and the business will grow automatically.

Although defect reduction is undoubtedly important, it is not sufficient to drive growth on its own. It is possible to improve your products and services continuously, to reduce defects and costs, and to streamline operations and still to go out of business. For example, Schwinn, the 97-year-old bicycle manufacturer, was one of the most revered names in its industry, yet in 1992 it was forced to file for bankruptcy. According to *Forbes,* "Schwinn was obsessed with cutting costs, instead of innovation."[3] There are many cases of companies that focused on cost reduction and failed to recognize changes in the marketplace, only to go out of business.

W. Edwards Deming realized that improvements in quality lead to cost reductions and improved competitive position (see Figure 1.2).

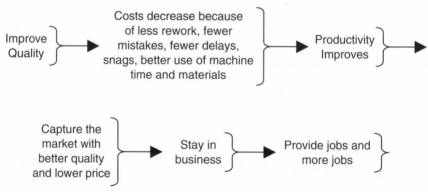

Figure 1.2   W. Edwards Deming's Quality Chain Reaction[4]

Focusing on quality sets off a chain of events that lead to productivity improvements and ultimately improved market share.

"The consumer is the most important part of the production line. Quality should be aimed at the needs of the consumer, present and future."[5] "Quality" in this context is often interpreted erroneously as *freedom from deficiencies*, but organizations must also focus on customers' *future* needs. Companies that focus exclusively on current market needs, at the expense of efforts to predict future market trends, run the risk of obsolescence. "The moral is that it is necessary to innovate, to predict needs of the customer, give him more."[6]

The emphasis on problem solving, combined with an obsessive pressure for cost reduction, can create a very insular improvement program in which people lack the opportunity to understand their customers, let alone predict their future needs. It creates an "if it's not broken, don't fix it" culture in which improvements are made only when problems occur. Problems need to be dealt with when they arise, but identifying organizational strengths and improving them further could achieve far more dramatic gains and improvements. To innovate new products and services, we must focus on what the customers' priorities will be tomorrow, not just the problems of today. We must take an "if it is not broken, fix it" approach to process improvement.

Delivering growth for an organization requires a different view of quality, which encompasses both the customers' current and future needs. This view should assess the added value that products and services bring to the marketplace. In addition to performance requirements, the term "quality" should reflect the commercial relevance of products and services. In this context, "a product or service possesses quality if it helps somebody and enjoys a sustainable market."[7] This definition of quality requires organizations to move away from focusing solely on eliminating deficiencies to understanding their customers' business models and continuously searching for ways to add value.

This expanded view of quality creates major changes in the classical Six Sigma approach. First, it creates a greater need for customer centricity. Developing an understanding of a customer's future needs requires an in-depth knowledge of the forces at work in the customer's industry, including changes in the business environment, technological changes, and concepts of (customer) systems economics and revenue enhancement. The organization needs to look at the customer's problems and priorities through the customer's eyes and continuously ask:

> **Six Sigma for Growth Key Questions**
>
> ❖ How can we profitably add value to our customers?
>
> ❖ How are our customers changing?
>
> ❖ What will they value in future?

Figure 1.3   Central Growth Questions

These questions form the basis of the Six Sigma for Growth approach. It is by asking them that we are able to uncover opportunities to profitably add value to our customers and enhance business performance—both theirs and our own. These questions are considered in more depth in the following chapters.

Six Sigma for Growth aims to understand customers and to become sophisticated about *their* businesses. This is more than conducting the occasional customer satisfaction survey or the typical market research study. It requires a deep understanding of customer problems and future trends to make it possible to develop offerings that customers will value. Such offerings not only solve customer problems today but also help the customer become more competitive in the future.

It is through such win-win relationships with customers that companies such as General Electric are banking on delivering sustained future growth. GE's At the Customer, For the Customer ACFC program is a leading example of how Six Sigma methods can be used to deliver sustained growth. Other approaches adopted by IBM, Oracle, and Cisco Systems, to name a few, are banking on solution selling as a means to drive business growth. This approach is often built upon Six Sigma or Design for Six Sigma methods and is discussed in greater depth in the following sections. These initiatives developed from the realization that simply solving internal problems cannot deliver sustained growth. Six Sigma for Growth expands the focus from reducing costs to customer-centric innovation—and so profitably adding value to customers. Today, many customers and shareholders will pay a premium for innovation and customized solutions to their problems.

Leading Six Sigma companies are transforming traditional notions of Six Sigma by focusing its powerful methodologies on revenue and business growth. The transformation involves moving outside the organization and applying Six Sigma tools to customer processes, enabling customers to succeed while making profits for the firm itself. We will now look in more depth at how some leading Six Sigma companies are focusing Six Sigma on growth.

HONEYWELL'S SIX SIGMA PLUS
GROWTH PROGRAM

Honeywell International (formerly AlliedSignal) has been at the forefront of Six Sigma development since the early 1990s. Initially, AlliedSignal's Six Sigma program was centered on manufacturing and operational productivity, and delivered huge productivity gains. The initiative was so successful that it made the company a benchmark for improving productivity by using Six Sigma.

Since its inception, Honeywell's Six Sigma framework has been expanded and modified to suit the requirements of the business and the marketplace. The merger between AlliedSignal and Honeywell, and the later failed merger attempt with General Electric fundamentally changed Honeywell's approach to Six Sigma. Honeywell started to look for a means to grow the business and turned to Six Sigma to achieve it. The Six Sigma program was customized and eventually evolved into Honeywell's Six Sigma Plus for Growth.

In its new program, Honeywell has concentrated on the sales, marketing, product development, business, and strategy development processes and has created a methodology and tool set to apply Six Sigma in these environments. The result is a combination of traditional Six Sigma tools, customer and market research, and program management tools that are integrated into a growth road map that follows a DMAIC methodology. It is an approach that marketing and sales people can relate to and use in what they do every day.

Honeywell uses a strategic approach that challenges people involved in growth initiatives to define their business as 10% of the opportunity space. Teams are then asked to identify the remaining 90% and to see where and how much of the 90% the company can address. The company also uses a tactical approach for teams that are developing an offering with a very specific value proposition. The output of this is a customer-centric, market-validated value proposition. The tactical method works on a case-by-case, offering-by-offering approach, in contrast to the strategic method that looks at the potential market overall, assesses customers and the competition, develops and validates hypotheses, and eventually produces recommendations to move the business from one area to another. Finally, Honeywell uses a third level in designing the offering, where Design for Six Sigma engineers use DFSS tools on specific offerings.

Growth projects are tied to the strategic plan, which very clearly defines what the business will be doing in the next three to five years. This translates into an annual operating plan that highlights very specific opportunities that are targeted year by year. As a result, each team working on a business strategy or an offering development is linked to the strategic plan, annual operating plan, or both.

GENERAL ELECTRIC'S APPROACH TO GROWTH

General Electric is well known for its willingness to implement radical initiatives. The most recent of these is aimed at accelerating growth through sales force improvements and customer centricity. To achieve this General Electric has introduced its "At the Customer, For the Customer" (ACFC) and "Sales Force Effectiveness" (SFE) programs both of which are founded on Six Sigma methods (See Figure 1.4).

As a widely diversified conglomerate, GE has many businesses operating in poorly performing industries, and overall growth has slowed during the last few years. The challenge is to gain market share and improve productivity and profitability in these difficult markets. ACFC puts GE's massive resources and know-how to work on improving selected clients' own productivity. For example, when a new hospital and research center was planned in Florida, GE was just one of several firms tendering for the supply of equipment and services. Unlike the competition, GE offered a host of value-adding benefits, from helping to design the workplace to providing a better-integrated clinical information system, and was awarded the contract. In another poorly performing market, plastics, GE is helping U.S. manufacturers to shift production to low-cost regions such as China.

ACFC puts Six Sigma Black Belts to work directly with the customers. ACFC's goal is to make GE's customers more efficient and

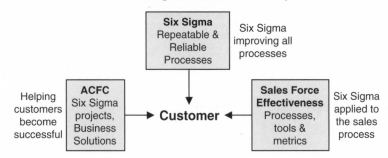

Figure 1.4   Six Sigma Driving Business Growth at General Electric[8]

cost effective by using the company's vast expertise. GE offers to send over Black Belt specialists from its Six Sigma program to work for months at a time on problems that may have nothing to do with GE products. This is more than simply becoming customer-centric—GE's avowed intention is to become embedded in their ACFC customers. ACFC's long-term approach requires GE to acquire a very thorough knowledge of how its customers run their businesses. Developing an understanding of the customer's business allows companies such as GE to develop new products and services—often beyond current offerings—that help customers while improving GE's business performance. The ultimate goal of creating such close ties with customers is to establish mutually beneficial relationships that enhance competitive position and drive growth.

Developing a close partnership with a customer is not always easy. Customers do not always respond well to the suggestion that GE's Six Sigma Black Belts should gain access to the inner workings of their own operations. And GE has its own criteria for selecting which customers to help—they must have a management that is willing and able to implement the sophisticated reforms that the Six Sigma approach can offer. Selected customers are companies that are likely to generate greater profits for GE once the solutions are in place. GE offers to work on specific, clearly defined problems that customers cannot solve themselves and that will produce easily measurable profitability gains for the customer. With such tangible propositions on offer, 30% to 40% of GE's customers are now involved in ACFC programs.

According to GE's CEO, Jeffrey R. Immelt, ACFC is intended to embed the firm in its customers' operations, offering them ways to improve their own profitability and, ultimately, GE's. "I'm not doing projects for the sake of doing projects," says Immelt, "The people in the field believe, as do I, that if you're doing this you're going to get better growth."

Immelt emphasizes the importance of constantly training the sales force and the need to "break down every ounce of arrogance" within the company. He believes that GE has very valuable resources, in terms of industry knowledge and best practices, that no other competitor can offer. He sees ACFC's prime function as making these resources available to appropriate customers. Offering these services is costly—Six Sigma Black Belts are not cheap to feed—but GE is prepared to make the investment. By making its customers as efficient as GE itself, Immelt hopes to improve growth rates over the long term.

Sales Force Effectiveness drives improvement in sales processes. The intent is to make these processes reliable and repeatable and looks at areas such as deal management, reducing non-value-added activities, and improving sales conversion rates.

GE has expanded Six Sigma's scope to include sales force improvements (discussed in more detail in the following sections) and to help customers through collaborative efforts. The focus has shifted from an emphasis on customer acquisition to customer care, from trying to profit on each transaction to profiting by helping customers and managing the entire product life cycle. It is no longer about selling a product but instead about identifying and profitably meeting the customers' real needs.

SIX SIGMA'S EXPANSION INTO CUSTOMER-FACING FUNCTIONS

There has been considerable effort in recent years in bringing Six Sigma to customer-facing business functions such as sales, marketing, service, engineering, and credit. This is critical to gaining an understanding of customer issues and proactively looking for opportunities to profitably add value. Customer touch points—moments when we interact with the customer—become a valuable source of information that can drive future product developments and innovation. Customer-facing functions are the front line of the business, and companies must continually strive to understand their customers' needs and seek opportunities to add value.

The work of the pioneering Six Sigma companies has revealed many insights into how its application varies according to business function. Six Sigma's value in manufacturing is very clear, but in other areas, such as sales and marketing, difficulties have emerged. Many of these difficulties are cultural. For example, it is not always evident to sales-oriented people that Six Sigma's rigorous approach is appropriate for their fields of expertise.

Experience contradicts this perception—Six Sigma does indeed have value in all business functions if it is intelligently applied. Increasingly, Six Sigma is finding applications in sales and marketing functions. Initiatives such as sales force effectiveness (SFE) are aimed at simplifying the selling process and making it reliable and repeatable. Six Sigma tools such as Design of Experiments (DOE) are increasingly being used by marketing to improve the return on investments for advertising campaigns.

As a major part of the front end, the sales force's close cooperation with the rest of the company is clearly vital when undertaking radical changes—such as the move to Six Sigma for Growth or solution selling. However, in cases such as Xerox's (see page 28) the sales force has become an obstacle in the drive to add value. Part of the problem is that the sales force often views its role as simply being a talking brochure whose function is to tell customers about the company's offerings and emphasize their benefits. Performance tends to be measured in terms of revenue, so a unit that beats revenue targets may believe that it is successfully creating value. This may be misleading—increased revenue for the company is not necessarily the same thing as creating value for the customer.

Over the last two decades, customers have changed their focus from the core product or service itself to broader issues, such as customization, improved support, more efficient purchasing systems, and the search for solutions to their own problems. Customers often have a wide choice of suppliers to choose from, and they want more than the basic offering. In this context, the sales force must proactively look for ways of creating value for the customer rather than rigidly pushing a generic offer. This change in the marketplace is leading many companies to rethink the role of the sales force from simply selling products to selling solutions and creating new offerings that customers value.

Six Sigma for Growth aims to create value beyond the products and services themselves. It aims to help sales people understand their customers, their problems and what they value, and then to seek ways to commercialize on it. At their simplest level, Six Sigma tools allow sales people to understand a customer's business, identify customer problems, quantify potential improvements, and then work to develop new offerings. This entails working closely with customers to develop mutually agreed-upon answers to recognized problems.

Generally speaking, there are two ways that Six Sigma can be applied to the sales force:

1. Add value to customers

2. Reduce costs

Increasing value means that sales people must act more like consultants and proactively look for ways to help customers above and beyond the product or service itself. Such efforts are now a major focus of many organizations that are looking to achieve profitable growth through a solution-selling business model. Reducing costs in this context means removing non-value-added activities from the sales process and making it easier and cheaper for customers to buy your products.

Not all customers respond well to a consultative approach aimed at creating value by adding benefits such as solutions. Usually, this is because their primary goal is to reduce purchase costs. In these cases, the way to add value is to reduce the costs of selling to them, for example, by offering online purchasing systems or telesales. The key here is to correctly identify the type of each customer—do they want more benefits or a lower cost?—and adjust the offering and sales approach accordingly.

This may entail a departure from the traditional ways of segmenting customers by account size or geography. One approach is to segment customers by their buying behavior, creating a unique view of the market and allowing tailored sales approaches for each segment. Take the case of customers that require electronic components. One customer segment may only want cheap components that are easy to purchase and are hassle-free, but manufactured to a high standard. In this situation, there is little that a sales force can do to create value or new benefits, and customers usually welcome the elimination of the sales force's salaries and commissions from the cost of the product. Even retail consumers are conscious that a product sold by a sales person who visits them at home is likely to be more expensive than a similar product sold online or at an out-of-town store.

Another electronic component customer segment may, on the other hand, want a supplier that possesses other competencies, which can create benefits beyond the product itself. This may include R&D capabilities, developing solutions to business issues, or even the ability to do more value-added assemblies. Clearly, the sales force must be aware of its customer needs. Approaching a price-orientated customer with a benefit-driven sales approach or vice versa, approaching a benefit-driven customer with a price-focused sales presentation will be a waste of the sales force's efforts and ultimately lead to customer dissatisfaction.

To streamline sales and marketing efforts, effective market segmentation is critical. In companies with poor segmentation strategies it is not uncommon to find the majority of the sales force effort focused on segments that generate only a small portion of the profits. In some cases, considerable sales force effort and resources are focused on nonprofitable segments. Projects aimed at studying profitability per segment and reallocating sales efforts to profitable segments can often raise sales and reduce costs at the same time.

Six Sigma initiatives such as sales force effectiveness (SFE) look to develop tailored sales approaches for different segments and to make the sales process itself more reliable and repeatable. There are many different ways to segment a market, and segmenting by buying behavior is not for everyone. Some firms have achieved notable success with this method, while others have found it difficult for their sales forces to implement and sustain. Some industries are not well suited to such segmentation, and in other instances, difficulties arise in developing the required understanding of customers and their internal procedures and behaviors. (See Figure 1.5.)

Applying Six Sigma to Sales

Add value to customers

❖ Solution selling

❖ Value-added services

❖ Build partnerships with customers

Reduce costs

❖ Reduce sales transaction costs

❖ Make it easier to buy products

Figure 1.5   Adding Value or Reducing Costs in the Sales Effort

SALES FORCE ADDING VALUE BY INCREASING BENEFITS

Customers who want benefits and solutions to their problems offer greater opportunities for the sales force to exercise its skills in adding value. For this segment, the value is in how the offering is used, rather than the product or service itself. These customers are generally willing to cooperate extensively with the supplier in developing bespoke solutions. For benefits-driven customers, Six Sigma efforts should be focused on understanding the client and trying to develop value-added offerings where a premium can be charged.

Typically, when seeking to increase benefits, Six Sigma for Growth efforts are focused on:

• Engaging with the customers on joint projects and helping customers understand their problems, issues, and opportunities

• Developing a tailored sales approach for different customer segments

• Working to reduce non-value-added sales force activities so that the sales force can spend more time working with customers

• Improving sales force effectiveness (see Figure 1.6) and reallocating sales force resources to areas which provide the highest return

SALES FORCE ADDING VALUE BY REDUCING COSTS

The customer segments that seek price reduction generally view the offering as a commodity; if one supplier cannot offer a sufficiently low price, they will look elsewhere for one who can. Ease of purchase is still a consideration because this may reduce the customer's overall costs. For the seller, the focus has to be on how to reduce these overall costs by lowering the product price, reducing the customer's risk—for example, by offering guarantees—or, as mentioned, making the offering easier to purchase.

For cost-oriented customers, Six Sigma efforts are best placed in reducing costs and risks, and eliminating waste in the customer's buying procedure. The central concern is how the supplier can strip costs out of the sales process and make the purchase process quicker, cheaper, easier, and hassle free for the customer.

Typically, Six Sigma for Growth efforts in this context are focused on:

- Reducing non-value-added activities and costs of the current sales process

- Lowering the costs of product acquisition

- Streamlining back-of-house operations

- Improving ease of product acquisition

SALES FORCE EFFECTIVENESS

Six Sigma is having a major impact on the sales force. In addition to helping companies move from a product-centric to a more solution-orientated sales approach, many organizations such as General Electric—with their sales force effectiveness (SFE) program—have gained substantial improvements by making the sales process itself more effective.

Sales force improvement efforts typically look at two areas:

1. *Effectiveness*: improving sales hit rates or success rates in closing sales transactions. This is typically done by improving conversion rates from lead generation to confirmed sale.

Sales Force Improvement Areas

Effectiveness

- ❖ Lead generation
- ❖ Account planning
- ❖ Lead management
- ❖ Profitability enhancement
- ❖ Account sales strategy
- ❖ Campaigns and promotions
- ❖ Product configuration

Efficiency

- ❖ Time and activity management
- ❖ Opportunity tracking
- ❖ Problem resolution
- ❖ Efficiency tools (automated quotations, product information)
- ❖ Competency and skills development

Figure 1.6   Six Sigma and Sales Force Effectiveness and Efficiency

2. *Efficiency*: improving the sales process itself. Projects usually focus on mapping the existing sales process and seeking ways to remove variability and non-value-added activities. (See Figure 1.6.)

Sales force problems are often misdiagnosed and poorly treated. The thinking may be that in order to improve sales all that is needed is to change the quotas and compensation for each sales person without any changes in the sales approach, product mix, or customer base. Six Sigma allows a far more rigorous method to improving the sales effort by using techniques such as sales force effectiveness.

One approach to using Six Sigma methods to improve the sales process is shown in Figure 1.7. This approach:

- Segments the market based on strategic factors such as growth potential, profitability, or customer value (benefits or cost)

- Develops tailored sales approaches based on customer needs for each key segment

- Develops sales force skills through training; tracks and continually improves training effectiveness

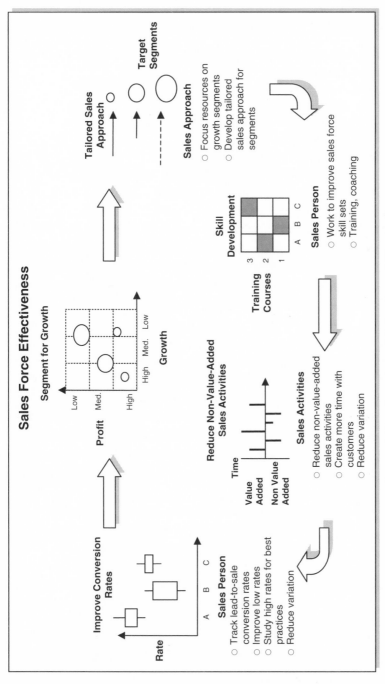

Figure 1.7 Overview of Sales Force Effectiveness

• Reduces non-value-added activities in the sales process so the sales force can spend time selling; helps sales people be more productive

• Works with the sales team to analyze sales conversion rates and improve them further

IMPROVING KEY SALES METRICS

Not all sales people were created equal. Some so-called super sales people seem to be able to sell anything; others seem to need more help. One important principle in sales force improvement is to create repeatable and reliable sales processes that help all sales people do a better job. Many super sales people may feel that there is no need for a clearly defined sales process, but they usually comprise only a small portion of the sales force. The majority of sales people will benefit significantly from a good sales process. Studying sales metrics such as conversion rates (that quantify the amount of sales successes from initial lead to signed purchase order) can offer significant insights into what makes great sales people so effective and highlights opportunities to help poor performers.

Looking at conversion rates for each sales person (or some other appropriate metric) and conducting a hypothesis test establishes whether there is a statistically significant difference between sales people. If there is such a statistically significant difference, we are then rightfully able to ask why. Six Sigma methods such as hypothesis testing and control charts can offer unique insights into sales performance.

Study the best sales people. What makes them so good? Can we adapt their techniques and methods, and make them part of the sales process? Great sales people may, for example, have a skillful way of making cold calls on prospective customers. By understanding their approach, it is possible to develop sales tools, such as a cold call script that less confident sales people can refer to during a cold call.

Study the worst sales people. What makes them so bad? Is it possible to understand why their performance is bad and help them improve? Is it a problem specific to the sales person, or has he simply been given a bad sales territory?

The Six Sigma approach looks for the root causes that drive sales performance. Once these drivers have been found, they are studied and improved. Simply changing a sales person's compensation or bonus scheme—a typical reaction to poor sales performance—often fails to address the underlying causes. Worst still, such efforts often assume that sales people need to be motivated to work harder—that they are currently not working as hard as they could. More often than not, this is wrong; sales people are working as best they can; the problem lies not with the sales person but with the product or process itself.

Improvements made by studying the sales force and modifying the sales process should result in higher conversion rates and hence revenue. Six Sigma efforts tie directly to overall success metrics and can definitively show that the improvements have been effective. If the improvements made have not enhanced conversion rates, margin, or whatever to key metric is, then the issue needs to be studied again until improvements are realized.

TAILORING THE SALES APPROACH

There are many ways to segment a market. Many advocates of sales force effectiveness feel the best way to segment is based on profitability or growth potential. This allows us to examine the sales resources being applied to each segment and often reveals significant resources being applied to segments that are not profitable. Reallocating resources from a nonprofitable segment to a profitable one can quickly lead to significant margin and revenue improvements.

It is possible to further refine this and then look at segment factors such as buying behavior. Some customers may have distinct methods by which they procure products and services. Matching the sales approach to the customers' buying methods often leads to significant gains in revenue. The result is a customized sales approach for each segment aimed at maximizing the sales effectiveness for target customers.

One of the problems with most segmentation methods is that they have been oversimplified. This can, in some instances, actually hide growth opportunities. In other cases companies are targeting market segments that do not actually exist, in the sense that the customer group does not exhibit the distinct characteristics that were assumed in the segmentation process. Naturally, such errors lead to a significant waste of effort in the form of marketing and sales efforts.

Six Sigma methods bring a rigorous approach to segmentation (see page 156). Typically this involves the following steps:

- Develop a hypothesis about how potential segments are defined

- Collect the relevant data for each segment

- Analyze data and test the hypothesis using statistical tools such as analysis of variance (ANOVA)

- Determine if there is a statistically significant difference between segments

Such analysis ensures that market segments are real, in that they are statistically different from other groups.

REDUCE NON-VALUE-ADDED SALES ACTIVITIES

It is not uncommon to find that sales people don't actually spend much time selling. This problem is rarely caused by a lack of skill or motivation, and more often than not is due to bureaucratic procedures or to poor process and support services. Streamlining order entry, account planning, lead qualification, sales reports, and other sales processes can free up significant amounts of time, which could then be spent face to face with customers.

Many organizations have never considered studying the sales process in order to reduce non-value-added activities. There are often quick wins with simple improvements that can lead to significant gains. Often, such improvements can be made without any new investments or additional resources.

Process observation is often a good way to study how sales people spend their time. This can be done using a stopwatch and check sheet to record activities for a period of time. As with its industrial engineering equivalent—time and motion studies—care needs to be taken doing such studies, to ensure that the data is correct and the sales people are willing participants.

The order entry and confirmation process at one firm consumed an average of 20% of the sales person's time. Streamlining the process led to a 15% reduction in the time spent completing such paper work, which meant sales people could spend 15% more time selling to customers.

SKILL DEVELOPMENT AND CONVERSION RATES

Identifying skill gaps and training requirements for sales people is an important step in raising the overall sales force effectiveness.

Studying sales metrics such as conversion rates can identify opportunities to help individual sales people to improve their performance. Statistical methods, such as hypothesis testing and control charts, can distinguish between systemic problems and specific issues—sometimes referred to as common and special causes. If such analysis reveals the need for training, programs can be developed that should lead to demonstrable improvements in performance metrics such as conversion rates. Training effectiveness is judged by improvements in sales metrics.

SIX SIGMA AND SOLUTION SELLING

In recent years, many companies have experienced difficulties in sustaining growth in the face of increased competition and a consequent trend toward the commoditization of what were once high-premium items—computer hardware and software, for example, have plunged in price. In response, major corporations across a wide range of industries are changing to selling solutions to their customers' problems rather than offering stand alone products and services. Solution selling aims to create powerful value propositions—typically, a combination of products and services and in some instances even merging customer and supplier operations—aimed at solving customers' business problems. Not surprisingly, this requires a deep understanding of the customer's business that goes beyond subjective opinions, and as such, many organizations have developed solutions selling approaches based on rigorous Six Sigma methods such as DMAIC (Define, Measure, Analyze, Improve, and Control) or DMADV (Define, Measure, Analyze, Design, and Validate).

Six Sigma Solutions Selling

❖ Creates unique value propositions for customers

❖ Uses customer business metrics to gauge success, not product price metrics

❖ Requires a consultative-type sales approach often based on Six Sigma methods

❖ Uses different approach to pricing, based on value created for the customer

❖ Solution development is a cross-functional effort and requires strong organizational alignment

❖ Often collaborative in nature and requires a deep understanding of the customer's business

---

Figure 1.8   Solution Selling Overview

Solution selling enables firms to offer their clients attractive customized propositions while keeping margins high. By using their proprietary knowledge they can add value while raising the barriers against competitors. Better still, this strategy entails relatively low capital investment.

These advantages are recognized by the stock market, and firms such as IBM, which derives nearly half of its revenue from selling solutions, have seen their stock price soar.

A solution is a mutually agreed-upon answer to a recognized problem. As such, solution selling starts with understanding what the customer's problems are. The sales force does not push a specific predetermined product. After working with customers to understand and diagnose the nature of the problem, a solution is developed, aimed at solving the problem. The solution could be a completely customized offering or a bundle of existing products and services. At any rate, what is created is a unique value proposition for customers. In some instances, the price of such value propositions is based on customer metrics such as cost reductions or increases in revenue.

Solution selling puts enormous pressures on traditional product-centric organizations. Internally, it requires a radically different sales approach, to which many organizations are simply not able to adapt. Developing customized solutions also requires close alignment between various functional groups and tight control of the development process. Externally, it requires gaining a comprehensive knowledge of customers' business issues and using customer metrics to gauge success, not simply product price and performance metrics. Six Sigma, as a strategic change initiative, provides an organization with means to overcome these challenges.

The transition from a product-based—or service-based—company to a solutions seller requires drastic organizational change. Front-end units must now develop even closer relationships with customers to identify problems to solve, and part of the solution may even entail using a competitor's products and services. This is an anathema to back-end units who have traditionally expected to push their own products rather than be pulled by the customer's needs.

Designing an effective solution may also require sharing sensitive information both internally and with other firms, and challenging the integrity of brands. The best customers may prove to be newer firms and in some cases old and prestigious customers may have to be abandoned altogether.

PROVIDING GUARANTEES

Why should a customer pay a premium for a solution? Many solution-selling companies think that by bundling their existing products they are offering solutions, but a solution that truly adds value solves a real customer problem.

A compelling answer to customer objections arises when the solutions provider offers a well-defined guarantee, taking risks and responsibilities off the customer's hands. Instead of offering, say, a simple warranty on the life of a machine, the solutions provider gives a wide guarantee defined in terms of the customer's needs and assumes a broad range of risks. Ultimately, selling solutions means committing the firm to the customer's own business performance. To do this successfully, the process of analyzing the customer's problem and designing the solution must be extremely thorough. Six Sigma's rigorous methodology is ideally suited for this.

CREATING A SOLUTION-SELLING ORGANIZATION

Radical changes are hard to implement, but Six Sigma helps to ease the implementation pain that organizations feel. Typically, this is achieved by creating a select team of talented people, led by Black

Belts, to explore the idea, test the concept, and prove that it works before it is rolled out to the rest of the organization. As a vehicle for strategic change, Six Sigma can provide a framework by which to engage with customers directly and to create a road map in which organizations can assimilate the new solution-selling model, creating a transition road map from the current business approach to a solution offer.

In many cases, companies adopt solution selling for a limited range of selected products and services, while retaining their traditional marketing approaches in other areas. This greatly reduces the risk; some firms that have opted for a total change to solution selling have suffered serious setbacks. For example, Xerox encountered major difficulties in retraining its sales force to sell document solutions rather than photocopiers during the 1990s and in harmonizing the front end with the back end. Although Xerox's strategy made sense, its execution was unsuccessful. Applying Six Sigma as a vehicle for strategic change helps to bridge the difficult gap between strategy and execution

The commitment to see such a radical change through has to come from the top: this is undoubtedly a top-down process. Senior managers must work hard to ensure full cooperation between the front and back ends, hiring outside talent and removing resistant employees where necessary. They must foster new internal channels of communication and accountability—a process ideally suited to Six Sigma—and in particular, they must persuade units running dominant product lines to participate fully. Front-end teams must be infinitely adaptable, rotating team members as the project progresses.

Tailor-made solutions may be great for the customer, but they may be expensive and time-consuming to develop, and there is a danger of low profits, especially if there is an increased assumption of risk. Successful solutions sellers are finding ways to resell existing packages by offering them in different markets or creating pre-prepared modules that can be adapted at low cost for new customers. Profit lies in repeatability. To achieve this, the design team must generate large numbers of potential solutions and then study and filter them to find the ones that are repeatable. This is a major role for the back end—designing solution elements that can be codified, standardized, scaled up or down, and combined in many different ways. This is a major factor in achieving the goal of offsetting development costs and increasing profits.

One addition to the traditional DMADV approach required for solution-selling is in the final step, Validate and Replicate, where teams look for opportunities to replicate any new offerings to the customers or markets.

CHANGING FROM PRODUCT SELLING TO SOLUTION SELLING

As discussed above, the change to solution selling, sometimes known as consultative selling or value-added selling strategies, may require drastic internal reorganization. To achieve the prize of developing unique offerings that beat the competition and enjoy a price premium, the organization has to commit itself to a major reform that is difficult to execute. The risks are high. For this reason, companies need to explore the strategy very carefully, testing every aspect of it, before deciding to go ahead. Even if, as is likely, the firm will continue to serve some customer segments in the traditional way, the change will have profound effects throughout the organization.

When undertaking such a drastic transformation, Six Sigma provides a vehicle of strategic change, analyzing how the new sales process works, building on successes and rolling out the new approach to the organization as a whole. Typically, the approach would be to first segment the market and identify customers interested in solutions, then to select a few high-potential Black Belt candidates who are able to work collaboratively with customers. The Black Belts' function is twofold, first to develop solutions for customers and second to design new internal solution-selling approaches.

Solution selling tends to require a long sales cycle. Launching specific Six Sigma solution projects often relieves pressure on the existing sales force, which is typically focused and compensated on short sales cycles. A principal aim of the Six Sigma project is to make the solution-selling approach repeatable and reliable. Once the Black Belts have successfully completed a solution-selling project, they are placed back in the sales force—acting as solution-selling champions— and new Black Belt candidates are selected. Thus, the existing sales force is gradually trained in effective solution-selling methods without disrupting more traditional ongoing sales operations.

In major strategic change initiatives such as moving from a product-selling to a solution-selling organization, Six Sigma efforts are focused on:

- Designing a new sales approach (Design for Six Sigma)

- Engaging with customers on joint projects

- Implementing changes to the sales process on a limited basis through Black Belt and Green Belt projects

- Moving the new selling processes to the larger sales force

SIX SIGMA FOR MARKETING

Six Sigma's expanded focus now addresses the problem of how to improve the marketing return on investment (ROI). The advent of the Internet and other new media has vastly increased both the range of marketing communication techniques and the volume of customer data. This has been a mixed blessing for customers and marketers because much is being wasted in an explosion of selling approaches—customers, for instance, do not appreciate having to wade through oceans of irrelevant marketing messages to obtain the information they want at a website, while at the same time a large proportion of marketing budgets is spent on ineffective efforts.

Sophisticated statistical tools for measuring the effectiveness of campaigns have been available for decades, but most companies do not take full advantage of them. This has been partly because such tests are traditionally perceived as costly—in fact, modern statistical software has greatly reduced costs in recent years—and partly because many marketing decision makers are insufficiently familiar with the power of statistical analysis. Six Sigma brings the requisite expertise and, even more importantly, can help to win the support of managers who are reluctant to accept that a statistician's interpretation of the data may be more accurate than their own.

Often, cause and correlation are misunderstood. Just because two variables are correlated, it does not necessarily mean that one is causing the other to occur. In complex systems such as the financial markets or supermarket retailing, it is very easy to mistake correlation for causation and to build a marketing campaign on entirely false premises.

Another common blind spot is the failure to identify the effects of a single variable in offerings that combine many variables. Typically, one offering is found to be superior to another by analysis of the historical data, but without establishing whether a new combination of variables might produce an even better response in the market.

Using relatively low-cost experimental design techniques that are at the heart of Six Sigma methods can improve response rates significantly. Experimental design tests the effects of individual variables and combinations of them and can model thousands of possible scenarios. It can tell you, for example, whether the fact that an offer was for a limited time contributed to more sales, or whether consumers were actually responding to some other element. In the 1970s, Nobel Prize winner Daniel McFadden used experimental design to forecast accurately the market share of San Francisco commuter travel that a new rail system, BART, would be able to capture and also to optimize the location of planned stations to maximize revenue.

Experimental design is rigorous and can produce startlingly accurate forecasts. It is especially useful in markets with a large number of customers and products—such as retailing—where the potential number of variables is commensurately large. Combinations of offering attributes such as price level, selling message, and promotional offer can be tested exhaustively to discover the optimal approach for a given market segment.

Unproven preconceptions, such as "lowering the price will not increase volume sufficiently to increase profits," can be tested for their accuracy as part of a continuous process of understanding ever-changing market segments.

Consumer-based companies such as Cable & Wireless and AOL are discarding the bombardment approach in favor of better market testing, using the vast range of proven statistical techniques that are available, including:

- *Experimental design* testing the effects of variables

- *Multivariable methods* techniques to investigate the interaction of variables in the offering

- *Regression and correlation* used to infer relationships between variables

- *Simulation* used for complex modeling where solutions cannot be analyzed statistically

- *Stochastic methods* test hypotheses of market structure and produce conditional predictions

- *Causal models* good for measuring consumer behavior

- *Deterministic methods* used to establish optimum combination of variables

Six Sigma techniques have been applied with great success in other business processes for many years but have come late to marketing, despite the fact that the complexity of marketing phenomena is far too great for it to be adequately addressed by intuitive methods. Many companies are now developing Six Sigma programs tailored specifically to sales and marketing functions with the aim of enhancing their performance and improving the ROI.

IMPROVING SALES AND DISTRIBUTION CHANNELS

The channels and partners by which a company markets, sells and distributes its products and services form the lifelines of the business. A company's channel decisions directly affect:

- Customers

- Strength against competitors

- Profit margins

- Costs

- Internal processes and functions

Once seen solely as a marketing function, channel management is now a strategic imperative for senior management. In any number of categories, it is the channel, not the product, that has become pivotal in the buying decision. In areas where there are few product differences, or where the differences are perceived to be of minor importance, the key differentiating value often comes from the means of acquisition—the channel. Many of today's leading companies, such as Dell, have achieved outstanding rates of growth and profitability through strategic channel management.

A central premise of Six Sigma for Growth is that organizations must strive to profitably create value for the customer, and this is also true for channels. Indeed, if channels do not create customer value, they will begin to erode value for suppliers who use them, and they may even threaten a supplier's competitiveness. This requires a change in thinking for many organizations that have historically thought about the value channels create for them—not about the value created for the customers.

Extending Six Sigma to the channel is an excellent way to enhance value for the customer. Six Sigma projects aimed at margin improvement, streamlining channel operations, and improving channel competency and channel sales force effectiveness can yield substantial improvements for all parties. There are two distinct ways in which Six Sigma for Growth can be applied to increase the value creation potential of channels:

1. Channel optimization

2. Developing new channels

CHANNEL OPTIMIZATION

Channels, as with any business process must be continuously scrutinized for improvement opportunities. From a cost management perspective, substantial improvements can be gained when all the firms in the business network adopt best practices and work together to reduce total costs and to add value to the ultimate customer. Many organizations however, have taken a hands-off approach to channels, which can often lead to a loss in value to the end users. Every supplier using channels needs to play an active role in improving the value that each channel is creating for customers. There are usually many opportunities to improve channel operations—either their efficiency or effectiveness—by focusing on individual elements of the channel.

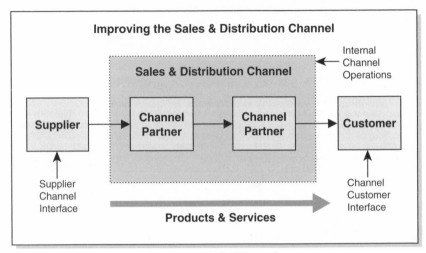

Figure 1.9   Six Sigma and Channel Improvements

One approach to improving the channel performance is to extend Six Sigma initiatives to the channel. This usually entails working on cross-organizational improvement projects and having Six Sigma resources focused on the overall channel performance. Typical Six Sigma for Growth projects include:

- *Supplier to channel interfaces.* Supplier projects aimed at targeting inefficiencies between the supplier and the channel. This may involve improving logistics and inventories or introducing electronic commerce initiatives with the aim of reducing transaction processing costs, increasing the accuracy of data exchange, reducing uncertainty, and improving relations.

- *Internal channel operations.* Targeting inefficiencies within the channel. These can be collaborative projects aimed at helping the channels run their business, developing their internal business processes, and reducing costs.

- *Customer interface.* Projects here are often focused on improving the sales force effectiveness, improving product knowledge and competency, looking at price and discount optimization, product positioning, marketing effectiveness, and determining the optimal product mix.

Six Sigma & the Channel

❖ Six Sigma initiatives extended to include sales and distribution channels

❖ Channels must add value to the ultimate customer

❖ Suppliers and channel partners work together to create solutions to customer problems

❖ Inter-organizational cost management aimed at reducing total costs

---

Figure 1.10   Six Sigma and the Sales and Distribution Channel

DEVELOPING NEW CHANNELS

Given the rapidly changing nature of the marketplace, rethinking and redesigning channels is becoming a regular activity for many organizations. Six Sigma methods can be used effectively to develop completely new channels.

The approach starts with developing a clear understanding of needs, behaviors, and economics of different customer segments; this is the foundation of channel development. By aligning channel capabilities with the needs and purchasing behaviors of target customers, companies are able to attract and retain relationships with customers.

Customer knowledge must be supplemented with a detailed understanding of the value-added activities required to identify, sell, and support target customers. The result is a sales and distribution channel focused not only on market coverage but also on what value they bring to the end customer.

CASE STUDY: IMPROVING MARGINS BY OPTIMIZING THE CHANNEL

A well-known company making telecommunications equipment found that its profit margins had been declining steadily for several months. The company sells its products through a complex distribution channel that includes resellers, and logistics and inventory handlers. In some cases, resellers sell to other resellers, forming several layers of intermediaries spread across many different locations.

As is often the case, the firm's channel system had grown haphazardly over the years. Often, the technology of its products was in such great demand that all parties in the channel were able to make sizable profits. The main problem was how to get products to the customer rapidly, and price was rarely an issue. The company never really paid much attention to its channel until it noticed a slow and steady decline in the margins.

A Six Sigma team was set up to investigate the root causes of the margin erosion and to improve them. The team quickly went to work to document and map the existing sales and distribution channels. The approach to process mapping was to show the product flow from the supplier through the resellers to the ultimate customers. Inventory and logistics process were included, and a picture of the existing sales and distribution channel was developed.

Joint Six Sigma projects and workshops helped each channel member understand the big picture of the sales and distribution channel, and to find ways to improve its overall effectiveness. Each activity in the process maps was scrutinized for the value it provided for the ultimate customer and how it could impact margins. Several areas were identified:

- *Non-value-added activities.* Logistics and inventory movements were not optimized. In many cases, it was possible to ship products directly to the customer rather than through several storage locations. It was estimated that excess inventories and logistics costs led to a 2% reduction in the overall margin.

- *Reseller layers.* Products were being sold through a series of resellers. Eliminating a number of them would yield an extra 3% in margins.

- *Sales commissions.* Resellers gave discounts very easily because only a small portion of their commission was based on margin. Resellers focused on gaining revenue by lowering the price (reducing the margin). The Six Sigma team proposed a revised commission system to prevent this.

- *Sales skills.* Distributors' sales skills were poor. Resellers tended to offer customers the cheapest products, not necessarily the ones that would give the best performance for the customer.

Value-based selling techniques were needed so that resellers could gauge the customers' real requirements and not simply promote the cheapest system.

- *Pricing policy*. Many resellers were providing customers with incorrect prices. Pricing policy had not been fully understood by the resellers.

- *Channel stuffing*. Some sales teams were selling as much inventory as they could into the distribution channel to meet quarterly revenue goals. To make the sales, they had to offer steep discounts to the resellers. Resellers disliked the practice because it raised their costs and exposed them to the risk of keeping obsolete inventories. Channel stuffing had always been frowned upon by this company but had never seemed to go away. The Six Sigma team was the first to quantify the effects of this practice in terms of margin—estimating it to be a huge 8%. Put in these terms, leadership was able to gauge the extent of the problem and put procedures in place to guarantee it didn't happen again.

The Six Sigma team was successful in identifying a number of unrelated reasons for the margin erosion. These root causes were systematically addressed through collaborative projects with resellers. Teams worked to improve the overall profitability and value created for the ultimate customer. A win-win attitude was central to all members in the channel working successfully together. Within three months, the margin decline had halted, and by the following quarter profit margins were higher than they had ever been.

CHAPTER 2

Six Sigma Fundamentals

Six Sigma is the most important management training we've ever had. It's better than going to Harvard Business School. It's better than going to Crotonville. It teaches you how to think differently.
—Jack Welch[1]

SIX SIGMA TODAY

Six Sigma is quite different today from what it was 15 years ago. As it has evolved, it has come to encompass a wide range of activities. Today, a company's Six Sigma program may be one of a number of things: a quality goal; a strategy; a business philosophy; a process-improvement tool kit. Organizations have learned that to maximize its effectiveness, a Six Sigma initiative must be customized to suit

---

The Evolved Six Sigma Approach

Six Sigma is a comprehensive and flexible system for achieving, sustaining, and maximizing business success. Six Sigma is uniquely driven to deliver value to customers and the business through:

❖ A close understanding of the customers *present* and *future* needs

❖ The disciplined use of facts, data, and rigorous analysis

❖ Diligent attention to managing improving, and reinventing business processes

---

Figure 2.1   Six Sigma Approach Defined

the particular needs of the business. For this reason, Six Sigma tool sets and deployment approaches vary significantly.

Six Sigma's rapid development into different applications sometimes causes confusion over what Six Sigma really is, so perhaps it is useful here to propose an updated definition. Six Sigma can be defined today as shown in Figure 2.1.

Although Six Sigma has expanded its scope, it remains, at its core, a systematic combination of proven quality principles and techniques for process improvement. As Six Sigma has gained popularity and found its way into other functional groups within organizations, it has developed a strategic aspect aimed at driving change initiatives across the entire organization. Hence, many organizations now refer to Six Sigma as a "vehicle for strategic change" or a "strategic change initiative."

A key feature that distinguishes Six Sigma from other improvement initiatives, such as Total Quality Management and Quality Circles, has been the focus on customers and key business issues. Simply put, Six Sigma aims to identify key business issues, select talented people, and allocate resources to areas that will yield the greatest value to the business.

This is a far cry from previous quality approaches that advocated improvement simply for improvement's sake. It is this combination of an effective process improvement methodology and a strategic business direction that has made Six Sigma so effective.

FINDING ROOT CAUSES

A fundamental principle in Six Sigma is that in order to solve problems effectively and reduce waste you need to go upstream to find the root causes of poor performance. Managing a process by its outputs is far less effective than identifying and managing the inputs or root causes. When Six Sigma was first introduced, this was a radical concept. It was the time of mass production when quality was "inspected" into products. Quality control inspectors sifted through mountains of finished goods inventories looking for nonconforming parts. The dependence on mass inspection and the capital costs of inspection equipment made organizations unable to compete against their Japanese counterparts whose approach to quality focused on finding defects *before* they occurred, not after.

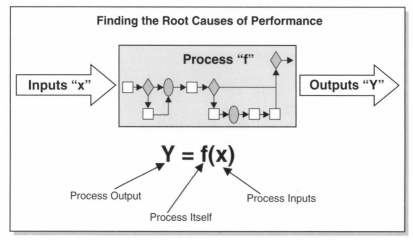

Figure 2.2   Y = f(x). Output is a Function of the Process and its Inputs

Catching defects after they occur is inherently wasteful, and Six Sigma methods offered organizations a way to understand processes and determine the upstream factors that lead to defects. Identifying these root causes and controlling them is by far the more effective approach.

Six Sigma is very much concerned with understanding processes and their inputs and outputs. This approach is expressed in the Figure 2.2 where "Y" represents the output of a process, "f" the process and "x" the inputs.

Six Sigma projects typically work back from the outputs of a process to understanding the process itself, and then ultimately to identify the key factors that affect the output of the process. Once the root causes are identified, steps are taken to modify them so that the process output conforms to customer requirements. This sequence of working upstream from the outputs of a process is set out in the Define, Measure, Analyze, Improve, and Control (DMAIC) process improvement sequence. Six Sigma is an effective process improvement tool set because of this methodical cause-and-effect analysis of processes.

In addition to being an effective problem-solving methodology, Six Sigma is also:

- A quality goal

- A culture and philosophy

- A vehicle for strategic change

- A tool set

QUALITY GOAL

Many companies still think that 99% good quality is a great achievement. Judged by historical standards, they are correct. In the years after the Second World War, demand vastly exceeded supply. The main concern of organizations was to make products rapidly and ship them out to eager customers. Customers cared more about obtaining a product than the quality of the product itself.

Today, supply has exceeded demand in many markets, and quality standards have been raised dramatically. For example, one out of every hundred flights not making it to its destination or one lost parcel out of every hundred is hardly considered good. Customers have come to expect ever-increasing standards of quality. A 99% success rate is now unacceptable, and can cause large financial losses. Unfortunately, many companies have not even reached this level of quality. Quality experts such as Joseph Juran suggest that poor quality costs consume between 20% to 40% of the effort expended by industry. Such costs include those associated with defective products, inspection costs, and other non-value-added activities. Instead of 99%, world-class companies today strive to achieve 99.9999998% good quality, equating to 3.4 defects per million, which is the definition of Six Sigma quality levels.

Figure 2.3 illustrates Six Sigma quality. The figure shows the normal distribution that describes the statistical properties of many naturally occurring populations. In this case, the distribution represents the performance of companies' products and services and is sometimes referred to as the voice of the process. Specification limits, which are requirements from the customer, are also highlighted in this diagram. These limits are referred to as the voice of the customer. In essence, Six Sigma compares the performance of products with the customer's requirements. Looking at the diagram, it is clear that the spread of the data or the variation in our products is important. Variation reduction is a central theme in Six Sigma. Less variation equates to a smaller chance of defects and less waste. In statistics, variation is measured using the standard deviation,

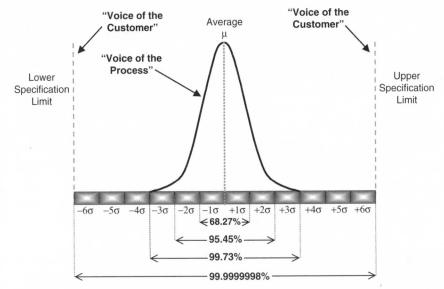

Figure 2.3   Centered Normal Distribution—Six Sigma Performance

which is sometimes referred to as sigma. As can be seen in the figure, six standard deviations on either side of the average equates to 99.9999998% good quality, or a Six Sigma quality level.

Variation reduction is a key concept in Six Sigma. How is this relevant to business growth? Quite simply, customers notice the variation in the products and services they purchase. For example, if one auto mechanic tells you that the repairs to your car could take between 20 minutes and one day, and a second auto mechanic tells you that it will take between 20 minutes and one hour, you are likely to prefer the latter service, assuming that the quality of both is equal in other respects.

Inconsistent performance is immediately apparent to customers and is often a destabilizing influence on them. Importantly, the ability to reduce variation also implies a deep understanding of the key factors that influence a process and its output. In short, in order to reduce variation you must really understand the process, and this in turn results in higher performance in the eyes of the customer.

Six Sigma is a specific quality goal. To achieve it means meeting customer requirements 99.9999998% of the time. The Six Sigma standard forces an understanding of customer requirements, provides a metric that compares performance with these requirements, and sets an ambitious quality goal.

It has been adopted by many organizations as a key measure, but using Six Sigma (or Six Sigma Scores) to manage business process performance is not universally accepted. Some organizations have found it difficult to implement. Forrest W. Breyfogle notes that creating a "one-size-fits-all" metric, such as sigma quality level, can lead to frustration, falsification of measurements and "playing games with the numbers."[2] Certainly, using the wrong metric and setting arbitrary goals are counterproductive. Sadly, many organizations have a history of managing business by such arbitrary goals and failing to develop a culture of continuous improvement. Such failures have led to criticism, such as W. Edwards Deming's comment that "conformance to specifications, Zero Defects, Six Sigma Quality, and other nostrums, all miss the point."[3]

To be effective, sigma metrics must be used appropriately. The main focus should be on continuously reducing variation and improving processes. It is essential to choose suitable metrics for specific cases, and in some instances other performance metrics such as Cpk or PPM are more applicable. What is important is that the selected metric compares the process performance with customer requirements. It is only through such comparisons that we are able to offer improved levels of quality to our customers.

A Culture and Philosophy

Establishing numerical goals is only a small part of the story. Six Sigma is also a means to communicate a vision and develop a culture that prizes continuous improvement and customer focus. The aim is to create a business in which people naturally look for ways to improve processes and take action. In this sense, Six Sigma is as much about people excellence as technical and business excellence. People's creativity, teamwork, and dedication are a powerful part of the Six Sigma culture.

Effectively applied, Six Sigma instills a unique culture into an organization. General Electric uses Six Sigma as a leadership development program. High-potential candidates are selected for important Black Belt projects and upon successful completion are promoted within the organization. Furthermore, people cannot be promoted to a management level unless they have completed a Green Belt project. The message is clear; leading customer-centric improvement will get you

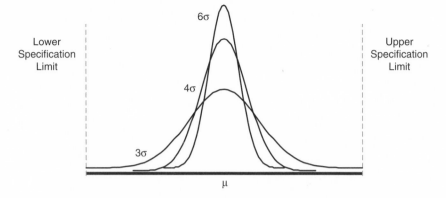

Sigma Level	Acceptable %	Defective PPM	Capability Cpk
1	68.27	317,300	0.33
2	95.45	45,500	0.67
3	99.73	2700	1.00
4	99.9937	63	1.33
5	99.999943	0.57	1.67
6	99.9999998	0.002	2.00

Figure 2.4   Improving Sigma Levels

promoted. If constantly reinforced, after a while this message becomes so ingrained in an organization that it changes—to use a GE term—its "DNA." When this happens, continuous improvement becomes part of the basic company values and culture.

A VEHICLE FOR STRATEGIC CHANGE

Six Sigma creates a framework by which an organization can embrace change. In today's constantly changing marketplace, the ability to change is widely thought to be the most important competitive weapon for business.

The notion of Six Sigma being a vehicle for strategic change is often overlooked by Six Sigma practitioners. The tendency may be to focus on the Six Sigma tool set and its suitability to specific projects, rather than to its organizational or strategic aspects.

As a vehicle for strategic change, Six Sigma provides an organization with a means to transform itself. The vehicle is the Six Sigma organization with its Master Black Belts, Black Belts, and Green Belts, and reporting structure, which is given direction by medium and long-term strategic goals.

Six Sigma projects are the tactical moves necessary to reach these strategic goals. For example, consider a company wishing to transform its sales force from a product-centric model to a more consultative solution-selling approach. The company would call upon its Six Sigma organization to develop the new selling model, then implement it through Black Belt and Green Belt projects. Once the new model proves to be effective, it would be rolled out to the whole organization. An aerospace company might decide, for instance, that to remain competitive in the coming years it needs to reduce the time taken to design and build aircraft engines—from five years to one. Such a strategy requires changes across the entire organization, from design teams to procurement and manufacturing. To achieve this goal, the Six Sigma organization would be called upon to develop a change road map and to provide a means to manage and drive the company-wide change initiative.

The strategic change aspect of Six Sigma has led many organizations to expand the tool set. It is not uncommon to see Six Sigma initiatives using Design for Six Sigma to handle design issues, Lean Enterprise to look at things such as cycle time reduction and waste elimination, and Total Productive Maintenance to look at improving overall equipment effectiveness. Others have even included Activity Based Management for finance and Six Sigma for Growth for sales and marketing. Simply put, the Six Sigma framework employs whatever tools are needed to transform the organization.

SIX SIGMA TOOL SETS

Six Sigma combines tools and methodologies that have been around for many years and have proven to be very effective. Originally, the tool set was primarily based on statistical methods applied to solving specific problems. Six Sigma evolved to meet the changing needs of organizations, and today, depending on the organization and the approach taken, the tool sets can include:

• Six Sigma (DMAIC)

• Design for Six Sigma

- Lean Enterprise

- Total Productive Maintenance

- Six Sigma for Sales

The following is a brief overview of each improvement methodology.

SIX SIGMA (DMAIC)

The Six Sigma DMAIC methodology uses proven process improvement and statistical tools. These tools are used to define problems, identify root causes, and then find optimal solutions. The focus

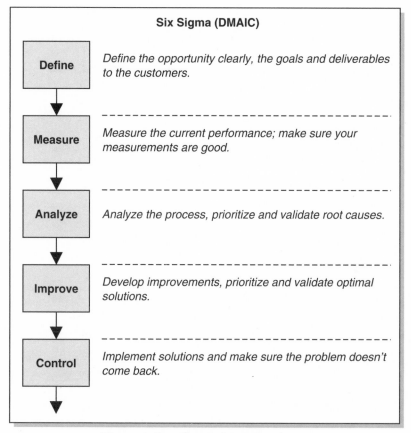

Six Sigma (DMAIC)

Define	Define the opportunity clearly, the goals and deliverables to the customers.
Measure	Measure the current performance; make sure your measurements are good.
Analyze	Analyze the process, prioritize and validate root causes.
Improve	Develop improvements, prioritize and validate optimal solutions.
Control	Implement solutions and make sure the problem doesn't come back.

Figure 2.5   Classical DMAIC Steps

is on reducing defects and variation and generating bottom-line savings. Six Sigma DMAIC is typically used for improving existing processes, products, or services.

Projects are usually led by Green Belts, Black Belts, or Master Black Belts.

DESIGN FOR SIX SIGMA (DFSS)

DFSS combines statistical and design tools in a methodology that aims to understand customer requirements and then develop a product or service—and the means to deliver it—that meets those requirements (see Figure 2.6). It is used to create new processes, products and services or redesign those which need major modifications. Again, projects are usually led by Green Belts, Black Belts or Master Black Belts.

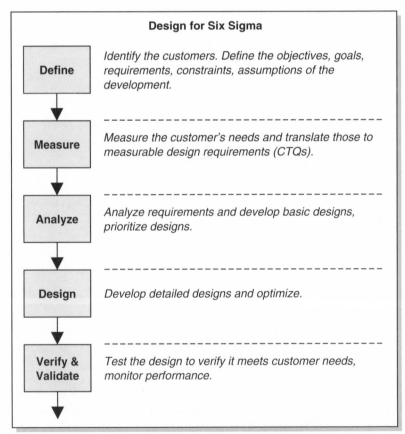

Design for Six Sigma

| Define | Identify the customers. Define the objectives, goals, requirements, constraints, assumptions of the development. |

| Measure | Measure the customer's needs and translate those to measurable design requirements (CTQs). |

| Analyze | Analyze requirements and develop basic designs, prioritize designs. |

| Design | Develop detailed designs and optimize. |

| Verify & Validate | Test the design to verify it meets customer needs, monitor performance. |

Figure 2.6   Design for Six Sigma DMADV Steps

Lean Enterprise

Taiichi Ohno is often credited with the creation of the Toyota Just-in-Time (JIT) production system. The JIT system is regarded by many to be the greatest contribution to the manufacturing world since Henry Ford's mass production. Many Six Sigma initiatives today include Lean, which is based on the JIT production system. It involves the systematic identification and elimination of waste and is sometimes referred to as wasteology. Waste is generally broken into different categories (Overproduction, Excess Inventory, Transportation, Waiting, Unnecessary Motion, Overprocessing, Correction and some also include Complexity and Bureaucracy), but at its highest level are simply things that consume resources and do not add value. The term "Lean Enterprise" is often used to denote that the initiative is being applied internally and to the entire value chain of external customers and suppliers.

Lean tools include:

- Flow manufacturing

- Multiprocess handling

- Kanban

- Manpower reduction

- Visual control

- Leveling (Heijunka)

- Changeover

- Standard operations

- Jidoka: Human automation

- 5S

- Poka Yoke (mistake-proofing)

Lean manufacturing is a powerful methodology, (see Figure 2.7) and many organizations have integrated it into their Six Sigma management frameworks. Methods such as Six Sigma DMAIC and Lean are complementary and address different issues at different stages during the improvement process.

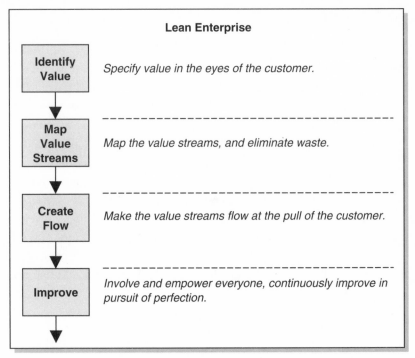

Figure 2.7   Lean Enterprise Steps

Many organizations today talk about "Six Sigma reducing the variation and Lean shifting the mean (average)." This is an oversimplification since JIT has always talked about removing waste ("muda" in the Japanese), stress ("muri"), and inconsistency or variation ("mura") or the three Ms.[4] Organizations with Lean programs use Lean Experts and Lean Masters to lead projects.

TOTAL PRODUCTIVE MAINTENANCE

Total Productive Maintenance (TPM) builds upon aspects of the Toyota production system but focuses on machine and equipment effectiveness (see Figure 2.8). TPM is productive maintenance that is carried out in small group activities by all employees. The focus is on reducing losses associated with poor machine performance, unscheduled downtime, and defect reduction. These losses are defined as:

- *Breakdowns:* Loss associated with machine breakdown and unplanned stoppages

- *Setup and adjustment:* Loss associated with machine setups and adjustments resulting in machine downtime

- *Minor stoppages:* Loss associated with jamming, idle time, and downtime less than 10 minutes

- *Quality:* Loss associated with producing defective products

- *Speed:* Loss associated with equipment running at reduced operating speeds

- *Yield:* Raw material losses due to startup and poor machine performance (mold flash, burrs, etc.)

TPM is particularly useful in highly automated production environments in which machine effectiveness is paramount. TPM practitioners are sometimes referred to as TPM Experts and TPM Masters.

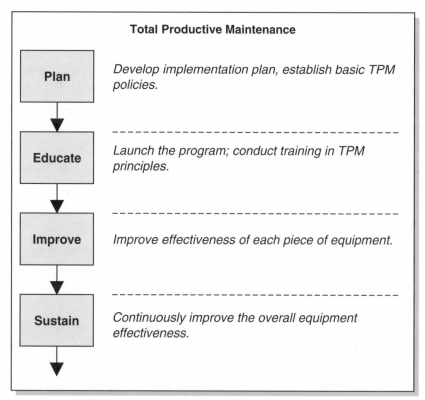

Figure 2.8   Total Productive Maintenance Steps

SIX SIGMA FOR SALES

Recently some organizations have developed tailored programs for sales and marketing based on either DMAIC or DMADV. In some instances, the approach uses simple tools such as process maps, cause and effect matrices, and failure mode effects analysis. Once the customer processes have been mapped, problems and opportunities to enhance value are studied. This allows sales people to gain a deeper understanding of customer processes and develops a solution selling culture within the organization. Such simple techniques can be very effective.

The DMAIC approach (discussed in greater depth in Chapter 5, page 141), used in some sale organizations, essentially looks for gaps between what the customer is expecting and what he is being given. It involves looking at the marketplace, developing an effective segmentation approach, and then focusing in on key segments. Key segments are analyzed for "root value drivers" (a similar notion to "root causes"). Key value drivers are then studied for gaps and improvements made to enhance the overall value to customers. This approach looks at improving existing products and services. A Design for Six Sigma approach (see chapter 6, page 163) is applicable when designing completely new offerings for customers or, as is discussed in detail later in this book, developing solutions to customer problems.

- *DMAIC for Growth*: Studies what customers value and looks for potential improvements in existing products and services to increase sales.

- *DMADV for Growth*: Profitably solves customer problems by developing new products and services or making major changes in existing offerings. This is often the basis of so called solution-selling approaches.

Typically, these are one-week training courses for Green Belts aimed at providing customer-facing people with tools that solve customer problems (solution selling) or improve sales force effectiveness.

Over the years, the Six Sigma tool set has expanded to meet the needs of the marketplace. This is a healthy situation, which is to be expected of any good improvement methodology. What is important is that organizations are receptive to changes in the marketplace and that they utilize the tools and methodologies that will help achieve their goals. In practice, this can require a combination of both approaches, depending on the specific organization or projects at hand.

SOLVING THE WRONG PROBLEMS

One valuable lesson Six Sigma has to offer is that *information* is more important than *data*. The basic principle behind statistical sampling techniques is to minimize the amount of data collected and maximize the information gained from it. To be effective, great care must be taken in collecting and interpreting data. In particular, selecting the right data for a Six Sigma project requires careful thought, to ensure that the correct opportunity is being analyzed and that the project is genuinely in line with the company's strategic goals. We need to be careful that we do not solve the wrong problem. In statistical terminology, finding the correct solution for the wrong problem is sometimes humorously referred to as a "type III" error. It is a remarkably common occurrence.

Consider a company that manufactures car seats. By conducting some Six Sigma projects, the company can reduce the costs associated with wasted fabric in the material-cutting process. Certainly, there are significant savings to be had from such an exercise, but as long as the focus is solely on reducing material waste, the Six Sigma project will have diminishing returns. Contrast this with a broader focus on car interiors and their alignment with market characteristics to encourage customers to choose their products over the competition. New breakthrough designs using new materials and processes will be largely ignored if the Cost of Poor Quality (COPQ) becomes the overriding goal for the business process. Business processes must account for both cost control and investment in capital to increase growth.

Taking another example, consider the metal flaps that you open when you fill your car with gasoline. Some car manufacturers have a variety of different shapes and sizes of flaps for different vehicles. Numerous costly metal stamping tools are needed to produce such a wide variety of these metal parts, as well as various fixtures for painting and large in-process and finished goods inventories.

Six Sigma projects could be initiated to help reduce metal stamping defects, reduce inventories, and streamline the supply chain. The fact is that very few customers actually care about the shape and size of these flaps. Focusing Six Sigma efforts on understanding what customers truly value would quickly lead to the variety of such parts being reduced, perhaps to a single standardized version which would result in huge cost savings.

The point is that the metrics you use to drive the Six Sigma efforts must be selected intelligently. In many instances, it is a false assumption that reducing costs and defects will invariably lead to top-line growth. Indeed, focusing solely on reducing costs can lead to commoditization of products and services, and drive the organization into a spiral of increasing competition and diminishing profits. Instead, it is often better to focus the Six Sigma efforts directly on higher-level metrics such as market share, margin, and top-line growth, or at developing new markets. If, during the course of the project, it is found that specific cost reduction actions are required, Six Sigma projects can be initiated, and the benefits of such initiatives can be linked to these metrics.

SUSTAINING SIX SIGMA

Most Fortune 500 companies now have various forms of Six Sigma initiative and are concerned with how to sustain them. It is not uncommon to hear accounts of Six Sigma programs that were successful for a while and then started to fall apart, or of pockets of success and failure within large organizations. Each organization has a unique environment, and it is difficult to develop a recipe for sustainability. Things that work in a centralized organization like General Electric simply won't work in more decentralized ones like Johnson & Johnson. Neither is better or worse, it is just that they are different.

The two key ingredients for sustainability are:

• A clear and urgent need for the initiative

• The initiative is supportive and aligned to the organization's strategic goals

Recently, the executive vice president of sales for a well-known company rolled his eyes when asked about Six Sigma in his sales organization and commented that "the Six Sigma folks are caught up in their own world." In essence, what was happening was that his firm's Six Sigma people had established the initiative purely as a cost-cutting tool. Six Sigma projects that generated revenue were unconsciously discouraged.

It may not be a wise tactic to ask busy sales people to reduce the time they spend selling in order to find ways to cut costs. It might generate savings in the early stages, but sooner or later Six Sigma will be put on the backburner, and the focus will return to the primary revenue-generating goals.

Six Sigma must help the sales organization achieve its goals. When Six Sigma efforts are aligned to the goals—in the previous example, focusing on projects that generate revenue—people naturally become excited and supportive. When the Six Sigma efforts are not aligned to the organization's goals, it quickly becomes a second priority or even a burden to the organization.

There are numerous reasons why an established Six Sigma initiative may not be aligned or delivering the type of results that would ensure sustainability. The following are just a few:

COMMITTED LEADERSHIP

W. Edwards Deming was one of the first to highlight that improvement in quality and competitive position cannot be delegated. It is senior leadership that creates and manages business systems, and it must lead change efforts. Lack of commitment was a problem back in the 1950s and still is today.

Committed leadership is critical to sustaining Six Sigma. Top management must support the effort and actively participate, not just give the occasional speech or token gesture. Such participation only comes when Six Sigma is, as mentioned, a means to achieve the organization's goals and not perceived as some unrelated activity that gets in the way of people's jobs.

POOR PROJECT SELECTION

Six Sigma teams must ensure that improvement projects are selected wisely to yield maximum results for the business. Companies that do not have a good approach to project selection often find it difficult to sustain the initiative. In some companies, Black Belts are left to select projects themselves, which can lead to their working on secondary issues or on projects that make no difference to the organization at all. In others, Six Sigma efforts are exclusively focused on the issues of the day and become very narrowly focused and reactive. When resources—Black Belts' time and effort—are focused on areas that make no difference to the business, it is natural for others to become skeptical about the initiative.

It is important to have an effective means of selecting projects and ensuring that there is a pipeline of critical projects to keep the initiative going. One of the best ways to ensure that a Six Sigma initiative stays on track is to manage proactive measures such as forecasted benefits from the project pipeline. Leadership's role is to identify and build the pipeline of projects that drive the efforts for the next 12 months. In large Six Sigma deployments across many business units and locations, pipeline management is critical. Periodic Six Sigma reviews with leadership should be focused on the size and nature of projected benefits, not on reactive issues of the day. This drives the correct behaviors and allows the initiative to be proactively managed.

MANAGEMENT MOBILITY

Job hopping by senior managers is common. It is a serious threat to the sustainability of a Six Sigma program. Typically, if the executive that was leading the initiative is transferred or quits, and the new leader is unfamiliar or uncomfortable with the past initiatives, even if they have been successful, the project is squashed.

There have been numerous cases when new leadership systematically undoes all the previous work, much to the bewilderment of the employees. This may be because the new leadership do not understand Six Sigma, or that they wish to put their own stamp on the program. This has become so much of an issue in one major blue chip Six Sigma company that it is now considering screening new leadership for their commitment to sustaining specific Six Sigma initiatives.

COMPLACENCY

Six Sigma initiatives are difficult. They require an organization to question itself fundamentally and to reinvent the way it has always done business. If a company has been very successful, it is natural to think that this success will continue and that such reinvention is unnecessary. In many ways, gaining commitment to change is easiest when times are bad and there is an urgent need. When times are good, people are less inclined to commit to such changes, even if there is a future threat.

FALSE STARTS

This occurs when managers switch initiatives according to the fad of the day. "False starts are deceptive. They give satisfaction, something new to show for effort, but they lead to frustration, despair, disappointment, and delay."[5] It is not uncommon to hear employees say things like "we tried this before and it didn't work" or "don't worry, this fad will be over in a few years when the boss finds a new thing." Although such comments are counterproductive to a Six Sigma initiative, they are in many instances grounded in truth.

It is important to consider such sustainability issues early on in the Six Sigma deployment. Anticipating such issues and taking proactive measures are even more necessary when Six Sigma initiatives are expanded to growth initiatives with customers.

BUREAUCRACY

Some Six Sigma programs are very bureaucratic, either because of bad initial design or because they have deteriorated over time. In one large company, the benefits realized from Six Sigma projects take weeks and even months to be calculated. The process involves many people, each of whom reviews the benefits and calculation methods. These are then discussed and reviewed again. The time it takes to calculate and verify the project benefits is longer than the project itself in some cases. This approach is very much an accounting perspective, trying to link projects to the company's accounting ledger. It would be more effective to assess benefits from a *financial* perspective, using ratios such as return on investment (ROI).

Another company had lengthy procedures for approving expenditures. Improvement teams needing to purchase goods found that they had to wait weeks to have selected vendors placed on the approved vendor list, to obtain three quotes, and to get approval signatures. Fortunately, the executives in this company acknowledged the problem and implemented a credit card system whereby employees could purchase up to $500 for improvement materials without prior approval. Subsequently, a Six Sigma team member purchased a $40 set of plastic containers to protect valuable aircraft engine turbine blades, resulting in a $38,000 reduction in material scrap.

Efforts must be made to make all processes value-added, fast, efficient, and reliable. Policies that benefit customers or comply with safety or government regulations should be adhered to, but many policies that are unproductive can be streamlined or removed completely.

CHAPTER 3

Six Sigma for Growth: Overview

The best Six Sigma projects begin not inside the business but outside of it, focused on answering the question: how can we make our customers more competitive? What is critical to our customers' success? ... One thing we have discovered with certainty is that anything we do that makes the customer more successful inevitably results in a financial return for us

—Jack Welch

To achieve profitable growth, some companies are exporting Six Sigma by embedding it into their customers' businesses, sometimes to solve customers' problems that are completely unrelated to the company's own offerings—as is sometimes the case with GE's At the Customer, For the Customer program.

This is a dramatic change from the classical Six Sigma approach. Placing Six Sigma resources externally to solve customers' problems, even if they are unrelated to your own products and services, calls into question the Six Sigma axiom that projects must tie directly to critical business metrics.

In some instances, projects may help customers but not deliver quantifiable results for the supplier's business—yet, in the view of Jack Welch, "one thing we have discovered with certainty is that anything we do that makes the customer more successful inevitably results in a financial return for us." For General Electric, this

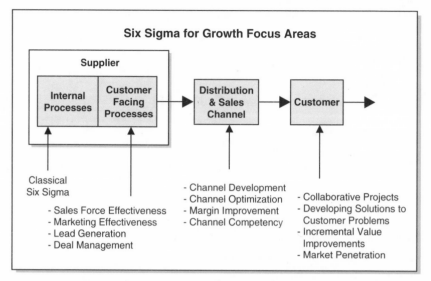

Figure 3.1   Six Sigma for Growth Focus Areas

approach is certainly paying off. Its aerospace group actively helps airlines improve their business performance and reduce their costs and inventories in order to make their businesses more competitive. The result is that GE differentiates itself in the marketplace and becomes a valued supplier to which the competition has huge challenges trying to match.

This approach may not be appropriate for everyone. It requires considerable resources that few organizations can afford. For companies with sufficient resources, however, it can be highly effective, provided that the right customers are selected and clear opportunities are identified (in the Discovery Phase, see pp. 87). Many of the world's leading companies are adopting a solution-selling approach to their key customers, which incorporates projects aimed at making customers successful.

Increasingly, organizations are using Six Sigma methodologies in the following areas (See Figure 3.1):

- *Customer-facing processes:* Sales force improvement and optimization, marketing effectiveness, lead generation, deal management and analyzing customer touch points—moments when you interact with customers—for improvement opportunities.

- *Sales and distribution channels:* Channel development and optimization, margin improvement, channel competency. Moving Six Sigma beyond the organization's boundaries to include the sales and distribution channels.

- *Joint ventures with the customer:* Collaborative projects, solution selling, market penetration projects. Working directly with customers on projects aimed at generating benefits for both parties.

Six Sigma for Growth, as envisaged in this book, originated as a tailored Six Sigma program for sales, marketing, and business development. Companies such as Motorola, Xerox, Honeywell, and General Electric were among the first to develop such programs, often as a result of persistent feedback that the standard Six Sigma training catered only to manufacturing and that transactional examples were not sufficient to bridge the gap.

Six Sigma methods apply equally to operational and transactional processes, but in many ways the critics were right. What was required was a Six Sigma approach that would be embraced by sales and marketing people and help them in their everyday work.

The expansion of Six Sigma from its traditional manufacturing base to other areas in the organization led to many joint Six Sigma projects between customers and suppliers. Many of these projects resulted in significant benefits for both parties and helped them develop stronger ties.

Collaborative efforts have opened up a vast spectrum of ways to profitably add value to customers. For example, GE Aircraft Engines (GEAE) moved from offering just its products—engines and spare parts—to providing customers with wing-to-wing maintenance of an aircraft. GEAE has excellent repair and overhaul facilities, but it found that there were many factors beyond its control that kept an aircraft grounded. In order to shorten such downtime, GEAE took over responsibility for the aircraft's engine maintenance from landing to takeoff, substantially improving the aircraft's uptime.

In pharmaceuticals, this approach has led many organizations to rethink their business from selling medicine to patient care—adding value to patients, doctors, and hospitals—throughout the entire treatment cycle. This has expanded companies' view of the market-place and has opened the way for sustained growth.

These companies have applied Six Sigma as a means to under-stand customers and their activities and to find ways in which to add value profitably, either by helping customers solve their prob-lems—the basic idea behind solution selling—or by improving and enhancing value in existing offerings. These two approaches are implemented by:

- D^2MAIC: Improving and optimizing value created with existing offerings (Discovery, Define, Measure, Analyze, Improve and Control)

- D^2MADV: Developing new offerings that profitably solve customer problems (Discovery, Define, Measure, Analyze, Design and Validate)

Many of the best projects help customers improve their business performance through innovative new offerings. Such offerings may be built around specific products or on peripheral customer activi-ties that surround the product. GEAE's wing-to-wing offering was not so much based on the actual product—engines—but on the hassles that customers face in maintaining them. The focus is on problems that result in significant losses—in this case, lost flying time— for which customers are willing to pay a premium to solve.

To identify opportunities to add value, Six Sigma practitioners must become experts in the customers' business and understand their issues and total economic picture. This is more than listening to the voice of the customer or the occasional customer survey. It involves becoming sophisticated about the customers' activities and internal processes. It requires firms to develop continuous com-munication channels and work collaboratively with customers on important issues. GE's At the Customer, For the Customer (ACFC) program is an excellent example of the use of Six Sigma methods to strengthen ties with customers and work toward mutual success.

THE TOTAL ECONOMIC PICTURE

Gaining a comprehensive understanding of the customer's business and total economics is a key concept in Six Sigma for Growth. By understanding customers' issues, problems, and expenditures, it is possible to develop new offerings that they value. Such offerings may be built on specific products and services or may help customers in completely new ways in unrelated peripheral activities and costs.

For many companies, business stops the moment a product reaches the customer. Once the product has been shipped, few companies take the extra step of understanding fully how the products are used by their customers.

The customer has to bear many costs associated with purchased products and services. Often, the purchase cost itself is a small part of the customer's total costs. For example, it has been estimated that 40% to 50% of all information technology spending is on maintaining existing systems. This has many IT companies focusing on developing new offerings in an effort to gain customer wallet share.

Figure 3.2 illustrates the potential scale of the issue where a customer has purchased a piece of equipment. There is a wide range of ongoing expenditure related to the customer's use of the product, from maintenance and repair to operator training. Energy costs or consumables may be major factors. In many cases, the customer may not consciously associate some of these costs directly with the use of the equipment. The aim is not only to address the customer's perception of costs but also to define the total economic picture in an effort to identify areas where the supplier can offer value-adding solutions. For example, can you, the supplier, offer the customer:

- A better financing deal on big-ticket items?

- A service and training package that includes guaranteed annual maximum downtime?

- A better distribution and delivery method?

- A better, more efficient procurement system?

- Added value in ways that distinguish the customer's offerings from the competition's?

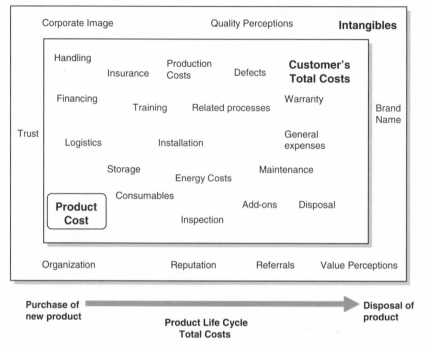

Figure 3.2   Customer's Total Economic Picture

Gaining a thorough understanding of the customer's business allows you to identify opportunities to improve the customer's total economics. In some instances, this can be done by working with customers, using Six Sigma methods such as core and peripheral activity mapping and brainstorming to generate a wide list of related customer costs and activities. Once the total economics have been detailed, it is possible to look systematically at each customer activity and analyze it for ways of expanding your offering and adding value.

Opportunities to add value through a new offering may be obvious and easy to implement. Such opportunities can quickly yield benefits for both parties. In other instances, the problem or cost identified may require considerable design effort. As the offering is likely to be new, or require a major change in an existing product or service, it is best to follow a rigorous Design for Six Sigma (DFSS) approach. The DFSS approach ensures that the new offerings will profitably meet the customer's requirement and be sustainable.

THE SIX SIGMA FOR GROWTH APPROACH

The Six Sigma for Growth approach presented in this book builds upon the traditional Six Sigma methods of DMAIC (Define, Measure, Analyze, Improve, and Control) and Design for Six Sigma, DMADV (Define, Measure, Analyze, Design, and Validate.)

The approach is to enhance value, either by improving existing offerings or by developing new ones, and making customers more competitive. Instead of focusing exclusively on requirements—a reactive approach—customers' processes are studied proactively for ways to add value. This may entail applying Six Sigma tools to understand the customer's internal processes and then systematically studying customer activity for opportunities to add value. For example, a customer may keep significant quantities of inventory, which could be reduced by a new logistics offering. Often, customers may not be aware of such opportunities and are unable to articulate their requirements. The onus is on the Six Sigma practitioners to uncover such opportunities.

Understanding the Customer's Total Economics

❖ How do our customers use our product & services?

❖ What are our customers' pain points?

❖ What are their total costs?

❖ Do they have quality problems?

❖ What hassles and problems do they face?

❖ What would make our customers more competitive?

❖ What business risks and challenges do our customers face?

❖ What non-value-added activities does our customer engage in?

❖ What is the future direction of our customers' business?

❖ Can I help my customer's core and peripheral activities?

Figure 3.3   Understanding the Customer's Total Economics

The first step in the Six Sigma for Growth approach, the Discovery Phase, aims to generate growth opportunities. These opportunities are identified, prioritized, and refined to become the basis of growth projects. The Discovery Phase works as a funnel, looking from a very high level to identify opportunities and gradually converting them into commercial offerings.

Often, significant growth opportunities can be found in the form of quick wins by applying simple Six Sigma tools such as:

- Mapping the customer's processes

- Studying the maps for cause-and-effect relationships that are critical to quality measures

- Looking for potential failure modes in the process

- Proposing a solution that improves the customer's processes

Some organizations that are using Six Sigma methods to drive growth ask their sales people to complete process maps of each of their key customers' businesses. These process maps are scrutinized by the growth teams for ways in which to add value profitably.

Growth projects aimed at working with customers or developing offerings to solve customer problems can be costly. It is wise to focus such Six Sigma for Growth efforts on market segments that are strategically important or that have good prospects for long-term growth. Several important additions to the traditional Six Sigma approach are required. These additions are concerned with identifying growth opportunities, managing collaborative projects with customers, and seeking ways to replicate solutions to other customers. In short, the focus is on offering development *and* commercialization. The first of the new additions is the Discovery Phase.

In the Discovery Phase, the team searches the marketplace for growth opportunities, assesses and prioritizes them, and then targets a select few. It is a rigorous project selection methodology that results in specific Six Sigma for Growth projects. The approach taken in the Discovery Phase is derived from the work of Peter Drucker and others whose innovation focus areas are useful to identifying growth opportunities.

The Funnel Effect

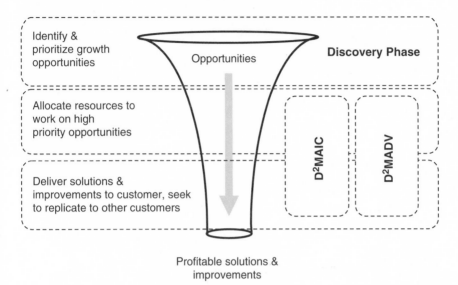

Profitable solutions &
improvements

Figure 3.4   Funnel Effect

The reason for the creation of a separate Discovery Phase is to augment the effort in opportunity identification and project selection. Many Six Sigma companies today have difficulty in selecting internal projects, let alone projects with customers. Things become more complex when you move beyond your organization's boundaries, so project selection becomes even more critical. Making substantial efforts to identify good projects pays off, increasing the success rate and optimizing the value added.

Figure 3.5 outlines the Six Sigma for Growth approach. Projects are identified in the Discovery Phase and then become the subject of improvement efforts through either a D²MAIC or a D²MADV approach depending on whether improvements are made to existing offerings or completely new offerings are required.

Other important additions include growth plans, quantifying the customers' total economics, opportunity identification matrices, and significant additions to the last step in the classical Six Sigma approaches. The final phase now emphasizes the search to replicate any solutions developed to other areas, or other customers.

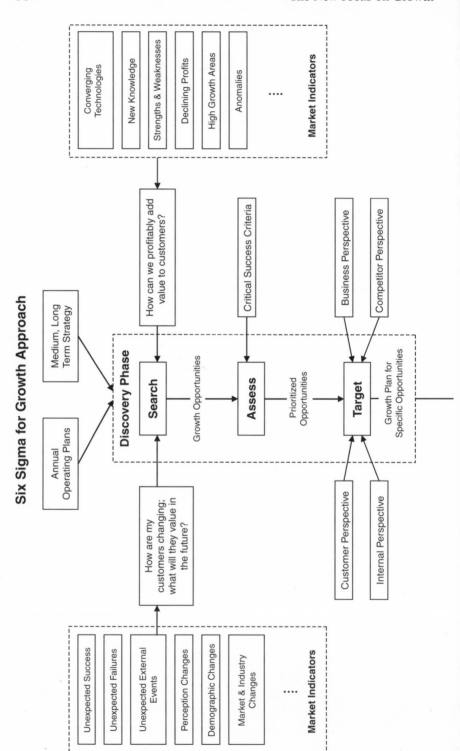

Six Sigma for Growth Approach

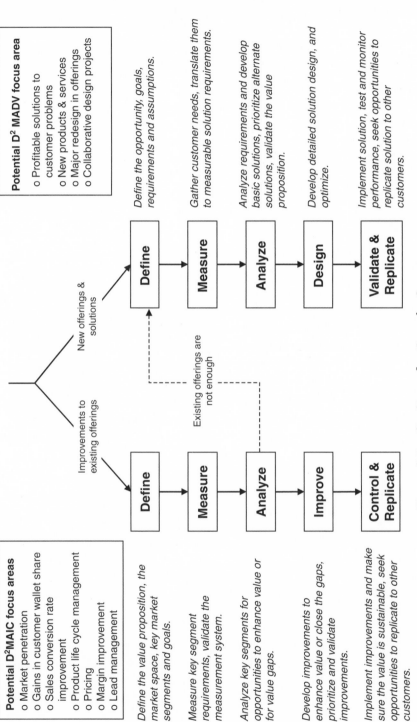

Potential D² MADV focus area
o Profitable solutions to customer problems
o New products & services
o Major redesign in offerings
o Collaborative design projects

Define the opportunity, goals, requirements and assumptions.

Gather customer needs, translate them to measurable solution requirements.

Analyze requirements and develop basic solutions, prioritize alternate solutions, validate the value proposition.

Develop detailed solution design, and optimize.

Implement solution, test and monitor performance, seek opportunities to replicate solution to other customers.

Define

Measure

Analyze

Design

Validate & Replicate

New offerings & solutions

Existing offerings are not enough

Improvements to existing offerings

Define

Measure

Analyze

Improve

Control & Replicate

Potential D²MAIC focus areas
o Market penetration
o Gains in customer wallet share
o Sales conversion rate improvement
o Product life cycle management
o Pricing
o Margin improvement
o Lead management

Define the value proposition, the market space, key market segments and goals.

Measure key segment requirements, validate the measurement system.

Analyze key segments for opportunities to enhance value or for value gaps.

Develop improvements to enhance value or close the gaps, prioritize and validate improvements.

Implement improvements and make sure the value is sustainable, seek opportunities to replicate to other customers.

Figure 3.5   Six Sigma for Growth: Overview

MAKING GROWTH PART OF THE CULTURE

Ultimately, all company employees should be attuned to the needs of the customer and the business. They must be empowered and equipped with the tools needed to implement improvements. The ideal is to achieve a growth-oriented culture in which everyone naturally looks for improvements in their areas to the point that improvement and day-to-day work are indistinguishable.

Achieving an all-pervasive culture of improvement is extraordinarily difficult. Furthermore, the marketplace is changing very quickly, and day-to-day improvements in limited areas are often not enough. When an organization finds, for example, that its customers are now looking for sales people to help understand problems and propose solutions—a radical change in the sales approach—it can be virtually impossible for the old sales organization to cope. One way to proceed is to create a completely separate sales team, equipped with Six Sigma tools, and have them lead the way.

The Six Sigma's organization of Master Black Belts, Black Belts, and Green Belts is now playing a vital role in many large companies. Its objective is to help corporations to reinvent themselves—a strategic change initiative—and to nurture and grow a culture for change. It is not simply a matter of assigning Black Belts to work on initiatives while the rest of the workforce remains unengaged. Many firms now maintain a full-time Six Sigma organization within the firm to train, oversee, and advise on any improvement activities, whether or not they are formally defined projects. The emphasis is on fostering cross-functional cooperation and value-adding behavior among all employees, providing them with the reinforcement they need to achieve valuable results.

Avoiding Suboptimization

There are numerous ways to create a Six Sigma management structure, depending on the size, business model, and strategic requirements of an organization. One approach is to place Black Belts within functional groups such as production, procurement, human resources, and sales and marketing, and have them report to functional leaders. For example, a Black Belt assigned to production would report to the head of production and would naturally focus on improvement opportunities within that particular function.

Improvements within a function, however, may not always translate to improvements to the organization as a whole or for its ultimate customers. It is possible for improvements within a specific function to be detrimental to the organization as a whole. For example, suppose that a procurement department reduces material costs by purchasing from the cheapest supplier. Although the material costs are reduced and procurement has achieved savings, if the materials are of lower quality, they may cause a higher rate of scrap and rework in production.

In such instances it is not uncommon for the total costs to the organization to increase. Another example would be the common practice of the sales department pushing finished goods to the marketplace at the end of each month (channel stuffing). Typically, at the end of the month finished goods are shipped to distributors or customers, whether they want them or not. This is done to achieve the month's revenue goals and usually leads to loss of margin and substantial increases in operating costs.

Improving one area to the detriment of the whole is sometimes referred to as suboptimization. In organizations that are arranged and managed in functional groups (sales, production, procurement, etc), very few people are able to see the business as a whole and suboptimization can occur very easily. As noted by W. Edwards Deming, "the obligation of any component is to contribute to the system, not to maximize its own production, profit, sales, nor any other competitive measure."[1]

To avoid suboptimization, Six Sigma projects should be selected so that they benefit both the company as a whole and the ultimate customers. It is possible for Black Belts within a specific function to work for the benefit of the company as a whole, but this demands a very comprehensive system to manage metrics and periodically assign goals to each function. Such systems require considerable effort to maintain and can become very bureaucratic.

Another approach is to view a business in the context of core processes that create products and services for the ultimate customer and to select projects that improve the overall performance of the process. As can be seen in Figure 3.6, there are two distinct ways to view an organization; by function or by core process.

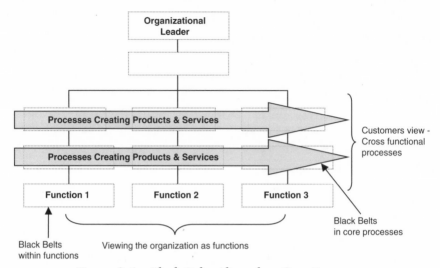

Figure 3.6   Black Belts Aligned to Core Processes

Creating a Six Sigma structure around functional groups can make managing large cross-functional projects very difficult. For example, it is not uncommon for each functional group to be given savings targets and to be held accountable for achieving them. With the often-obsessive push for savings, each function looks for its biggest opportunities and may refuse to work on larger cross-functional projects. Why would procurement choose suppliers of raw materials based on quality—reducing the overall costs to the organization —if its performance is judged solely by reducing purchasing costs? In many instances, reducing the total costs may require procurement to increase its material costs. There have been cases where Black Belts within functions have refused to work on important cross-functional projects because they were unable to show benefits for their own functional group. Organizing Six Sigma by function has sometimes led to such gross inefficiencies and lost opportunities. It is often more effective to assign Black Belts to cross-functional core processes.

Deploying a Six Sigma program around core processes usually leads to an organization chart like that in Figure 3.7. In this approach, Black Belts report directly to process owners and have an indirect reporting (a dotted line) to a Master Black Belt. Process

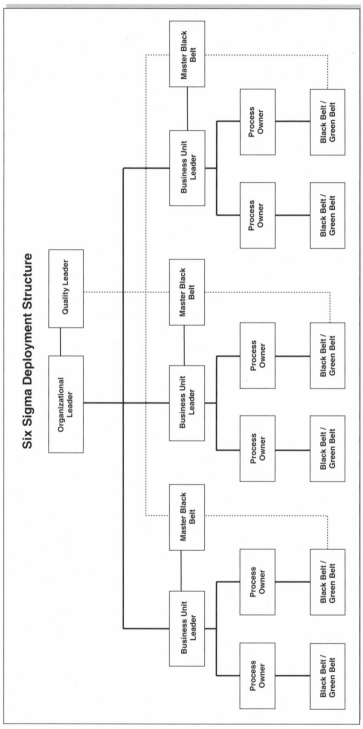

Figure 3.7 Typical Six Sigma Organization Structure

owners are selected from the management team and have ownership over critical business processes.

Many companies are currently trying to create organizational structures based on such core and supporting processes. Few have managed to do this effectively, chiefly because they have not identified the core processes clearly and because of the difficulties associated with cross-functional management. It is essential to identify such processes during the initial Six Sigma deployment. Once the core processes have been identified, process owners can then be called upon to support Six Sigma activities.

GROWTH DEPLOYMENT STRUCTURE

To focus Six Sigma on profitable growth, the organization must be aligned with the marketplace. One approach is to segment the marketplace by strategic and growth potential and then to create Segment Master Black Belts (Figure 3.8). In this instance, the Six Sigma structure remains cross-functional. The development of new offerings must be managed by the Six Sigma teams with the support of various functions. Identifying a growth opportunity is only half the battle. For commercial success, efforts from several different functional groups need to be co-ordinated.

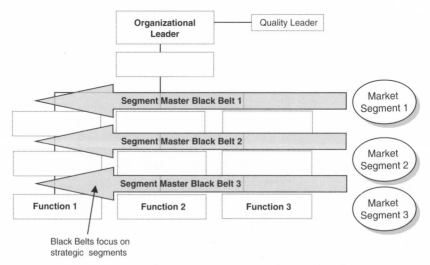

Figure 3.8   Aligning Six Sigma to the Marketplace

When Six Sigma management structure is aligned to market segments, there are several key roles:

QUALITY LEADER

The Quality Leader oversees Six Sigma efforts for the whole organization or, in some cases, a specific market segment. The Quality Leader is primarily responsible for the strategic aspects of the Six Sigma effort and advises the executive team on project selection and resource allocation. Quality Leaders are usually seasoned Six Sigma practitioners and may handle large cross-regional projects. Their role is to:

- Advise senior executives on Six Sigma strategies

- Oversee the Six Sigma program for an organization or key market segments

- Be the most senior point of contact for customers regarding collaborative Six Sigma efforts

- Develop project selection criteria

PROJECT SPONSOR OR CHAMPION

The Project Sponsor is an executive who has a vested interest in the project and the authority to ensure the project team is successful. The Project Sponsor's role is to act as an advocate of the project, removing barriers and providing financial and organizational support:

- Initiates the project

- Sets project goals and keeps the project on track

- Allocates resources

- Provides direction and removes barriers

- Reviews the team's progress

- Holds the team accountable for the project results

MASTER BLACK BELTS

Master Black Belts (MBBs) focus on specific market segments and oversee cross-functional projects. The development of new products or services typically requires the involvement of different functional groups. Master Black Belts can report directly to the Six Sigma Director or, more often, to the vice president overseeing all operations for the region. In the latter case, the MBB is "dotted line" to the Six Sigma Director. Ideally, the MBB is selected for his Six Sigma expertise and knowledge of the segment in question. The role of the MBBs is to:

- Lead internal and customer projects and coach multiple Black Belts

- Supply technical expertise in Six Sigma methods

- Have extensive knowledge of target market segments

- Provide guidance in project selection

- Formulate Six Sigma strategies for senior management

- Conduct Six Sigma training for Black Belts, Green Belts, and executives

- Develop a Six Sigma community and share best practices among different groups

BLACK BELTS

Black Belts (BBs) are full-time Six Sigma personnel who work on projects in a specific segment.

Some companies have difficulty in justifying the cost of full-time BBs. This is usually due to:

- *Poor project selection.* Careful selection is central to a project's success, yet some firms take a haphazard approach. The investment of full-time BBs in working on projects that are crucial to the business is likely to be amply rewarded by better returns in the long run.

• *A misalignment of the effort with the organizational goals.* For example, it is a clear misalignment to ask a sales person to lead a project aimed at cutting costs and judge his performance by increased revenue.

Ideally, the BB reports to the Master Black Belt or to a leader with cross-functional responsibility. If Black Belts report to a functional leader, they will tend to be assigned to projects that are significant only to that particular function. This is fine if the function in question has projects that will yield significant returns, but often the most important projects are cross-functional. Asking a functional BB to handle a cross-functional project can lead to sustainability issues.

The BB's role is to:

• Lead growth projects on a full-time basis

• Be trained and experienced in Six Sigma methods

• Work comfortably in a customer environment

• Train and mentor Green Belts

• Schedule and lead project meetings

• Oversee data collection and analysis

• Track and report project progress to leadership

• Calculate project benefits

GREEN BELTS

Green Belts (GBs) work on Six Sigma projects on a part-time basis within a functional group. A good rule of thumb is that they should spend approximately 20% of their time on projects. On joint projects, teams typically comprise internal and customer Green Belts. Once again, good project selection is vital, and it is advisable to assign GBs to projects that are aligned to their primary responsibility.

Many Six Sigma companies now insist that all managers participate in a Green Belt project. This is an excellent way of raising awareness of the Six Sigma program, provided there is a pipeline of projects that can yield significant results. Care needs to be taken to ensure that each Green Belt has projects, or else conducting wholesale training of management in Six Sigma methods can actually have a negative effect. Without practical experience on projects, training may be viewed more as an exercise that gets in the way of "real work."

A GB:

- Is trained in Six Sigma methods

- Spends at least 20% of time on projects

- Participates in team meetings and action items

- Collects data and assist in analysis

- Implements improvements

PROCESS OWNERS

Process Owners (POs) are senior managers who oversee core business processes. In the case of collaborative projects, Process Owners may be from the company itself or from a customer. They support the project by communicating the Six Sigma vision, obtaining approval for any process changes, and ensuring that any improvements are implemented and sustained.

POs:

- Provide resources for improvement projects

- Select team members

- Remove barriers and obtain approvals for improvement actions

- Ensure improvements are implemented and sustained

BREAKING DOWN THE SILOS
BETWEEN ORGANIZATIONS

One of the powerful principles of Six Sigma is that the business should be seen through the eyes of the customer. This creates a process view that cuts across the functional silos in an organization (see Figure 3.6). This has resulted in dramatic improvements in productivity and quality because more often than not improvement opportunities appear not *within* a particular function but *between* them. That is, the interface or boundary between each functional silo was ineffective and inefficient—the right hand didn't know what the left hand was doing. Engineering designed products that it felt were great only to find that manufacturing was unable to produce them. Procurement selected suppliers at the lowest cost only to find that poor materials created huge downstream quality problems. By looking at the organization as a set of cross-functional processes, the silos work together more efficiently. The result is huge productivity gains that are unimaginable inside any individual silo.

The recent emphasis on bringing Six Sigma to the customer through collaborative projects and initiatives has brought to light another area where huge gains in productivity can be found. In addition to cutting across functional silos, radical improvements can be had by cutting across *organizational silos*. Just as inefficiencies exist at the interface or boundaries between internal functions, so too inefficiencies exist at the interface between organizations. Working collaboratively with customers on issues that are important to both organizations cuts across these organizational silos and can result in huge gains, which the individual companies could not have achieved themselves.

What exactly do these external opportunities look like? Perhaps not surprisingly, they are similar to the inefficiencies that exist internally. Here are a few typical examples:

1. *Inventory and logistics waste.* Often, both organizations have duplicate inventories, warehousing, logistics and distribution processes. Collaborative efforts (see page 175 for case study) can reduce duplication, streamline processes, and reduce overall costs. Many logistics companies now, for example, partner with their customers and not only handle all of the logistics operations, inventory management, and warehousing but often perform other value-added services such as local packing and assembly. This creates a win-win relationship in which both organizations achieve gains.

2. *Communication and transactional processes.* It can take months for paperwork such as purchase orders to flow from one organization to another. Honeywell found for example that, by streamlining the

way it worked with some airlines customers, it was able to slash the time and costs associated with generating and approving such purchase orders. The result was gains for both the airlines and Honeywell.

3. *Design and development.* As was the case with internal design silos, customers today often design new products and services independently only to find out later that suppliers are unable to produce them. This creates huge waste in the form of redesign efforts and lost time. Intel and Applied Material avoid this by working together and concurrently developing the chips and the machines that will manufacture them. This reduces costs for both companies and yields competitive gains for both.

4. *Leveraging competence.* Organizations frequently have duplicate research and design efforts. Huge cost reductions can be had by optimizing such R&D spending across organizations. Johnson Controls was able to provide its automotive customers superior value by leveraging its core competency of car interior research and design. This allowed the automakers to outsource the car interior R&D—reducing their costs significantly—and allowed them to focus on producing cars.

Working with customers and breaking down organizational silos is not a new concept. What is new is that as business and the marketplace are changing, the ways in which companies can work together are proliferating. Organizations work together in ways that would have been unimaginable 10 years ago. To identify and capitalize on these opportunities, organizations must actively work to break down silos and develop much closer customer-supplier relationships.

For Six Sigma companies, it means that performance gains must be sought with the customers, across the organizational boundaries and not just internally. Instead of focusing projects exclusively on internal improvements, organizations must work together, through mutual change to achieve even greater levels of performance.

Working with customers in such close collaboration is not without a potential downside. Such partnerships can and have gone wrong. Six Sigma projects should be carefully selected (as outlined in the Discovery Phase—Growth Plan p. 119) so that they yield benefits for both organizations and risks are identified and mitigated.

In addition to the external risks associated with collaborative efforts, there are also internal risks. Who creates the process by which organizations work together? Who will take responsibility to ensure collaborative efforts work and are sustainable? Who will cut across the internal functional silos and the external ones? Six Sigma teams, Black Belts, and Master Black Belts have filled this role internally and can be called upon to do the same externally (depicted in Figure 3.8) across organizational silos.

TRAINING CUSTOMERS AND SUPPLIERS IN SIX SIGMA

Joint Six Sigma initiatives between customers and suppliers are now common. Many Six Sigma companies require suppliers to undergo Six Sigma training and to work on joint projects. Some sales organizations are looking to extend their Six Sigma programs to their sales channel partners and the ultimate users of products. This sets the ground for collaborative projects along the entire sales channel, which can lead to improvements in the competitive position of the entire value chain.

Expanding Six Sigma beyond the organization's boundaries can increase the costs of the initiative substantially. Travel and hotel costs alone can become prohibitively expensive. It is possible to lower these costs by having larger class sizes, but this usually results in extended periods between classes. It is not reasonable to ask a customer or distribution channel partner to pay thousands of dollars and have them wait months between classroom training sessions. It is important to keep such costs down, for example by using:

- eLearning tools
- Web-based project tracking tools

eLEARNING

When effectively combined with classroom training, eLearning offers an excellent way to train partners and customers and reduce overall costs. It allows anyone to undergo training at any time, from any location with an Internet connection. The costs of such systems have dropped significantly, and the quality can be excellent. Many systems have comprehensive learning management tools that can track students' understanding of the material online and recommend areas where they need extra tuition.

As well as controlling costs, an important benefit of such systems is that they decrease the time spent teaching and increase mentoring and coaching time. Often, training modules are self-explanatory and what students need is one-on-one guidance on how to apply the tools to their particular projects.

PROJECT TRACKING

Tools are very useful for tracking and monitoring projects across organizational boundaries. Such web-based tools allow ease of access to project information such as savings and revenue forecasts, project milestones, and overall status. Some also have the functionality—useful for large organizations—of tracking a pipeline of projects and potential gains.

SIX SIGMA READINESS ASSESSMENT

Sustainability issues are even more important if the Six Sigma initiative is expanded to encompass customers or partners in a distribution channel. It is not advisable to set customer expectations with the promise of joint Six Sigma projects and then fail to deliver on them. For major joint Six Sigma initiatives, it is best to conduct a readiness assessment of the partner or customer prior to any substantial commitments.

The readiness assessment detailed in the Appendix is a useful tool for gauging an organization's readiness to adopt a Six Sigma initiative. Depending on the nature of the Six Sigma initiative—a one-off project or a full deployment—the assessment can be used in whole or in part to understand whether an organization meets certain key requirements that help ensure success.

This assessment assumes that the organization in question is new to Six Sigma. If the collaborative effort is between companies with existing Six Sigma programs, a slightly different assessment is required.

This assessment looks at the current effectiveness of the Six Sigma program and addresses any gaps that may exist. One organization may assume, for instance, that Black Belts are full-time, and the other may not. Clarifying such differences from the outset helps ensure teams work smoothly together.

The assessment is divided into the following sections:

- *Process management.* Do they have clearly defined processes and a management system around them?

- *Customers and commitment.* How well do they know their customers' requirements? Is there a compelling need for change, and are they committed to change?

- *Employee focus.* Are employees willing to accept and participate in improvements?

- *Improvement approach.* Is there any existing approach to improvement, how successful has it been?

- *Accountability and incentives.* Are there clear accountability and incentive systems?

- *Measures and data.* Does the organization have effective data collection systems in place? Are decisions data driven?

- *Collaboration and resources.* Are they willing to collaborate and, if necessary, share internal information and intellectual property? Will they commit resources to the initiative?

The assessment is conducted, and a score issued for each of the above sections. Typically, the minimum points required are decided prior to customer engagements by the Six Sigma leadership team. The total points are tallied and compared with the minimum required number. Such assessments help to mitigate the risk of joint Six Sigma projects by raising important issues early on.

Six Sigma is changing from its traditional focus on internal bottom-line metrics and is now driving business growth. In Part One of this book we examined how this change is being led by several pioneering companies that are banking on Six Sigma to sustain growth.

In Part Two, an approach is outlined for helping companies with existing Six Sigma programs refocus them on top-line growth. Six Sigma for Growth methodologies and selected tools are examined in more detail, starting with a discussion of the newly introduced step, the Discovery Phase, which is designed to ensure that the best opportunities are identified and selected as growth projects.

PART II

The Growth Tool Set

CHAPTER 4

The Discovery Phase

*The customer rarely buys what the company thinks
it sells.*
                                    —Peter Drucker

INTRODUCTION TO DISCOVERY

Six Sigma for Growth introduces a new initial step, the Discovery
Phase, which begins with a broad and methodical search for growth
opportunities, proceeds through a rigorous assessment process, and
finally targets selected opportunities for development as Six Sigma
projects.

The Discovery Phase is a market-sensing process that takes a hard
look at the marketplace—existing, lost, and potential market segments—to find growth opportunities. These opportunities may be
enhancements to existing products and services, or completely new
offerings. Market sensing is a continuous activity if it is to remain up
to date, and uses information from a broad range of sources, some
of which are outlined in this chapter.

This phase has been introduced into the classical Six Sigma
approach to solve the problems many companies face in selecting
projects. It has developed from the introduction of a separate project
selection step by several leading Six Sigma organizations. Typically,
this separate step is called a "Recognize" or "Identify" phase (for
example, RDMAIC—Recognize, Define, Measure, Analyze, Improve
and Control).

Companies developed a more rigorous approach to project selection out of necessity. Selecting the wrong projects wastes time, effort, and resources. In the long term, consistently poor selection can turn an effective Six Sigma initiative into a burden to the company. One large automotive component supplier had full-time Black Belts working on reducing stationery costs—clearly a secondary issue—when it was in desperate need of revenue-generating projects. How did this happen? The Black Belts were given instructions to select projects that would reduce costs, and they acted accordingly. Every organization has problems and areas where costs can be reduced; the challenge is to focus on those that are most important to the business. If projects are not aligned to the organization's top priorities, its short-term annual operating plans, and longer-term strategy, they may be difficult to sustain. The need for a rigorous approach to project selection is especially important in projects with customers and projects that directly affect customer value propositions.

The Discovery Phase addresses these issues by a rigorous approach to project selection that proceeds in the context of the company's short-, medium-, and long-term strategies. The organization's leaders must actively participate in the Discovery Phase. It is they who see the organization as a whole and understand its greatest challenges. It is their responsibility to ensure that Six Sigma resources are focused on the most important issues of the business.

In essence, the search for growth opportunities that will form the basis of Six Sigma projects rests on studying the marketplace and asking the following questions:

• How can we profitably add value to our customers?

• How are our customers changing?

• What will they value in the future?

The term "customers" is used here in the broadest sense of the word and refers to any group that would value the offering. It is important not to focus exclusively on existing customers and wherever possible to expand the market view to include potential and lost customers as well.

HOW CAN WE PROFITABLY ADD VALUE
TO OUR CUSTOMERS?

Even in today's climate of customer-centric business, there are still companies in a wide range of industries that have no idea who their customers are. It is not uncommon to hear of situations where, for example, products are delivered to the end users through complex distribution channels, and the manufacturer never really has close contact with its ultimate customers. Or perhaps a product is in such demand that customers come to the manufacturer, and the primary concern is to get products out the door. This is typical of high-growth periods in an industry.

Many companies that were habituated to high demand are now struggling to move from a product-centric to a customer-centric business approach and are in the throes of trying to create new value-added products and services that extend far beyond existing offerings.

Closely analyzing how customers use your products through techniques such as process observation and expanded market mapping can often reveal opportunities to add value. These opportunities may lie in the product and service itself or the issues and customer pain points that surround the offering. A deep understanding of customers' businesses and their total economics can be achieved through collaborative projects and partnerships, information from customer-facing groups such as sales and marketing, or, in the case of General Electric's At the Customer, For the Customer (ACFC) program, Black Belts working for extended periods with the customer. Some pharmaceutical companies gain such information through Green Belts who interact with customers (patients and health care workers) and develop process maps that identify customers' activities at each stage of the treatment cycle. These maps, which detail costs, unmet needs, and problem areas are studied for opportunities to add value.

HOW ARE MY CUSTOMERS CHANGING; WHAT WILL
THEY VALUE IN THE FUTURE?

Change brings opportunity. It is at the root of creating new products and services and is fundamental to innovation. Assessing changes must be part of a deliberate process that can convert them into concepts for new products, services, customers, and/or markets.

This assessment of future directions separates Six Sigma for Growth from the traditional Six Sigma approach. Traditionally, the aim of Six Sigma was primarily to meet customer requirements, reduce defects, and deliver more consistent products and services. We certainly do not want to have dissatisfied customers, but even satisfied customers will switch to a competitor when innovative new products and services are offered. For example, the manufacturers of vacuum tubes had happy loyal customers. Each year, they worked to improve vacuum tubes, making them smaller and smaller. When William Shockley and others from Bell Telephone Laboratories developed the integrated circuit, hitherto happy and loyal customers deserted the vacuum tube and ran for the pocket radio. Simply meeting customers' requirements is only half the story—it is also necessary to innovate, predict the needs of the customers, and give them more.

Careful detective work must be done to gain an understanding of the future direction of customers and the marketplace. Such information comes from multiple sources, including different levels in the customer's organization. In some instances it is possible to predict future trends quite accurately, but in others "the best way to predict the future is to invent it."

One way to invent the future is to study each activity in the customer's processes and scrutinize it for ways to introduce possible changes. What will each activity look like in five years? Will it still be required? Will it become more important? How can we shape the future of the business?

DISCOVERY PHASE OVERVIEW

The Discovery Phase starts by obtaining a clear understanding of the company's medium and long-term strategic plans (typically two to five years) as well as its short-term annual operating plans (what needs to be achieved this year). These plans answer the questions "what do we need to achieve this year? What areas are important to our future business?" They provide the overall direction for the Discovery Phase, which proceeds in three steps: Search, Assess, and Target (see Figure 4.1).

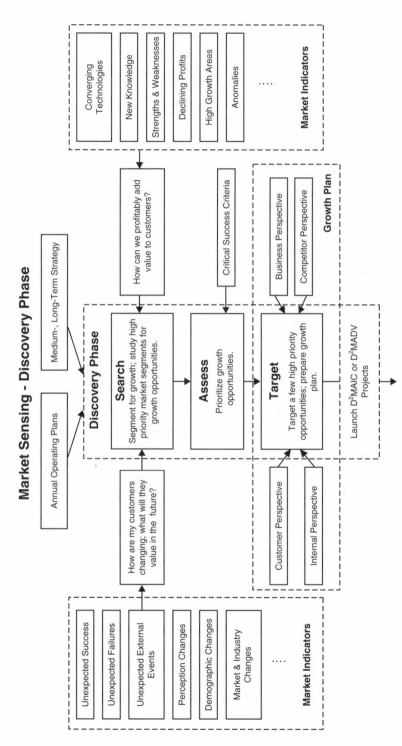

Figure 4.1 Discovery Phase Overview

SEARCH THE MARKETPLACE

The Search step selects growth market segments, the high-growth areas that are strategically important to the company. These segments are studied for growth opportunities. This may involve looking at the account plans of key customers, listening to the voice of the customer, or engaging directly with customers to identify issues they care most about.

Six Sigma for Growth focuses on key strategic market areas because of the high financial cost of development. Whether you are extending a Six Sigma initiative to the marketplace, developing solutions to customers' problems, or creating completely new offerings, the process is likely to require substantial investment. The Discovery Phase aims to select focus areas carefully to maximize the returns.

Opportunities are considered in the context of market segments wherever possible. This is to avoid the danger of developing customized offerings for specific customers, only to find later that they are not valued by the larger market.

To aid the search for growth opportunities, several systematic innovation techniques have been added to the classical Six Sigma approach. These approaches based on the work of Peter Drucker and Genrich Altshuller have been successfully utilized in numerous industries over the years, but are new additions to the Six Sigma tool kit.

The Search step creates and maintains a long list of opportunities in key growth segments. As with brainstorming, the quantity of ideas, at this stage, is more important than the quality of ideas.

With any good Six Sigma program, a pipeline of potential projects needs to be built and maintained by senior managers. Proactively managing the project pipeline makes it easier to allocate resources effectively, identify crucial focus areas, and sustain projects over the long term. A strong focus on the forecast benefits from a pipeline of projects keeps long-term goals in sight and motivates teams.

ASSESS GROWTH OPPORTUNITIES

The next step focuses on the quality of the opportunities and ideas that have been generated in the Search step. The Assess step develops selection criteria and uses them to rate each opportunity.

The result is a list of growth opportunities that have been prioritized against the organization's critical success measures.

Leadership sets the direction of the Six Sigma initiative by developing selection criteria and mandating that all projects must be prioritized against these criteria. If, for example, customer satisfaction is a top priority for the organization, it will be given a greater bias in the project selection criteria.

TARGET HIGH-IMPACT OPPORTUNITIES

A few high-priority opportunities are selected as Six Sigma for Growth projects. In the Target step, the team looks carefully at each of these and builds a Growth Plan that will guide the project through the development processes.

The Growth Plan describes the project from a customer perspective, a business perspective, an internal perspective, and a competitive perspective. Growth plans are updated during the course of the project and are reviewed by the leadership team at each project (tollgate) review.

Search the Marketplace

Segment for growth; study high-priority market segments for growth opportunities.

The Search step is a purposeful, systematic analysis of the marketplace, aimed at generating a large volume of growth opportunities. As discussed in the previous section, the Search step aims to provide detailed answers to the essential questions:

• How can we profitably add value to our customers?

• How are our customers changing?

• What will they value in the future?

The search for growth opportunities depends heavily on knowing your customers, their issues, and their future directions. Traditional market research and other reactive customer survey methods are often insufficient. Such methods are important, but they are discrete in nature and often fail to capture the customer's true situation.

Six Sigma for Growth aims to develop continuous communication channels with key customers wherever possible and to see customer problems through the customers' eyes. It is by learning about your customers' problems and unmet needs and becoming an expert in the customers' business that you are able to provide services and solutions that they value.

The search begins by analyzing the market for high-priority segments: those areas in the market that are important to the future direction of the company. These segments may comprise of existing, lost, or potential customers, and are studied in depth to identify specific growth opportunities. Such opportunities may lie with current products and services or in completely new areas.

As mentioned earlier, offerings with wide appeal and that are easy to replicate are the most likely to achieve high-profit growth. For this reason, the search for growth opportunities starts by identifying important market segments first, rather than searching for customer-specific opportunities. Looking at segments helps teams to develop offerings with a much wider market appeal that can be replicated to multiple customers.

There are numerous techniques for identifying growth opportunities, such as the structured innovation methods pioneered by Peter Drucker (see page 183). In the following sections, we examine typical strategies taken by Six Sigma companies to identify and prioritize market segments.

CURRENT MARKET ANALYSIS

More and more companies are becoming selective about the customers they want to serve. Firms now realize that market share and volume growth are not always the best indicator of a company's health. In fact, having a large share of an unprofitable market can quickly put you out of business. This may seem obvious, but is often overlooked in the heat of day-to-day operations. Markets can change very rapidly. A profitable product or service may suddenly become commoditized and loss-making. Companies need to remain vigilant for such changes and to respond by focusing efforts in areas that will deliver profitable growth.

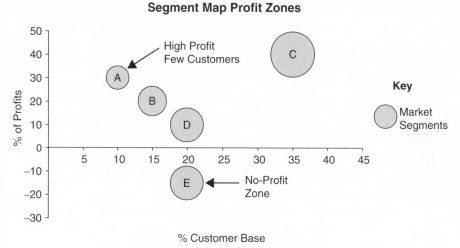

Figure 4.2   Market Segment Map

An examination of the customer base usually reveals wide variation in the profitability of specific segments. Typically, a small portion of the customer volume contributes a large percentage of profit (customer group A in Figure 4.2). These customers are precious gems, which must be constantly looked after to ensure continued business and to protect them against the advances from the competition. Other groups of customers may create losses for a company (customer group E). Such groups are usually customers for histori-cal reasons or have some future potential for profit. Without such potential, it may be best to change business terms with them or in the worst case cut business ties with them altogether.

Customer Groups B, C, and D contribute to the bulk of the com-pany's profit, and relationships with them need to be maintained and wherever possible enhanced. Customer group D's profit, how-ever, is relatively small and changes in margins could quickly move them into a no-profit zone.

The reason for analyzing the existing customer base for growth opportunities is that it is much easier to sell to an existing customer than to a new one. Existing customers are more likely to work col-laboratively on issues, and quick-win growth opportunities can often be found.

No-Profit Zones

No-profit zones are business activities that have become essentially unprofitable. This is often due to competition effects or changes in the power structure within an industry.

For example, long-term trends in food retailing have resulted in a major shift of power away from manufacturers and their brands to the major retailers themselves. Using a variety of techniques, including own-brand marketing, leading retailers are now in a position to squeeze manufacturers' profits severely without risking damage to the overall supply of goods.

Commoditization and overcapacity are obvious drivers of no-profit zones, yet their effects vary across industries. For instance, in the PC industry, it is the wholesalers who suffer most from wafer-thin margins. Rapidly changing customer values are constantly destroying markets and creating new ones, making it difficult for smaller players to stay profitable.

Sales growth and gains in market share are not, and have never been, synonymous with profitability—a fact that can easily be forgotten in planning an offering. It is easy in a business plan to paint an optimistic picture of markets and their economics, based on a shallow analysis of their real dynamics. For this reason, it is essential that the discussion of the markets in the plan be realistic and that it has been rigorously checked and tested by the proposers. Numerical figures can be wrong, and there is an abundance of inaccurate—often overoptimistic—data available for many industries. An over-reliance on figures, without fully understanding the forces that they represent, can lead to poor decisions. There is always uncertainty, especially in extrapolating from emerging trends, so it is essential that the project team be clear about what can and cannot be known about the markets under discussion.

Mapping customer segments against profit is one method used to look at the current market and to target key areas. If profits are already healthy and likely to remain so, the same approach can be used to map customers and revenue to target revenue-generating segments.

Tools such as the segment map are an excellent way to gain an understanding of the current status of the customer base. They can be constructed in various ways, including looking at product and service groups instead of customers.

FOCUSING SIX SIGMA ON KEY MARKET SEGMENTS

Six Sigma for Growth initiatives should be focused on high-priority market segments or on up-and-coming segments with growth potential. Wherever possible, segment maps should be constructed of the entire market (including current, lost, and potential customers). This requires a company to look at the entire marketplace to understand both the current *and* future shape of the business.

Current State Segment Maps. These describe current market segments in relation to the profits or revenue generated. They help identify segments that are in no-profit zones as well as segments that generate the bulk of a company's profits. Very profitable segments can be chosen as candidates for Six Sigma for Growth projects aimed at building closer ties with these customers and looking for ways to further enhance strategic positions, thereby keeping the competition at bay. Other segments in no-profit zones should be the focus of margin-enhancement projects or new offering development to move them back to profitability.

Future State Segment Maps. It is important not to just look at what the market is today but question what it will be tomorrow. Future states are typically explored by understanding trends in the marketplace and by the strategic direction of the company. There may be, for example, a trend in a particular industry to move away from product selling toward solution selling. Or the trend may be away from purchasing products toward leasing and pay-for-use, for example, charging hourly usage rates for aircraft engines. Such trends, combined with the organization's strategy, are used to develop maps that reflect future changes in offerings, customer segments, and profits.

Figure 4.3 illustrates situations that a Current and Future Segment Map may generate. In it, new offerings are being developed specifically for customer segment E. These new offerings are aimed at improving profit margins and moving this segment out of a no-profit zone (to E'). Six Sigma for Growth projects could be launched to develop and test these new offerings with a few select customers before introducing them to the whole market.

Customer segment C in the figure is faced with reducing profits and an increasing customer base. This may be because of an industry trend that products are becoming commoditized. Unless there are

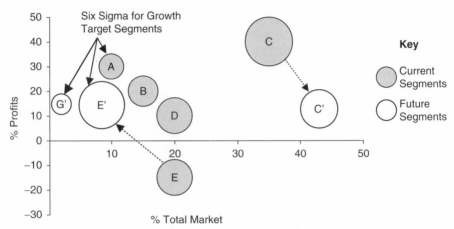

Figure 4.3   Current and Future Segment Map

clear opportunities to improve falling profits, Six Sigma efforts may be better applied elsewhere.

Suppose that a completely new offering can be developed for a small but highly profitable customer base. New customer segments such as G' can be very fruitful ground for such Six Sigma initiatives. They should be examined carefully and every effort made to capture this new segment.

MARKET SEGMENT MATRIX

Another useful method of looking at market segments, both current and potential, is to construct a segment matrix that compares the strategic importance of a particular segment with its growth potential.

Market segments that have the highest growth potential and are strategically important are targeted first.

SEGMENTING FOR GROWTH

One technique employed by companies such as Coca Cola, General Electric, and Gillette to help drive growth is to expand their view of the market. They view their business as only a small portion of the total market by including customers' related purchases, suppliers'

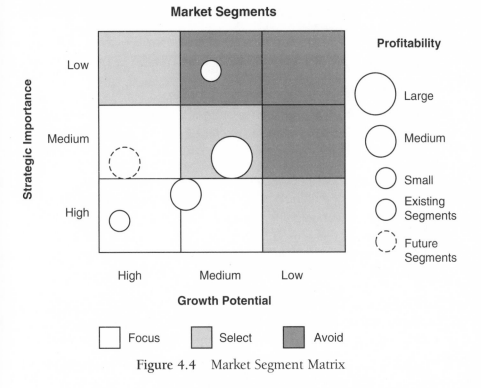

Figure 4.4   Market Segment Matrix

and competitors' businesses. The organization then challenges teams to find ways to gain market share.

This approach is very effective. Traditional ways of segmenting a market tend to be overly narrow and fail to identify the true potential for growth. Many growth opportunities emerge if we expand our conception of our overall market and define new segments within this expanded arena. For instance, instead of defining market share as, say, 40% of U.S. truck engines; it is more stimulating to see it as 3% of the global market for diesel engines. Or a manufacturer that controls 50% of the aircraft engines market in the United States may define its business as 1% of the global aerospace market.

The expanded definition of the market does not necessarily have to be geographical; it can be expanded into related businesses or into a broader class of business activity, including customers' related purchases, such as from shaving foam to male grooming products in general.

Once the expanded market has been broadly defined, it can be analyzed as follows:

- Provisionally identify segments in the expanded markets by looking at the customer's needs, values or behaviors.

- List all the products and services that could possibly be related to a customer's use of your core offering, and organize them into categories.

- Filter the newly defined segments by looking at how your company might be able to add value in these areas. For example, many products can be differentiated through packaging and other relatively minor changes: a luxury food item can be a seasonal Christmas item for one segment and a regular weekly purchase for another, with an entirely different image and price point.

- Estimate the total potential revenue and profit margins for each segment. It may emerge that you do not have adequate data on some of these segments. Plan how you will obtain this information.

- Once you have all the data you need, focus on the most promising segments—in terms of profit/added value and best fit to your existing capabilities—for further analysis.

Continue the process of developing possible segments by exploring new options—for example, small companies tend to have different

---

Segmenting for Growth

❖ How can we expand our definition of the market so that our share is only a few percent of the total?

❖ Can we segment this expanded market based on customer needs or behaviors?

❖ Which segments are attractive and which should be avoided?

❖ How can we address the needs of key segments?

❖ Do any customers in apparently unrelated segments actually have similar needs and will behave in a similar way to your marketing approaches?

Figure 4.5   Segmenting for Growth

needs from big ones: can small companies in different segments be grouped together in a new subsegment? Is there any special need, such as environmental protection, that cuts across several segments? Do customers in different businesses share similar values or priorities? Who is likely to pay the most for your offerings? Which customers are likely to stay loyal for many years?

There are numerous variables to consider before selecting the segments on which to focus efforts. As a final stage, the key questions must relate to how your firm can develop a strong competitive advantage; your firm must offer target segments highly attractive propositions that have the greatest potential for growth.

EXPANDING THE VIEW OF THE MARKET

Many organizations have realized that their traditional definition of their markets has been far too narrow—a legacy, perhaps, from the product-centric mentality of the past. Asking how to add value to customers, and also how customers are changing, leads to an expanded view of the market.

Many healthcare companies, for instance, are moving away from their traditional set of products to the full spectrum of patient care. Instead of driving sales for specific products, they aim to add value to patients throughout the entire disease cycle. This involves working closely with patients, doctors, and healthcare workers to develop market maps that start with patient diagnosis and end with treatment and recovery. Market maps highlight the activities of all parties who are directly or indirectly involved in the treatment cycle. Each group of stakeholders in the treatment cycle—patients, doctors, and caregivers—are seen as customers, and attention is paid to each group's requirements at every stage, analyzing unmet needs and highlighting them as opportunities to improve overall value.

In developing market maps, include any peripheral activities that the customer may engage in. This approach seeks ways to improve the product or service itself, but also looks for new things that solve customer problems and improve their overall performance.

American Express developed substantial business by studying how customers used their cards. Concentrating on business travelers, Amex examined the problems that its customers often encountered in travel situations. Business customers sometimes arrive late at a hotel and lose their room, so Amex introduced a late-arrival feature, guaranteeing the room reservation if you prebooked by Amex. Travelers often lose their wallets—so Amex offered a 24-hour replacement guarantee wherever the customer was located. Other new features included automatic car rental insurance and a Frequent Flyer air miles program. All these features genuinely add value for the customer and help to distinguish Amex from competing cards, justifying the premium cost.

EXPANDED MARKET MAPS

Expanded market maps provide a view of the market or opportunity space in which you wish to operate. In the early stages, it is preferable to keep a wide scope and encompass suppliers, competitors, distribution channels, and customers.

There are many ways to construct the maps, but in general two approaches are favored, Activity Mapping and Market Sector Mapping.

- *Activity Mapping.* This looks at the activities of customers and stakeholders. The examples mentioned above—mapping patient activities in the treatment cycle, or credit card holders and their purchasing activities—are methods of mapping customer activities.

- *Market Sector Mapping.* Sometimes referred to as "horizontal" growth, this is a recent approach that has been adopted by many companies. It maps all the activities required to produce, use, and maintain products along the entire product life cycle. In heavy industrial equipment, this would include looking at suppliers, production processes, distribution channels, after-market services, financing, and product trade-in or disposal.

The first step in developing a market map is to define the start and end points of the market you are studying. In the case of health care (Figure 4.6), the start point could be when a patient first notices symptoms, and the end point when treatment is complete and the patient recovers. In the aviation industry, the start point could be the moment the aircraft is purchased, and the end point when it is retired from service.

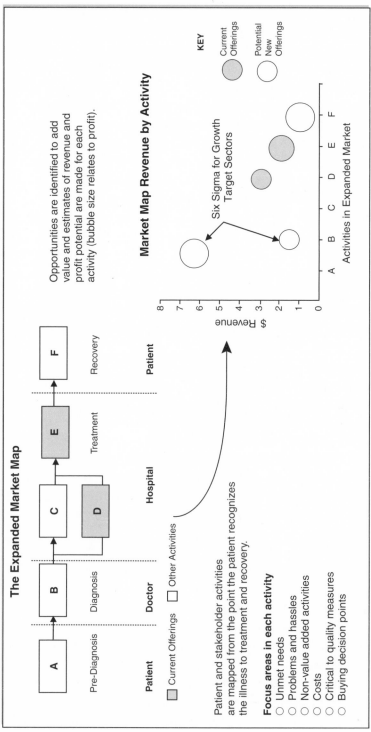

Figure 4.6   Expanded Market Map—Patient Treatment

It is usually better to take an expanded view of the market in the early stages and look beyond your traditional business areas. By looking at the larger market, you may uncover previously hidden opportunities. The scope of the map will be quickly reduced as promising areas are identified.

Once the scope of the map has been determined, the intermediary activities are documented. This is best done in a cross-functional team including customers and stakeholders. One effective tactic, utilized by several leading companies, is to hold workshops with members of key customer and stakeholder groups and invite them to generate process maps of their daily activities.

At this stage, the market map will still be at a relatively high level, but it is useful to make preliminary estimates of costs, time, and other measures that are critical to quality for each activity. Understanding the costs and other important factors at each stage is useful for determining the market size of any new offerings that may be developed. Each activity in the map is analyzed for growth opportunities, which then become focus areas to be studied in greater depth in the Six Sigma project.

The expanded market map (Figure 4.6) offers insights on how to add value to the existing business processes. It is useful for identifying unmet needs and non-value-added activities, and for developing solutions to central and peripheral activities. The size of the bubbles in Figure 4.6 indicates the estimated profit for each activity (the larger the bubble, the larger the expected profit).

Typically, one of the first insights to emerge is that you do not have a single customer for your product, but rather a sequence of customers, each of whom has different requirements and interests in your product.

Value creation requires us to extend our view of the market to multiple customers along the value chain. Frequently, it becomes evident that the customers' costs associated with the product or services are far greater than the initial purchase cost. For example, an estimated 50% of all information technology budgets are not spent on acquiring new products but on maintaining and supporting existing ones.

Gaining a slice of that 50% expenditure from the customer's IT wallet is now a major goal for many companies. Developing a clearer understanding of the customers' total costs and unmet needs and identifying non-value-added activities is an important part of the Define Phase and is discussed in more detail on page 146. At this stage, the map is still at a high level and ideally describes the complete market, including peripheral and indirect customer activities.

IDENTIFYING OPPORTUNITIES—MAPPING WORKSHOPS

As mentioned earlier, an effective approach to developing expanded market maps is to hold joint workshops with customers and stakeholders in order to understand activities at each stage and identify any unmet needs. The workshops allow participants to express themselves freely about the aspects of the business, including, but not limited to, specific product offerings that concern them the most. They can provide an unfiltered view of the customers' issues, which is often far more revealing than those generated by traditional focus groups and surveys.

The workshops should be conducted with groups that have similar interests because people from the same peer group are more likely to be frank about activities and underperforming areas. Workshops should not be limited to current customers or "easy" customers. Seek out demanding customers—lost and potential customers as well.

The output of the workshops is a detailed map of the activities at each stage in the value stream. In addition to mapping the activities at each stage, unmet needs, as well as value-added and non-value-added areas, are noted.

IDENTIFYING OPPORTUNITIES—ACCOUNT PLANNING

Account planning is an important part of the sales process that focuses on the customers' businesses—*their* issues and what matters to *them*—and seeks to devise specific sales actions to support goals. It is a great cross-functional event that can reveal opportunities for Six Sigma Growth projects.

Companies with a good account planning process hold review meetings on a regular basis; often monthly, and focus on sales opportunities for each account. These opportunities are prioritized and the appropriate sales actions are determined.

Account plans typically include the following:

- *Customer profiles:* Overview of the customer, executives and decision-makers, and key issues that the customers are facing

- *Opportunities:* Sales opportunities for each customer

- *Objectives:* Revenue targets for the account

- *Strategy:* The approach needed to achieve the revenue target

- *Tactics:* Specific actions necessary to achieve goals

Account planning in many organizations tends to be very product-centric and focuses mainly on increasing revenue for specific customers. These sessions can also be useful for discussing customer issues and directions and generating growth opportunities. These may be adaptations of existing products or completely new offerings.

IDENTIFYING OPPORTUNITIES—CUSTOMER/ SUPPLIER COLLABORATION

Once high-priority segments have been identified, they must be studied carefully for growth opportunities. Often, the best way to understand how to add value to customers is to engage with them directly and help them explore their business to find their greatest opportunities. This could be achieved by embedding Black Belts with the customer or by holding collaborative events such as joint Six Sigma programs with customers and suppliers.

As mentioned earlier, many Six Sigma companies, such as General Electric and Honeywell, now offer training or consulting services to their key customers in an effort to help build closer ties. Initially, many such direct engagements with customers worked out poorly since it soon became evident that such initiatives required both parties to commit substantial resources and that there was often little return on the investment. Now, instead of offering such services to all customers, organizations are more selective and work with customers that have the greatest growth potential.

Joint initiatives with customers are an excellent way to become "experts in the customer's business," which is a central theme of Six Sigma for Growth. For it to be effective, however, a thorough business assessment must be conducted prior to any substantial commitment of resources.

Joint Six Sigma programs demonstrate a commitment to customers and are generally very well received. They are a unique opportunity to add value for the customer and to gain an in-depth understanding of the customers' businesses and the issues they face. These issues can present significant opportunities for growth.

It is equally important, from a growth perspective, to extend such joint Six Sigma programs to suppliers as well as customers. Today, it is not enough that individual organizations are efficient; they must also be part of a highly efficient, innovative supplier network. Dramatic improvements can be made by collaborating with suppliers on joint issues.

Typically Six Sigma companies work with customers through the following outlets:

- *Leadership Seminars.* These one- or two-day sessions are held with the customer's leadership team and introduce the Six Sigma methodology. The group studies its applicability to its particular business situation. Typically, customers are asked to list their main business issues and key problem areas as prework for such programs, and these are discussed in depth during the seminar.

- *Workshops.* Once a particular project has been scoped, workshops are held to study in depth how the Six Sigma methodology would be applied. Such workshops are hands-on training events and can last up to two or three days.

- *Projects.* Working with the customer on projects, conducting training, and coaching teams. These are usually Green Belt or Black Belt projects and can last from three to six months.

- *Organizational Development.* This is much broader in scope than projects and aims at helping organizations develop their own internal Six Sigma organization. It usually includes extensive consultation, coaching, and training of customers' staff and leadership. It may even involve helping customers develop their own Master Black Belts and Six Sigma executives.

IDENTIFYING OPPORTUNITIES—BRAINSTORMING

As an adjunct to workshops with customers and stakeholders, brainstorming sessions can also generate many ideas to profitably add value for customers. The brainstorming group should be cross-functional, with people from sales, marketing, product development, purchasing, and so on. There are various brainstorming techniques that can be used; what is important at this stage is the number of ideas generated, not the quality of those ideas. Critiquing each idea will be done at a later stage.

To aid the brainstorming process, it is useful to revisit W. Edwards Deming, one of the founders of modern quality and leadership methods, who wrote that "the consumer is the most important part of the production line. Quality should be aimed at the needs of the consumer, present and future."[1] In other words, it is necessary to innovate and improve our existing offerings and to predict the future needs of the customer. The emphasis on considering the future needs of customers is a major change from traditional Six Sigma methods which tend to focus on current offerings and meeting existing customer requirements.

To create a more focused approach to brainstorming, it is beneficial to develop a list of market indicators. These indicators provide clues to growth opportunities and changes in markets and were originally developed by Peter Drucker as a systematic approach to innovation. These are detailed on page 183. During the brainstorming session, teams review each market indicator to see if it is applicable to any of their customers or offerings. This list should expand in various directions, depending on the needs of the particular businesses.

IDENTIFYING OPPORTUNITIES—VOICE OF THE PRODUCT

This approach is based on systematic innovation techniques pioneered by the talented inventor Genrich Altshuller. Adapted for business, the technique can be used for brainstorming value-adding modifications to existing offerings. The central question is:

• Are there ways we can modify our current offerings such that they will add value to the customer?

Unlike "classical" methods that rely on listening to the Voice of the Customer (VOC) to drive improvements and innovations, the Voice of the Product (VOP) takes the view that customers may not always be able to envisage improvements or articulate what new innovations they would value. The onus is on the improvement teams to understand the customers' requirements and business situations and to modify existing products and services or develop new offerings that will service them better.

This approach is based on structured innovation techniques that can lead to innovative ideas that can be missed by listening only to the voice of the customer. Customer focus groups may exhibit bias, either toward very small improvements to existing products and services or toward impracticable ideas.

The challenge is to find workable ideas that are different enough from existing offerings for customers to value. This systematic approach to innovation can generate a wealth of practical innovations.

The process starts by setting a framework: we are listening to the voice of existing products. First, list all the characteristics of the chosen product or service, including its components, appearance, life span, uses, the environments in which it is used, and so on.

Then, systematically apply a series of "paradigms for change" to the list of attributes to see how the product could be transformed.

There are five paradigms:

1. Multiplication

2. Subtraction

3. Division

4. Combining functions

5. Attribute dependency

These essential patterns of transformation emerged from the work of the Russian engineer Genrich Altshuller, who developed this approach to innovation in engineering. Each pattern defines a basic kind of physical change.

Multiplication

Can adding more than one of a particular attribute enhance the offering? In many cases, it can. For example, adding another blade to a razor gave us the Gillette twin blade, which gives a smoother shave because one blade raises the hairs while the second, set at a different angle, cuts them more cleanly than a single blade razor. Adding more of an existing feature can have surprising physical effects that may not emerge until they are tested. They may also improve ease of use—adding extra gauges to different parts of a construction tool, for instance, could make it easier to operate from different angles of sight.

Subtraction

Everybody thinks about what you could add to a product, but what if you took something away? Constantly adding features can turn a useful tool into an unmanageable monster, like so many remote control and hand-held IT devices. Hobbyists may love all those buttons and functions, but many customers only want the product to do a few things well and to be easy to use—and they don't want to spend half a day figuring out how it works. Subtracting elements can also lead to surprises and new uses.

Division

There are two main ways to divide a product: dividing by function and dividing in such a way that each piece retains all the functions of the whole. The first type is more obvious: separating the key board and mouse from a computer, for instance, by replacing cables with cordless technology gives users the added benefits of being able to operate their PC from a distance and dispensing with awkward wires. Some products—usually simple ones—can be divided in the second way: for example, cutting judo mats into small pieces that are rejoined by velcro has two valuable benefits: it enables users to size the mat easily according to the space available and makes transportation easier.

Combining Functions

Why have two buttons where one will do? As long as an innovation does not affect the ease of operation, product components can sometimes be used to do more than one job. A well-known example is an automobile's rear window demister that doubles as a radio aerial. This eliminates the need for an exterior aerial—often vandalized and easily broken—without loss of reception quality. Ease of use and no loss of quality are the important factors here.

Attribute Dependency

Once you have exhausted all the possibilities generated by applying the preceding four patterns for change, there's a final, more challenging pattern. Put simply, the term "attribute dependency" means systematically examining your listed product attributes to see how they relate to the environment in which they are used—including the users themselves. Color, weight, and appearance, for example, often have a relationship to the sex and age of their users and can be varied to appeal to different groups.

Many products are sensitive to temperature and humidity. Drivers experience different maintenance problems with their vehicles in the tropics from those they endure in the arctic. Some products have marked seasonal sales cycles. Could they be adapted or repackaged to serve a market at a different time of the year? For example, many luxury food products are strongly associated with the Christmas season, yet there may be customers for these goodies at other times, so long as the packaging doesn't mention Christmas.

DON'T FILTER TOO QUICKLY

As with brainstorming, this method may produce ideas that may be rejected immediately. This is a mistake. Each possibility first needs to be conceived in detail by a team of people from many different areas of expertise. It's a painstaking process requiring discipline to force oneself not simply to look at the obvious, but to examine each hypothetical innovation thoroughly in the search of potential benefits. It's the fact that the work is hard and initially even painful that gives this process the edge over other techniques for generating ideas, since it increases the chances of thinking of innovations that no one has ever thought of before.

Identifying Opportunities—Benchmarks

Benchmarking is the search for best practices that, when adopted, will help an organization achieve superior performance or open new opportunities for growth. It is a highly effective way to learn from the achievements of others.

There are several different approaches to benchmarking, which include:

- *Internal Benchmarking.* Looking for best practices within different areas of your own organization

- *Competitive Benchmarking.* Learning directly from your competitors

- *Industry Benchmarking.* Looking at wider trends within a specific industry

- *"Best in Class" Benchmarking.* Looking across different industries to completely new areas

Don't confine the search for benchmark processes to your competitors' businesses. Your suppliers, customers, and even firms in totally unrelated fields may have processes that you could use as benchmarks. Looking farther afield can often lead to highly innovative practices or processes.

Questions to ask:

- What are the leading companies doing in this industry?

- What are they doing in other industries?

- Can we adopt these best practices?

Identify all the processes in your business that are important to your customers and ask:

- Who is doing this better?

- Who is the very best at doing this?

- How could we improve on what they are doing?

Look at related processes that your company does not currently undertake and ask:

- How could we adopt and adapt these?

- Would they add value if we did so?

- Are there any advances in technology that we could bring to the customer?

Search Step Summary

The Search step should yield a rich selection of growth opportunities. The focus is on stimulating the way people think about their company, offerings, customers, and markets, and encouraging them to generate as many potential opportunities as possible. These may build upon current offerings or require developing completely new ones.

In the next step, Assess, the team studies each opportunity and evaluates its growth potential and feasibility.

Assess Growth Opportunities

Prioritize growth opportunities.

In the Assess step, the team makes a thorough appraisal of the growth opportunities generated in the Search step.

Careful, upfront assessment is one of the main factors determining a project's eventual success, as has been established by industry best practices. Projects with unrealistic goals or expectations, few available resources, or limited management support have little chance of success.

Many Six Sigma organizations struggle to identify growth opportunities and to select appropriate Six Sigma projects. Companies often find that projects they undertake have little or no bearing on the business, and the Six Sigma effort quickly loses effectiveness. These issues become even more challenging when projects cross organizational boundaries to include suppliers and customers.

Successful projects are not chosen by guesswork or to meet arbitrary goals. The process begins by establishing a clear strategic direction to provide a high-level guide for project selection. This guide, combined with the business goals, is translated into a set of selection criteria for rating each project and ensuring it is aligned with the organizational goals. This assessment aims to avoid situations in which projects become isolated from key business issues or fail to deliver the desired results.

The next task in the Assess step is to develop the critical success criteria. These criteria vary, depending on the nature of the business and the business unit goals. Some organizations, such as General Electric, control the critical-to-quality criteria and insist that every new Six Sigma project must meet one of these goals. Others need to develop their own assessment criteria. This is best done by the leadership team. Typically, the leadership team conducts a brainstorming session in which all criteria important to the business are listed and rated in order of importance.

In the case of joint projects with suppliers or customers, it is important that leadership from all parties be involved. The assessment criteria should be developed by members of each participating group. This often uncovers issues that must be addressed to prevent them from causing problems later.

Typical examples of selection criteria include:

Strategic Fit. Opportunities with the best chance of success are often aligned to an organization's strategic direction. This enables the company to channel its innovative efforts realistically in ways that will pay off in the market.

A key strategic decision may, for example, be choosing the customers the organization would like to serve. Clearly defined and carefully chosen market segments provide a clear direction for Six Sigma activities.

Other decisions may relate to the offerings the company wants to develop. These decisions are usually explicitly stated in the company's mid- to long-term strategic plans.

Return on Investment and Payback. Return on investment (ROI) is a major consideration in project selection. Payback (the time it takes to recoup the investment) is a less sophisticated measure, but is popular with decision makers. Some organizations specify that the total payback of investment for any Six Sigma project should be within one year of the project's completion. This is not unreasonable; many organizations implementing Six Sigma have obtained very high returns within the first year.

In addition to the internal return on investments, many organizations have begun to focus on projects that have a high ROI for their customers. General Electric publishes a QI number in its annual reports, indicating the amount of benefits it has generated for its customers. Other companies price their offerings based on the total benefits to the customer. This is naturally a very attractive proposition to customers and is a major theme in using Six Sigma to drive growth.

Risk Assessment. Risk mitigation is central to the Six Sigma for Growth approach. It is important to be aware of risks and to take steps proactively to minimize or eliminate them.

Typical considerations include the risks associated with entering new areas or in committing to major initiatives with customers. The risk to the customers or suppliers is also a key factor. Each phase in the development or improvement effort should contain a risk assessment. Typically, this is done through a Failure Modes Effects Analysis (FMEA).

Common sources of risk:

- *Business:* Investment, revenue, margin risk

- *Competitive:* How the competition will respond

- *Capability:* Setting customers' expectations and then failing to deliver

- *Internal to the Organization*

- *Health and Safety*

- *Compliance:* Government standards

- *Customer:* Risk to the customers that the new offering may pose

- *Legal:* Potential legal implications

The Chance of Success

If the Six Sigma teams are inexperienced or if the project is with a key customer, it is often important to rate projects on their likelihood of success. Setting customer expectations and then failing to meet them can damage a good relationship. Such joint projects need to be chosen carefully so that they have a good chance of success. Early successes build momentum, and once teams gain experience, they can quickly move on to more challenging projects.

Ease of Implementation

Opportunities that are easy to implement, are attractive. They require fewer resources and less time to develop, and are sometimes referred to as "low-hanging fruit." They are often found in processes that cross functional or organizational boundaries.

Customer Satisfaction

Recent studies have confirmed that satisfied customers have a much higher propensity to repurchase or continue business than dissatisfied ones. Major benefits can be gained by selecting projects that are targeted specifically at improving customer satisfaction.

Resource Availability

The best projects and greatest opportunities will be lost if the resources are not in place to see the project through to completion. In the case of joint projects, both companies need to have a clear understanding of the resources required before commencing the project.

OPPORTUNITY ASSESSMENT MATRIX

The opportunity assessment matrix (Figure 4.7) is an adaptation of a Quality Functional Deployment or House of Quality. It is a useful tool for prioritizing growth opportunities. The matrix rates each opportunity against the assessment criteria. This can be done by creating an opportunity assessment matrix in which columns are used for the assessment criteria and rows for the projects in question. Weights are assigned to each assessment criterion (1–10) in order of

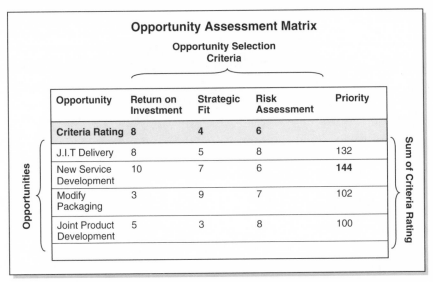

Figure 4.7 Opportunity Assessment Matrix

importance. Each opportunity is then studied to see how it relates to each criterion. Relating the opportunity to the criteria is again done by assigning a rating (1–10) in order of importance or, in the case of risk, severity.

Finally, the criteria weight and opportunity rating are multiplied together and summed to give an overall opportunity assessment number.

ATTRACTIVENESS VERSUS STRENGTHS

Another approach to prioritizing opportunities compares the opportunity attractiveness with business strengths (Figure 4.8). The opportunity attractiveness here can be a combination of factors, depending on the needs and priorities of the business. Business strengths refer to the organization's ability to capitalize on the opportunity.

Attractiveness

Financial
- Size of market

Strategic
- Improved competitive position

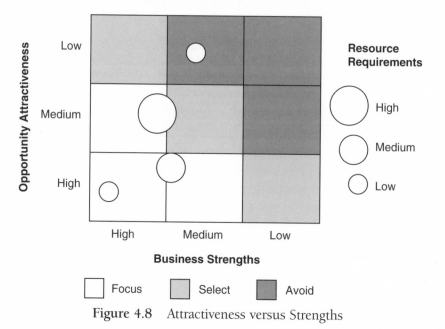

Figure 4.8   Attractiveness versus Strengths

- Growth rates   - Future market direction
- Revenue   - Customer impact
- Margins
- Return on investment

Business Strengths

Market   Technology
- Share   - Patents and copyrights
- Supply chain   - Process technology requirements
- Competitive strengths
- Organizational strengths

ASSESS STEP SUMMARY

In summary, the objective of the Assess step is to filter and prioritize the growth opportunities that were identified in the Search step.
This is done by comparing each opportunity against critical criteria
identified by the leadership team. This process usually leaves a few

high-priority growth opportunities that will be studied in more depth in the Target step.

Target High-Impact Opportunities

Target a few high-priority opportunities; prepare a growth plan.

The Target step explores, in detail, a few high-priority opportunities that resulted from the Assess step. This involves developing a clear understanding of the growth opportunity and preparing a Growth Plan that is the basis for subsequent Six Sigma projects.

When developing new offerings or collaborative ventures, a greater emphasis on planning is needed. Such projects may, for example, price new products on the value created for customers and not simply a product's unit cost, requiring very thorough analysis. In the case of collaborative projects, the projected value to each party must be made clear through an agreed-upon business plan before they commit resources.

The Growth Plan that is initiated in the Target step is developed throughout the subsequent D^2MAIC or D^2MADV phases of the project. The intricate details of the business often become clear only after a deeper understanding of the business is gained. The plan is reviewed at each project review tollgate, and a decision is made on whether or not to proceed with the project.

The plan that results from the Target step forms the basis of the growth project. This is passed to Six Sigma project teams who then officially launch the project with the Define Phase.

Six Sigma for Growth Plan

The two key planning documents for a project are the Growth Plan, discussed below and the Project Charter (developed in the Define Phase, page 199). The Growth Plan is a strategic planning document that details the rationale for the project, seen from four perspectives: the customer, the competitive environment, business, and the internal organization of the company. Looking at the opportunity from different perspectives challenges teams to think outside the box and injects realism into the plan. Traditional business plans are necessary but often focus on internal measures only and fail to take into account the overall impact of a new proposal.

In practice, no two organizations think about strategic planning in the same way. Some focus on financial plans for revenue and profit, others on products and services, others on market segments, and still others on an organization's internal capability. Views also vary between functional groups; finance people consider the financial perspective, sales and marketing consider the customer, human resources consider internal capability. The Growth Plan aims to tie together these different perspectives into a more holistic view.

Although the Growth Plan supplies an argued rationale, the Project Charter gives the details, focusing, as with any Six Sigma project, on specifics such as targets, team resources and project timelines.

The way in which these documents are used will vary from company to company and project to project. Some projects will be simple enough not to require such an intense planning effort, but most will involve comprehensive planning, especially those involving a high level of risk, or where both organizations commit to developing shared processes or partnerships.

In all cases, the plans should signal the importance of adhering to all relevant company policies, procedures, government regulations, and ethical standards.

The approach to planning outlined here is a guide and not an exhaustive list of planning requirements. Instead, the following section overviews each of the perspectives and certain key elements within them. Since the Growth Plan will vary from project to project and from company to company, each organization should build upon these elements and develop approaches relevant to its own business. The end result should be a standard of required information that will be used by all projects in a similar manner to a Project Charter (see Growth Plan example on page 202).

The typical Growth Plan (Figure 4.9) should contain the following key elements:

1. The customer's perspective

2. The business perspective

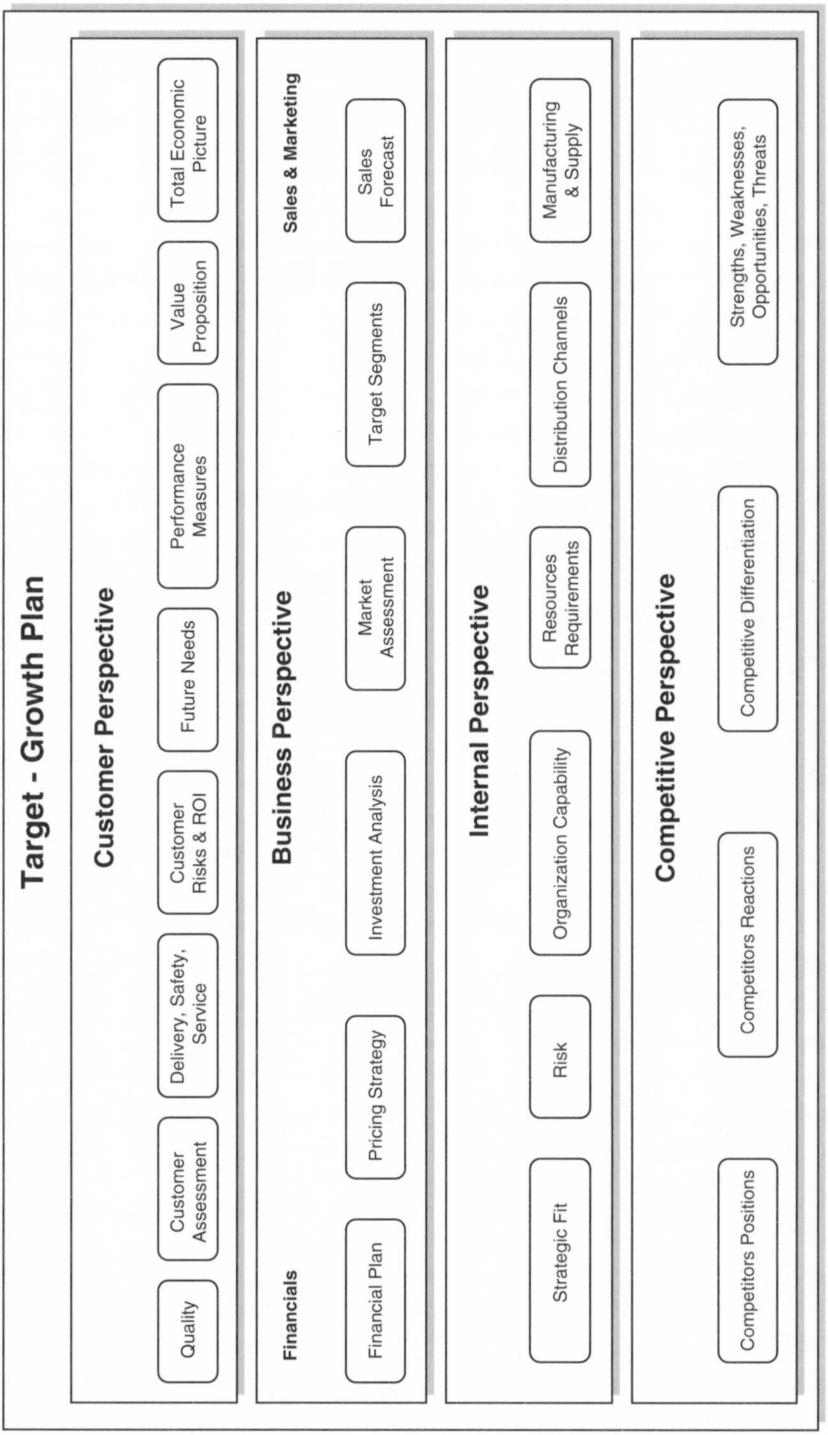

Figure 4.9 TARGET—Growth Plan

3. The internal perspective

4. The competitive perspective

THE CUSTOMER'S PERSPECTIVE

Who are the customers? Why would customers value the proposed offering? If customers were involved in the development of this Growth Plan—an excellent practice that should be adopted by more companies—what would they say?

This section describes the benefits the customer will gain from the new offering. It is expressed in their terms, using metrics customers care about. It may quantify improvements in the customers' total economic picture (see Chapter 3, p 63), or perhaps help them with a current or future need.

Customer Assessment

When we study the business carefully, we often find that instead of a single customer there is a complex network of people, organizations, and systems—all of which depend on our offerings. Typically there are several layers of customers—wholesalers, retailers, and end users—each of which have their own interests and requirements. Each customer in this sequence needs to be identified and its requirements assessed.

This assessment should highlight key customers for the new offering and group them by segment, explaining the rationale. Detail should also be given on how key customers buy, and how purchasing behavior may change in the future.

Once customers in the value chain have been identified, the assessment should explain why you see the selected customers as key to the new offering and should show how the selection has been optimized from the profit perspective.

Key areas include:

- Quantifying improvements in the customers' total economic picture

- Customers' quality issues with our offerings

- Customers' non-value-added activities

- Key customer needs for improved efficiency, to increase sales, profit, and productivity

- Customer problems and business issues

- Customers' future requirements and business direction

- Costs and return on investments for collaborative projects

The Value Proposition

The value proposition describes the offering from the customer's point of view. It describes the proposal and shows how it fulfils the identified customers' needs and adds value to their businesses. It answers the question "what will this do for the customer?"

The proposition should state if this is a new product or service, or an improvement to an existing offering. The value proposition should include the following:

- *Offering Description:* An overview of the new offering. This should specify, from the customers' perspective, the value that the new offering will bring. It should also outline any enhancements to existing company offerings and advantages over offerings from competitors.

- *Needs Assessment:* Highlight the specific customer needs this new offering will address.

- *Benefits:* Detail the quantifiable and intangible benefits the customer will gain from the offering. Quantifiable value aspects should include technical, competitive, or financial benefits to customers and the impact of the improvements on their total economic picture.

- *Features:* The term "features" typically refers to the measurable attributes of an offering. The proposition should give details of specific, measurable characteristics and attributes of the offering.

- *Price:* What is the pricing strategy, and why it will be attractive to customers? Effective pricing is critical to the success of any new offering. Different approaches to pricing are discussed in the following sections.

- *Quality:* The enhancements in quality over prior offerings—how does the new offering address these issues? What is the impact on customers?

- *Innovative Elements:* Overview all the innovations the offering includes.

- *Potential Future Variations and Roll-Outs:* Is the initial offering part of a multigenerational plan aimed at helping customers' businesses? If so, give details of each generation in terms of the vision, features, process, and methods (see multigenerational plans, page 219).

- *Collaborative Processes:* Describe any collaborative activities with customers and supplier, and show their potential effect on customers.

- *Life Cycle Management:* The value-added aspects of the management of the life cycle of the offering, including support, service and warranties.

The assessment explains in general terms how the offering will be perceived by customers and how it will be positioned in the target markets. In the case of tailor-made solutions, discuss how the offering can be designed so that it can be extended later to other customers and markets (the "replicate" phase of growth projects).

Developing a clear value proposition is an important aspect of growth projects. Careful analysis of the value proposition against specific customer requirements reveals gaps in the offering and is an important step in the Analyze Phase of D^2MAIC projects.

Performance Measures

From the outset, a clear understanding of how the customer will measure success needs to be developed:

- Specify how customers will measure success.

- Describe any arrangements for jointly measuring the success of the offering with customers.

• Show how you will reinforce customer satisfaction by ensuring that customers recognize good performance when it occurs.

Quality

Customers are the only worthwhile judge of quality. Quality needs to be defined in terms relevant to the customer. To do so:

• Give the details of any quality issues already highlighted.

• Identify and address any weak points or gaps.

• As before, give details of customer success metrics— how customers will measure the success or failure of the offering.

• Ask whether the performance of third parties is an issue? How can the company ensure high standards from third parties, and should any of these elements be "insourced" to maintain quality?

Delivery, Service, and Safety

Describe in detail the customers' needs in these areas:

• What are customers' expectations, and how can we exceed these?

• Are there any potential safety risks? How will these be reduced or eliminated?

Customer Risks and ROI

Are there any risks for the customer? As mentioned earlier, both parties must carefully manage risk in collaborative projects, such as solution development.

Particularly in the case of collaborative efforts, the customers may need to invest in the initiative. What will the customers' costs be? Does the initiative make sense to customers from the perspective of payback or return on investment?

Future Needs

Sustained growth requires understanding what the customer needs today and tomorrow.

- Describe trends among customers and how they are changing.

- Show how this offering will address these trends, and explore the need to adapting it or develop new offerings in the future.

- How long will this offering remain relevant to customers?

THE BUSINESS PERSPECTIVE

The business perspective considers the more traditional sales, marketing, and financial aspects of the proposal. It examines maximizing revenues, growth and profit for the company. It asks, "How are we going to make money from the proposal"?

Market Assessment

What economic sector and industry category are you addressing (such as manufacturing or industrial chemicals)? Identify targeted subsections of an industry such as plastics.

This assessment should describe the markets to which the offering is addressed, and show how the offering might be expanded to related areas in the future. Discuss the major industries involved, and give a general analysis of their economics and cyclical stage. Describe the defining characteristics of the industries and their products and services.

Analyze the absolute size and growth rates of all markets and industries discussed, and identify any special features. What are the demographics of the customers? Focus on presenting information in ways that are convincing to a knowledgeable reader. Avoid giving data from doubtful or controversial sources. Try to support all statements with good evidence.

Identify and discuss the key economic, social, legal, and political factors affecting the industries' performance.

Give evidence of historical trends of sales and profits, and the factors driving them. Discuss the future outlook for the industries, giving your reasons and stating all assumptions clearly. Make a convincing case for why your predictions are realistic.

Assess capacity. Are any of the industries/markets examined prone to overcapacity? Discuss emerging trends. Identify and explain in detail all relevant economic measures, such as leading indicators. Ask:

- Which are the most profitable areas now?

- Which are potentially highly profitable in the future?

- Where are the no-profit zones?

Target Segments

The Search step segmented the market, based on growth potential. The plan should highlight the chosen methods of segmentation and describe each segment, giving weight to their unique features and the major drivers of customer behavior. Rank segments by priority and explain the team's reasoning for this.

Give details of each segment's potential for launches, pilot offerings, and prelaunch trials.

Give a comparative analysis of the segments, including a description of their "psychographics," such as "early adopters," "value orientated."

Analyze the long-term growth potential for each segment. Describe any special skills and approaches required to target specific segments and estimate their relative costs.

How the Offering Makes Profits and Adds Value

Describe the profitability model for the offering and summarize sales revenue projections. Show how the offering adds value to your company.

Sales Forecast

The sales forecast can be included here to enable reviewers to assess its realism in the context of how the offering will be marketed.

Profitable sales volume is critical to the venture, and ultimately all other elements of the plan depend upon it, so knowledgeable readers will examine it closely. One useful approach is to prepare a number of sales forecasts for different scenarios, for example, a best case, a worst case, and a conservative scenario. The advantage of this is that it makes the distinction between different potential outcomes clearer, and suggests ways in which the business can respond rapidly to actual sales returns.

Pricing Strategy

Pricing is a much-neglected aspect of new offering design, but its dynamic effects on sales and profit are well understood. Pricing models are quantifiable and lend themselves easily to the Six Sigma approach, so there is no good reason for the design team to approach the topic with any less rigor than the other aspects of developing a new offering.

Typical pricing strategies include:

- *Market Penetration.* New offerings are priced low in an effort to gain market share. There is a risk of a price war with competitors.

- *Loss Leaders.* Setting the price of one offering lower and offsetting the loss by raising the price of others. Retailers often use this strategy to attract customers. Its success depends upon customers buying the other, higher-priced offerings as well as the loss leader.

- *Value Pricing.* Linking the price to a measurable financial gain that the customer receives. This is sometimes used in solution selling.

- *"Satisficing."* Setting prices to gain a modest return. Often used in competitive bidding.

- *Price Wars.* The lowest-cost producer of an offering can defeat the competition in a price-sensitive market.

- *Market Skimming.* An innovative offering may be rolled out slowly through market segments, targeting the highest payers first. IT-based products often use this strategy, being sold at high prices to early adopters before being offered more cheaply in the mass market.

Developments in accounting techniques such as Activity Based Pricing provide improved ways of combining cost information with sales and marketing data to optimize prices. The relationships between price and sales volume, and costs and sales volume, must be evaluated simultaneously.

A pricing assessment should fully describe all the assumptions made in developing prices and clearly define the planned pricing strategies. Give details of pricing models and value analysis. Analyze price elasticity by market segment. Describe any unusual market factors affecting prices. Discuss possible price responses by competitors and give details of how pricing strategy will change to meet the challenge.

Price and Cost

Many companies do not have sufficiently accurate cost information to price well, and can lose profits to competitors with better cost knowledge. Traditional methods of allocating costs can be arbitrary, leading to sales at prices that, unknown to the seller, actually result in a loss.

Costs can be adjusted at the product development stage much more easily than at later stages, and this is the best time to strive for optimum cost efficiency. Activity Based Costing analyses and defines the activities involved in manufacturing, distribution, sales, and so on, and assigns costs to each. This enables non-value-added activities to be eliminated and for all remaining activities to be accurately costed before setting a price.

This approach to costing reduces so-called fixed costs to a minimum, since many elements in traditional fixed costs are now identified as cost-driving activities. This prevents the assignment of an arbitrary share of the fixed cost overhead to an offering, which is a prime cause of inaccurate, often loss-making, price levels.

Price Elasticity

Price elasticity is simply the degree to which customers are sensitive to changes in the price of a specific offering, assuming that all other factors remain unchanged. For example, the price of cigarettes may be said to be inelastic if sales volumes do not change when prices increase. A number of factors affect elasticity, including:

- *The ability of a customer to purchase a substitute for the offering.*
  The more acceptable the substitutes, and the wider their availability, the more price elasticity there is in the offering.

- *Customer awareness of substitutes.* If customers are unaware of the availability of substitutes, they are less price-sensitive.

- *The effect of the price of the offering on the price of the customer's products and services.* Where customers use the offering to produce offerings of their own, if the percentage of the offering price to their total costs is high, it will be more price sensitive.

- *The price sensitivity of customers' offerings.* If customers' offerings are highly price sensitive, they will be price sensitive in turn to their suppliers.

- *The cost of switching suppliers.* If the cost to the customers of changing to another supplier is high, they will be less price sensitive.

- *Frequency of purchase.* The more frequently the customer buys the offering, the more information the customer will acquire, which will lead to greater price sensitivity.

- *Ease of comparison.* If a customer has difficulty in comparing the offering with substitutes, there will be less price sensitivity.

Low price elasticity implies a higher profit potential, so it is desirable, but many offerings will have high price sensitivity. The key is to correctly analyze all factors affecting price sensitivity and to set prices at a level that optimizes profits, altering prices as circumstances change.

The Financial Plan

The financial plan should state the financial goals of the offering and answer the following key questions:

- How much finance is needed?

- At what points in the development and marketing of the project will the finance be needed, and in what amounts?

- How will the finance be provided (e.g., cash, bank loans, trade credit, issue of corporate debt/equity)?

- Who will provide the finance?

State key financial goals for the project, such as:

- Growth rates for sales and profits
- Return on investment
- Payback/retirement of investment and/or loans
- Working capital needs

In addition, give details of:

- All the key assumptions made in constructing the financial plan.
- Pro forma cash budgets, balance sheets, and income statements for the project.
- Breakdowns for market segments, key customers, variations of the offering, and so on, where appropriate. Generally, the projections should be for three to five years, broken down by month and/or quarter.
- Investment projections for the same period.
- Quarterly profit/loss statements for the period to include all costs including tax. Provide breakdowns for variations in the offering and/or by major components where appropriate.
- Cash flow analysis for the period, stating clearly how it has been constructed.

Investment Analysis

Analyze the projected financial performance of the project, using appropriate standard investment and management ratios such as return on investment, return on capital employed, payback, compounded annual growth rates of revenues and profits, debtor days, creditor days, current assets to current liabilities, assets to sales, and return on sales. Comment on the results.

Provide a sensitivity analysis using a standard statistical technique such as Monte Carlo analysis. This is to show the likely variation of the projected outcomes.

Some Useful Financial Ratios

Financial ratios must be selected carefully for their relevance to the project. In essence, they are tools to gauge whether the project is financially feasible and progressing according to plan. Discuss your choice of ratios with a financial officer, and explore how to ensure that they can be interpreted clearly. Many ratios can be calculated in more than one way, so it is helpful to state the definitions of the ratios you are using in the plan.

Here are some commonly used ratios:

Return on Investment (ROI). Usually calculated as net operating income/total assets. Measures how many income dollars are earned per dollar of assets. The higher the ROI, the more profitable the operation.

Average Collection Period (ACP). (accounts receivable × 365)/net sales. Shows the average number of days it takes for your customers to pay. A rising ACP rate is generally a bad sign, since it means that the firm is extending more and more credit to its customers.

Debt Ratio. Total debt/total assets. Measures the leverage of the operation.

Inventory Turnover. Cost of sales/inventory. Gives the average number of times a year that inventory is produced/purchased and sold. The higher the turnover, the higher the firm's liquidity and profitability, all other things being equal.

Total Asset Turnover. Sales/total assets. Measures productivity in terms of how many sales dollars are produced by a dollar of assets. The higher the ratio, the more productive the assets.

THE INTERNAL PERSPECTIVE

Are we able to deliver what we have promised to the customer? What impact will it have on the way we run our business? What exactly do we need to do to make this proposal a success?

Even attractive and highly profitable projects are of little value if they are not aligned with the overall company strategy or cannot be properly executed for internal reasons. Looking at the proposed offering from an internal company perspective helps to ensure that the project does not detract from the company's aims and that the organization has—or can acquire—the resources and capacity to undertake it successfully.

In the early days of solution selling, some projects failed solely because of organizational problems. Personnel and processes were not realigned to cope with the new demands that solution selling imposed on them.

Strategic Fit

Strategic fit addresses how the proposed offering *supports* and is *supported by* the organization, its partners, and strategy.

Assess how the proposed offering can be integrated with existing strategic and operating plans for the entire company. Highlight any important issues, and discuss opportunity costs.

Resource Requirements

What resources will be required to ensure that the project is a success? These requirements—detailed here or in the Project Charter—should be estimated in terms of people, resources and time.

Manufacturing and Supply

Assess your company's ability to develop this offering and address the following questions:

- Is the offering technically feasible?

- What key technologies are needed?

- If strategic partners or suppliers will be used, who are they, and what will they contribute?

- Have agreements with these partners or suppliers been made?

Provide a road map for technological development of the offering.

Describe the plan for design. Discuss potential problems with technology, including trade-offs. Describe the current status of the relationships with essential suppliers, and give a plan for how these will be managed for the project.

Organizational Capabilities

Describe the business functions involved in the new offering, including all operations and the supply chain. Highlight any human resource issues, and show how they can be solved. Ask:

- What are the current capabilities of existing business units?

- Should any new units be created?

- What skills are required?

- What standards should be set?

- Will new people be hired?

- What criteria should be used?

Discuss how the organization of the project will affect the company as a whole, and how it can be integrated with the existing corporate structure.

Distribution Channels

Multiple marketing channels are difficult to control efficiently. There are often serious conflicts of interest between the company and its distributors because of pricing and cost differences in different channels.

Where the offering is high value-added, there is usually a strong case for controlling all distribution directly, despite the increased costs. Essentially, the reason to use third-party distributors is either to massively extend the reach or to reduce costs because of customer price sensitivity. In some cases, such as in specific foreign markets, there may be legal obligations to use third-party distribution channels.

Describe the combination of marketing channels to be used and ask:

- Can we "disintermediate" in any of these channels? How will this affect performance?

- Are there any channels in which we would like to disintermediate, but cannot because of the need to preserve the channel for other offerings? How might we solve this?

- Can we partially substitute a new channel for an existing one?

- How can we make the channels more efficient?

  Analyze the principal channel intermediaries, asking:

- Do they give satisfactory after-sales service?

- Is our company/brand image affected by their activities? If so, how?

- Are their locations appropriate for our target markets?

- Do they sell to our target markets?

- Is their sales force appropriately trained? Is it large enough?

- What is the size of their promotional budgets? How effective are they?

- Which intermediaries finance the holding of our stock? How do they manage their inventories?

- Do they carry competitors' products?

- Are they creditworthy?

Risk

Methods such as Failure Modes Effects Analysis (FMEA) should be used to list all the possible risks associated with the project, categorized by type (e.g., financial, health, environmental, antitrust, antidumping, political). Rank these by Risk Priority Number (RPN) and detail how they can be reduced or removed.

Highlight legal issues and obtain legal opinion for the major risks.

THE COMPETITIVE PERSPECTIVE

Who are the competitors? How are they performing in the eyes of the customer? How will they react to the proposed offering? How are we going to differentiate ourselves from the competition?

This assessment should be as objective as possible, highlighting major long-term issues, especially those that affect profitability.

Competitive Differentiation

Describe the differential benefits of the offering (those benefits that only your company provides). Rank them in order of their value to customers, overall and by segment. Give evidence for this, such as market surveys. Quantify the competitive advantage that these benefits offer the customer compared with competing offerings.

Discuss market entry. Can the offering be sustained over the medium to long term in these markets?

Competitors' Positions

Identify the competitors in each market, and show their relative positions. This is best done in tabular form (see Figure 4.10).

The main objectives of competitors within a given market may be classified as one of the following:

- *Entering the market.* Note the reasons, which may include defending against a threat in to other areas, building from strength, and exploiting new opportunities.

- *Building position.* Usually involves a change in strategy, often with more precise segmentation.

- *Maintaining position.* This may be aggressive or defensive.

- *Harvesting.* Maximizing profit is given priority over developing the market further. May involve the consolidation of activities.

Competitors' Positions				
Competitor	Markets	Products	Objectives	Position

Figure 4.10   Competitors' Positions

- *Leaving the market.* A company may eventually decide to leave a market altogether to pursue better opportunities, reduce risk, or eliminate costs.

Identifying a company's position in a market is not always clear cut. Here are some questions to ask:

MARKET LEADER

- Does the firm have the highest revenues or unit sales in this market?
- Is the firm defined as the market leader in the trade press? If so, why?
- Does the firm influence the performance of competitors? How?
- Does the firm influence the behavior of competitors? How?

STRONG POSITION

- Does the firm have high revenues and unit sales in this market?
- Does the firm perceive itself not to be vulnerable to competitors?
- Does it have a wide choice of strategies?
- Can it implement unorthodox strategies without damaging its position?

ADVANTAGEOUS POSITION

- Does the firm have unique competitive strengths in this market?
- Does it control certain niches?

DEFENSIBLE POSITION

- Is the firm profitable, but clearly not a major player in this market?
- Does the firm lack any dominant hold on a specific niche?

Weak

- Is the firm profitable in this market?

- Are sales declining?

- Does the firm lose in direct challenges from competitors?

- Do customers regard the firm's offering with derision?

Identify all competitors, major and minor, giving high-level data. Discuss potential future competitors, including possible new entrants to the market.

SWOT Analysis

Once you have defined the relative positions of competitors for each major market or market segment, you can now assess your own company's situation in this context.

SWOT is an analytical technique used to ascertain the business unit's present position in its markets, compared to its competitors. The aim is to show how the company and the present offering are different from others in the market. The "SWOT" acronym derives from the four angles from which it views the situation: "strengths," "weaknesses," "opportunities," and "threats."

Provide a SWOT analysis for each segment, summarizing the key factors. These summaries should be easy to read and helpful in capturing the practical issues that must be addressed. They should have a clear theme, enabling others to draw useful conclusions on which they can build.

A good SWOT analysis:

- Clearly explains our perception of the market

- States our marketing aims

- Identifies necessary actions

and tells us:

- What the customers need

- How they buy

- How we perform

- How our competitors are behaving

Strengths and Weaknesses

Identify the critical factors for success in the chosen markets. These may include:

- Product performance

- Degree of service

- Speed of service and delivery

- Price

Summarize the strengths and weaknesses of our competitors and ourselves in relation to these critical success factors. Include information on brands and brand perception in the markets. Give full information on trends and market share for all competing offerings.

Opportunities and Threats

Summarize the present and future effects of external influences such as:

- Government policies

- Regulations

- Taxation

- New technology

- Demographic trends

Define the major threats to the industry, and show how the major players respond to these threats. Discuss how your firm can counter the threats.

   Explain the strategic opportunity for your offering, why it exists, and how you will exploit it. Show how this will be profitable in the long term. Typically, the opportunity will be one or more of the following:

- Providing a better service

- Lowering costs/prices

- Creating a new/untapped market

- Fulfilling unsatisfied demand

- Introducing an innovative product or service

Competitors' Reactions

How will the competition react to the new offering? Competitors will not sit idly by while you take business away from them by providing customers with new offerings. Wherever possible, such reactions should be anticipated and preemptive action taken.

TARGET STEP SUMMARY

The Target step develops the Growth Plan that will be used throughout the growth project. It is usually clear at this point whether the opportunity is an improvement to an existing offering (hence requiring a D^2MAIC project) or whether it is a new offering requiring the D^2MADV approach. In the next chapter, the D^2MAIC methodology is discussed.

CHAPTER 5

D^2MAIC—A Breakthrough Approach to Growth

The value decade is upon us. If you can't sell top-quality product at the world's lowest price, you're going to be out of the game … the best way to hold your customers is to constantly figure out how to give them more for less.

—Jack Welch

The D^2MAIC approach adds value to customers by improvements to existing offerings. The aim is to grow by constantly seeking to give customers more for less while making profits for the firm. Projects are usually conducted by customer-facing groups such as sales, marketing and after-sales service or through collaborative efforts with customers.

Customer-facing groups—the people who serve and work with customers every day—are uniquely positioned to contribute to the growth effort. By working on customer problems or analyzing customers' activities proactively for value-adding opportunities, these groups play a vital role in achieving sustained growth because of their detailed understanding of the customers.

To capitalize on market opportunities using Six Sigma methods, more and more organizations are developing tailored approaches for sales, marketing, and product development groups. The objectives of these initiatives are typically two-fold: first, to improve internal customer-facing processes and second, to help customers directly.

One large chemical company began applying Six Sigma to its sales force in 2001. The focus of the initiative is firstly to improve customer processes and secondly to offer consulting services on technical issues. The company offers these services free of charge for key customers, in the hope of building a strong customer/supplier interdependence. It invites customers to attend Green Belt training sessions and offers the services of Black Belts to help improve customers' internal processes. As part of their basic Green Belt program, the company requires customer executives and salespeople to prepare process maps of their customer processes, estimate the costs of each customer activity, and highlight any unmet needs. Each customer activity is scrutinized for opportunities to add value by using tools such as the Cause and Effect matrix and Failure Modes Effects Analysis. Green Belts use the results of this analysis to propose solutions to customer problems. This helps the company move toward a more consultative sales approach, builds closer ties with customers, and shifts the customer focus away from price points to mutual value creation.

A telecommunications company that began its Six Sigma efforts in the sales force in 1998 is also focusing internally and on customer processes. In addition to streamlining its sales processes, this organization has taken the innovative step of helping *their* customers'

D^2MAIC Phases	
Discovery	Identify growth opportunities.
Define	Define the value proposition, the market space, key market segments and goals.
Measure	Measure key segment requirements. Validate the measurement system.
Analyze	Analyze key segments for opportunities to enhance value or for value gaps.
Improve	Develop improvements to enhance value, or close the gaps, prioritize and validate improvements.
Control & Replicate	Implement improvements and make sure the value is sustainable, seek opportunities to replicate to other customers.

Figure 5.1 D^2MAIC Phases. Enhancing Value of Existing Offerings

sales processes. Black Belts help customers improve the sales of their offerings, which in turn generates revenue for the customers and suppliers. Similar approaches have been developed by companies that rely on sales and distribution channels to help resellers improve sales revenues. An organization may, for example, work with its resellers on mutually beneficial projects aimed at making resellers more effective and hence improving revenues.

Offering such services to customers is costly. Organizations that are applying Six Sigma to help their customers typically select customers and opportunities very carefully (see page 87 Discovery Phase) before committing any resources.

The D²MAIC approach outlined in this book improves existing offerings and follows the phases highlighted in Figure 5.1.

Projects begin by defining a value proposition and then challenging teams to develop a comprehensive understanding of what customers require, both now and in the future. This is usually achieved through Voice of the Customer methods, customer workshops and idea-generation techniques such as brainstorming. The value proposition is then compared with customer requirements to enhance its features and identify areas where it falls short.

Typical projects include:

- Revenue enhancement with existing products and services

- Product life cycle management

- Channel improvement and optimization

- Collaborative projects with customers

- Gaining market share and market penetration

- Margin enhancement

- Pricing and price elasticity

- Gaining customer wallet share

- Demand generation effectiveness

D²MAIC—BREAKTHROUGHS IN GROWTH

The approach detailed in Figure 5.2 is new. It builds upon approaches developed by several leading Six Sigma companies that

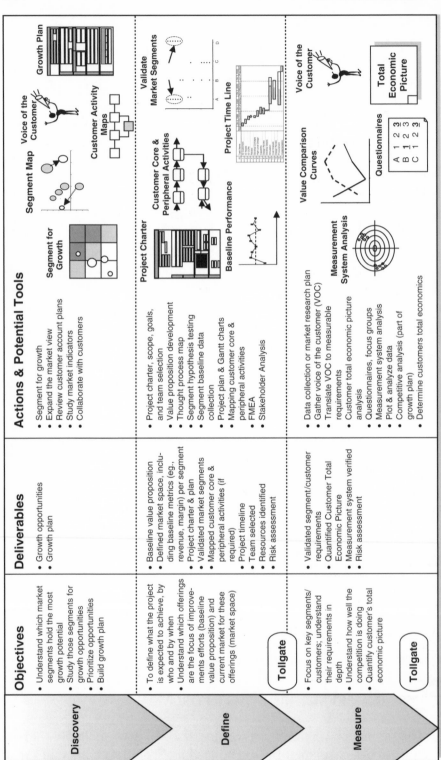

Objectives

Discovery
- Understand which market segments hold the most growth potential
- Study those segments for growth opportunities
- Prioritize opportunities
- Build growth plan

Define
- To define what the project is expected to achieve, by who and by when
- Understand which offerings are the focus of improvements efforts (baseline value proposition) and current market for these offerings (market space)

Measure
- Focus on key segments/customers; understand their requirements in depth
- Understand how well the competition is doing
- Quantify customer's total economic picture

Deliverables

Discovery
- Growth opportunities
- Growth plan

Define
- Baseline value proposition
- Defined market space, including baseline metrics (eg., revenue, margin) per segment
- Validated market segments
- Project charter & plan
- Mapped customer core & peripheral activities (if required)
- Project timeline
- Team selected
- Resources identified
- Risk assessment

Measure
- Validated segment/customer requirements
- Quantified Customer Total Economic Picture
- Measurement system verified
- Risk assessment

Actions & Potential Tools

Discovery
- Segment for growth
- Expand the market view
- Review customer account plans
- Study market indicators
- Collaborate with customers

Tools: Segment Map, Segment for Growth, Voice of the Customer, Customer Activity Maps, Growth Plan

Define
- Project charter, scope, goals, and team selection
- Value proposition development
- Thought process map
- Segment hypothesis testing
- Segment baseline data collection
- Project plan & Gantt charts
- Mapping customer core & peripheral activities
- FMEA
- Stakeholder Analysis

Tools: Project Charter, Customer Core & Peripheral Activities, Baseline Performance, Project Time Line, Validate Market Segments

Measure
- Data collection or market research plan
- Gather voice of the customer (VOC)
- Translate VOC to measurable requirements
- Customer total economic picture analysis
- Questionnaires, focus groups
- Measurement system analysis
- Plot & analyze data
- Competitive analysis (part of growth plan)
- Determine customers total economics

Tools: Measurement System Analysis, Value Comparison Curves, Voice of the Customer, Questionnaires, Total Economic Picture

Tollgate

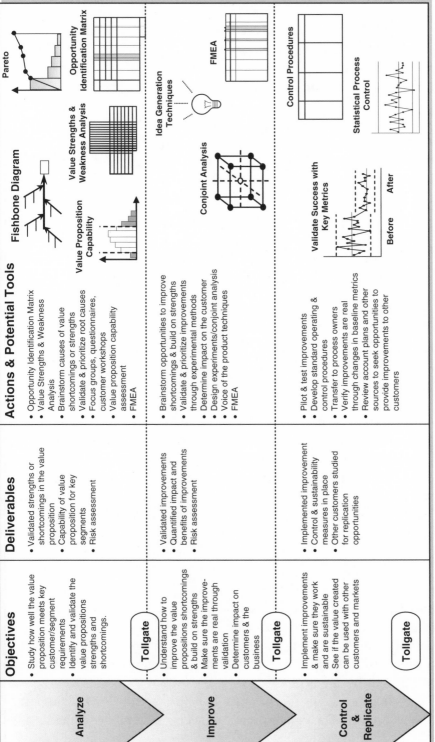

Figure 5.2 D²MAIC Detailed Overview

are focusing their efforts on growth. The tools mentioned are by no means an exhaustive list and are intended only as a high-level guide. The choice of tools depends very much on the nature of the business and the nature of the project at hand. As with any Six Sigma program, organizations must customize the approaches and tool set to their particular needs.

The Six Sigma D^2MAIC approach is an effective means of delivering value enhancing improvements in existing offerings. There are several modifications to the classical (DMAIC) approach, such as the integration of some marketing and competitive analysis tools as well as the creation of some new ones. Another significant difference is that project teams work directly with customers. Decisions made by growth teams affect key offering characteristics and the overall value proposition. They directly affect what customers buy and hence the organization's revenue and margins.

The Define Phase begins with an opportunity that has been identified in the Discovery Phase. It signals the commencement of improvement efforts as well as management's support for the initiative. D^2MAIC projects work to improve existing products and services, and can be collaborative efforts with customers. Improvements made by the team may affect product pricing or any number of the value proposition attributes and characteristics. They directly impact customers and their purchasing decisions, and as such success is measured in terms of returns to the business—revenue and margin.

"An opportunity that is well defined is half solved." The purpose of the Define Phase is to develop a clear understanding of the opportunity, the value proposition, and the market that will be addressed. Properly scoping the project allows teams to establish clearly the aims of the project at the outset.

A Project Charter and Growth Plan set out a clear opportunity statement, value proposition, and the project goals. In the case of collaborative projects, the Project Charter becomes the central document from which both organizations work. It details the project teams, the required resources, and timelines for both organizations. The Growth Plan addresses the business design—how we expect to profit from the improvements—and is updated throughout the various improvement phases.

Stakeholder analysis is conducted to help gauge the level of support for the project. For collaborative projects, stakeholder analysis is particularly important, given that there may be additional decision-making parties involved.

Defining the value proposition and market space are unique features of growth projects. Market definition through effective segmentation allows project teams to focus on high-priority areas and avoid others that may not yield significant returns. The project team begins market characterization by measuring the baseline performance and documenting different segments by using measures that reflect performance.

Baseline performance may be sales figures per market segment, product return rates, customer defection rates (sometimes referred to as customer churn), or measures that relate to the specific offering in question. Ultimately, the improvements made should be reflected in these baseline metrics.

In the case of projects aimed at customer processes (or activities), customer core and peripheral activity maps are used to develop a clear understanding of current customer activities. Such maps are also used to gauge the customer's total economic picture. Understanding the customer's total economics allows teams to judge the impact of any improvements made in terms of customer measures.

The Measure Phase seeks to understand the targeted customer requirements in detail. This involves Voice of the Customer methods (reactive, proactive, and continuous sources—see page 179). VOC information is translated by the team into measurable requirements. At this stage, the value proposition and the customer requirements are compared. Often, teams now find that, in the words of Peter Drucker, the customer is not buying what the company thinks it sells. Simply put, we ask the questions "What do our customers want?" and "What are we giving them?" Value gaps—areas where we fail to meet customer requirements—are prioritized and become the subject of further improvement efforts. Similarly, value strengths—the things we are good at and the customer cares about—are examined for opportunities to enhance them further. Focusing on strengths is just as important as focusing on deficiencies.

Wherever possible, efforts should be made to understand and quantify the customers' total economic picture, using process maps detailing customers' activities. Modifications or enhancements to the value proposition should be quantified in terms of the customer total economics. Value enhancements should help customers and be something they are willing to pay for. It is important to quantify these enhancements in a way that will help customers to understand their impact.

The Analyze Phase seeks to identify value gaps and strengths and then drill down to root causes. A customer may, for example, note that your product is difficult to use. Further analysis may reveal that training material or attached instructions are not clear. The objective is to identify and then validate—using rigorous methods—root causes that drive performance.

Hypotheses on possible causes are developed and tested. Appropriate statistical tools and techniques are used, such as histograms, box plots, multivariate analysis, correlation and regression, and hypothesis testing. In this way, the team confirms the determinants of value performance.

In the Improve Phase, the team studies the root causes and then develops improvements. Typically, several improvement concepts are generated and then prioritized. These solutions are systematically verified, using experimental or test methods. The team may plan and design experiments (DOEs) or use conjoint methods to verify solutions or optimize the offering. In the case of the product that customers found difficult to use, once the root cause is validated as poor instruction material, the team creates different versions of the instruction material and tests which is best through workshops or focus groups. The result should be a validated improvement.

The project team designs and documents the necessary controls to ensure that gains from the Six Sigma improvement effort can be held once the changes are implemented. Quality principles and techniques are used, including concepts such as feedback loops, mistake proofing, and statistical process control. Process documentation is updated, and process control plans are developed. Standard operating procedures (SOPs) and work instructions are revised accordingly.

Implementation is monitored, and process performance is audited over a period of time to ensure that gains are held.

The addition of a replicate step is important to ensure that any improvements in one area are transferred to other customers. For a development team, it is often easy to transfer such improvements to another customer or to another improvement team. By integrating this into the control phase, the sharing of best practices becomes part of the project.

GAPS AND ENHANCEMENTS IN VALUE

As with any Six Sigma project, the objective is to find root causes of the performance of the issue at hand. In projects such as market penetration—gaining revenue in existing markets—it is important to identify root value drivers, the aspects of the product or service that differentiate it from the competition and that customers value. The approach is to identify these value drivers from the customers' perspective, and then compare them with what they actually receive. Gaps or enhancements in value between customers' needs and what they actually receive become the focus of the improvement effort. The teams must ask two questions:

1. What are the customers getting that they don't or will not want?

2. What do they need now or in the future that they are not getting?

It is only when customers get what they need that we are providing the optimal offering. In such instances, we should ask how we can profitably give customers more. In other instances, we are either giving customers what they don't need or failing to meet their needs, in which case we need to optimize our offerings and align them to

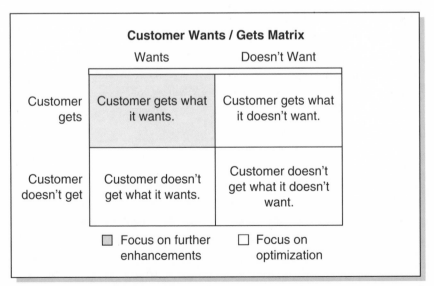

Figure 5.3 Analyzing Customer Needs versus What They Are Getting[1]

customer requirements. Talking to customers and using simple tools such as the needs/gets matrix can often reveal opportunities to add value for customers (see Figure 5.3).

Such comparisons require a thorough understanding of customers and their business as well as competitors' offerings. Value comparison curves (page 217) and conducting strength, weakness, opportunity, and threat (SWOT) analysis (page 138) can also reveal opportunities to add value. Competitors' positions, dissatisfaction with competitors' offerings and value driver gaps are then the focus of improvement efforts. As stated earlier, this is similar to the classical DMAIC approach that aims to identify root causes that drive process performance, but the root causes now include root value drivers and opportunities in areas that will profitably enhance value. These new gains in customer value are validated in terms of business metrics such as revenue, margin, and market share.

BASIC IMPROVEMENT APPROACH

D^2MAIC refers to a six-phase approach (Discovery, Define, Measure, Analyze, Improve, Control and Replicate). It is based on the classical DMAIC approach, which is generally standardized, although it is not uncommon to find slight differences:

MAIC	Measure, Analyze, Improve, and Control
DMAIC	Define, Measure, Analyze, Improve, and Control
RDMAIC	Recognize, Define, Measure, Analyze, Improve, and Control
DMAIIC	Define, Measure, Analyze, Innovate, Improve, and Control

Many other improvement models have been developed over the years. Most of these approaches are based on W. Edwards Deming's —Plan, Do, Study, Act (PDSA) cycle. Deming himself referred to this as the Shewhart Cycle, but it is more commonly known as the Deming Cycle (see Figure 5.4).

The DMAIC approach, based on the PDSA cycle, is a more common approach today and is synonymous with Six Sigma.

The cycle of learning and improvement applies equally to both problem and nonproblem areas. This is significant, because employing Six Sigma exclusively as a problem-solving tool is limiting. First, it encourages a narrow focus on reactive issues: the problems of the day. Second, it limits the scope of improvements. Why focus only on what is going wrong? Why not identify strengths and see if they can be further enhanced?

For example, an aerospace division of Honeywell found that its customers (airline companies) were on the whole satisfied with the time taken to repair aircraft engines. The industry standard for repair time was on average 45 days for smaller engines, and customers were willing to accept this. When asked about their requirements (Voice of the Customer), most were primarily concerned with the costs of engine repair. Honeywell had recognized, however, that airlines carried large quantities on inventories—spare parts—in order to ensure that planes kept flying. A faster repair and overhaul service would lead to a reduction in the airline's inventories, which in turn would generate huge savings for customers. The impact would be large enough that customers would be willing to pay a premium for a fast repair service. After careful consideration, the Honeywell Six Sigma group decided to focus on reducing the time taken to repair engines. Repair time was not seen as a problem area, but after Honeywell slashed it by 70%, customers were delighted. The dramatic improvement in repair time yielded a significant reduction

**The Shewhart Cycle for Learning and Improvement
The PDSA Cycle**

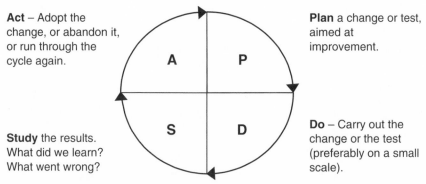

Act – Adopt the change, or abandon it, or run through the cycle again.

Plan a change or test, aimed at improvement.

Study the results. What did we learn? What went wrong?

Do – Carry out the change or the test (preferably on a small scale).

Figure 5.4   The Plan Do Study Act (PDSA) Cycle²

in the total costs to customers, so there was no objection to paying a premium for the faster service.

If Honeywell had focused on problem areas—engine repair costs—improvements would have only had minimal impact on customers and would have resulted in the margin erosion of Honeywell's products.

WHAT CUSTOMERS VALUE

Dr. Noriaki Kano of the Tokyo Science University has developed a framework that uses the customer's point of view to describe the characteristics of products and services. Dr. Kano suggests three kinds of characteristics:

Basic characteristics. These are must-have attributes of the offering that do not delight customers when present but cause anger if they are absent. The customers have every right, for example, to expect their mobile phones to receive calls. When they do receive a call, they don't celebrate, but if their phone is unable to receive calls, they get angry. For this type of basic characteristic, customers are usually able to tell you whether your offerings are up to standard.

Performance-related characteristics. The more of these characteristics there are, the less frustrated and eventually the more satisfied your customer becomes. For example, if the battery life on your mobile phone is less than expected, customers are likely to be dissatisfied. If the battery life is better than expected, customers are likely to boast about your products. Often these characteristics are related to speed, capacity, user-friendliness, value for money, and accessibility.

Delight characteristics. Even a minimal presence of these characteristics creates satisfaction among customers. From the customer's point of view, delight characteristics are enchanting surprises. For example, cameras in mobile phones have recently delighted consumers. Delighters may become commonplace features over time and may eventually become basic characteristics that customers insist upon; television remote controls are an example.

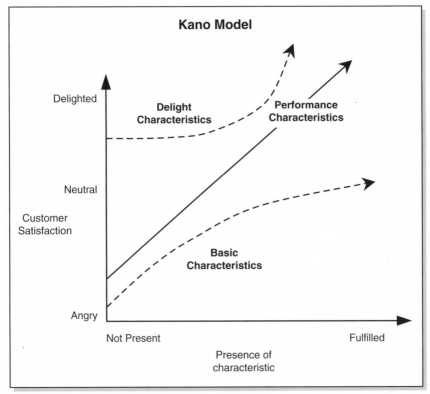

Figure 5.5 Kano Model

Delight characteristics create new markets and give a temporary competitive advantage to those who develop them. Once the novelty of the characteristic wears off and the competition includes it in their offerings, customers come to expect them. When this happens, the delight characteristics become performance characteristics. Eventually customers expect these performance characteristics as standard. When this happens, the performance characteristic becomes a basic characteristic.

This migration of characteristics is constant. To remain competitive, product developers must continually introduce new delight characteristics, provide more performance characteristics, and see that basic characteristics are always met.

There are some important lessons to be learned from Kano's model. First, customer satisfaction attributes are not all equal. Basic characteristics do not matter when they are present, but seriously detract from overall satisfaction when they are absent. In contrast, performance characteristics contribute to the overall satisfaction in an approximately linear fashion.

Second, simply responding to customer complaints is shown to be inadequate. Customer complaints are mostly linked to basic characteristics. A quality strategy aimed exclusively at removing problems in basic characteristics can never result in delighted customers. Such efforts will only lead to parity with the competition. Improvement efforts should be proactive and based on a deliberate policy of seeking out customers and potential customers to discover and characterize their needs, and then to innovate new value-added offerings that meet or surpass these needs.

CUSTOMER SATISFACTION AND LOYALTY IS NOT ENOUGH

W. Edwards Deming noted, "We certainly do not want to have an unhappy customer, but it will not suffice to have customers that are merely satisfied."[3]

It is good to have loyal customers—the people who are willing to wait in line for your products and services, and to recommend them to their friends. Loyal customers trust your products and services, and see them as higher value than those of other suppliers. Focusing on customer satisfaction and on building customer loyalty are important areas to which Six Sigma methods can contribute significantly. Studies have found that it cost 5 times more to gain a new customer than keep an existing one and 12 times more to regain a customer that had been lost.[4] Having loyal customers is clearly healthy for a business, but their future loyalty cannot be taken for granted. There is not necessarily any guarantee that customers will continue to purchase your offerings indefinitely. Efforts to improve customer satisfaction and build customer loyalty must be complemented with rigorous efforts to understand customer needs—both present and future—and create innovative new offerings. Customers are often not able to tell you what innovations they need. It is up to you to be proactive and figure out how to add value.

The business world abounds with stories of companies that were left behind because of competitor innovations. Floppy disk drive manufacturers, for example, had happy loyal customers that came back year after year to buy disk drives. Floppy disk drive manufacturers continued to produce drives with higher and higher performance levels and focused on improving customer satisfaction through quality improvements and improvements in logistics and support services. With the appearance of mass storage drives, rewritable CD and DVDs, however, formerly loyal floppy disk drive customers left in droves. Such disruptive technologies are often initially inferior, but good enough to win a large market share. Happy loyal customers will change suppliers very quickly when there is an innovation that creates more value for them.

In the past, the pace of innovation was much slower. In the eighteenth century, major innovations occurred once in a lifetime, but today such innovations are occurring on a daily basis. In the technology world, this phenomenon is sometimes referred to as disruptive technologies and can radically change marketplaces overnight. The challenge today is that such radical innovations are occurring more frequently than ever before and that simply focusing on customer satisfaction and loyalty, in the sense of improving existing products and services, is often not enough to guarantee survival.

In addition to the pace of change, many organizations today are facing another serious challenge: customers are becoming less loyal to suppliers. From the customers' perspective, there are typically several suppliers available with more or less the same offerings—the same product, features, price, and service. Why should they be loyal to one particular supplier over another? What's more, loyal customers will quickly change suppliers, given a superior offering from another supplier.

As Jack Welch has noted, the value decade is upon us. The only way to keep customers is to constantly figure out how to give them more for less. In other words, to be proactive and figure out how to add value before the competition does so.

Customer loyalty metrics serve an important function. Indexes such as customer retention and satisfaction are a good feedback mechanism for an organization, making sure customer requirements are being met. If certain market segments are found to be leaving the customer base (defections), Six Sigma initiatives can be used to find the root cause of the defections and then develop a method of regaining their business. Some organizations use special teams—sometimes referred

---

Customer Loyalty Metrics

❖ Defection rates

❖ Revenue per core customer

❖ Willingness to recommend

❖ Satisfaction

❖ Repurchase intent

❖ Repeat purchases

❖ Referrals by customer

❖ Customer loyalty indexes

Figure 5.6 Typical Customer Loyalty Measures

to as SWAT or Tiger teams—focused on regaining lost customers. In any industry, it is valuable to know which customers are leaving and why.

Sustained growth requires a more proactive approach. Meeting customer requirements and expectations only sets you on the same level as the competition. The customers' expectations of value are set by the marketplace—you and your competitors—not by customers themselves. As W. Edwards Deming put it, "The customer expects only what the producer has led him to expect."[5] In other words, what is required is not only to meet customer expectations (as quantified by loyalty measures) but also to proactively find ways to set them.

MARKET SEGMENTATION USING SIX SIGMA METHODS

Market segmentation allows an organization to focus on key segments and stay away from less attractive areas of the market. Understanding the value drivers in key market segments enables the creation of tailored offerings and specific sales approaches that add substantial value. Segmentation is best done for the entire market, not just for existing customers. New or upcoming segments may be significant growth opportunities that will be overlooked if only the existing customer base is segmented.

Poor segmentation can actually conceal growth opportunities. For example, if we assume that two distinct market segments exist when in fact they do not, we may develop tailored products and services inappropriately. Suppose it is assumed that younger people prefer different styles of shampoo bottle caps than older people (segments based on age groups). This may lead to the creation of numerous customized bottle caps, which require added resources and effort on the part of manufacturing and supply. If the assumption is false, and people don't really care about the style of shampoo bottle caps, the development is a massive waste.

It can be equally damaging to see a market as a homogenous group when in fact there are distinct segments within it. For example, if a company fails to recognize that one market segment prefers cameras in their mobile phones and another doesn't, it may lead them to promote camera-less phones to the entire market. The result is lost sales from the segment that wanted cameras.

Six Sigma methods can prove very valuable in segmenting markets. One approach is to:

- Develop some hypothesis about potential segments

- Determine the appropriate sample size and collect the relevant data for each segment (for a given value proposition)

- Analyze data and test the proposed segmentation using statistical tools such as graphical methods and hypothesis testing

- Determine if there is a statistically significant difference between segments

Data on potential segments can be collected through standard techniques such as focus groups and surveys.

Tools such as cluster analysis are effective in sorting customers into a smaller number of homogenous segments. Many organizations have now integrated these tools into the standard Six Sigma for sales and marketing curriculum. Naturally, given the importance of such segmentation decisions, it is critical to validate the results. Do the results make sense? Are they replicable? Are the segments acceptable by the key members of the business?

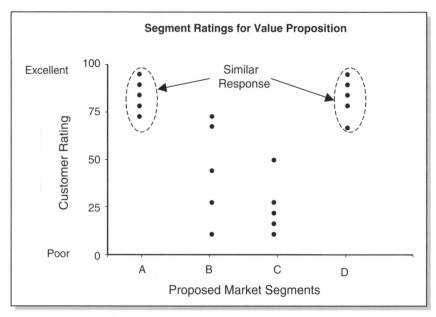

Figure 5.7   Validating Market Segments

Comparing D²MAIC with "Classical" Six Sigma DMAIC

D²MAIC differs from the classical Six Sigma DMAIC approach in the following ways:

- D²MAIC has a rigorous approach to project selection in the form of the Discovery Phase.

- The focus is directly on the ultimate customer and gaining a deep understanding of the customer's business and activities. Projects are directed at customers and are often collaborative events with customers.

- The concept of root causes is expanded to incorporate value drivers. Projects seek to profitably improve the value created for customers.

- Both problem and "nonproblem" or opportunity areas are the focus of improvement efforts.

- Consideration of customers' future needs and direction is important. With change comes opportunity; characterizing future needs is central to sustained growth.

- The concept of identifying customer core and peripheral activities and rigorously analyzing them for value creating opportunities.

- Understanding the customer's total economics and being able to develop improvements that can be measured in these terms.

- The incorporation of marketing tools such as cluster analysis and conjoint analysis.

- The Control and Replicate Phase seeks to ensure that added value is sustainable in the customer environment. It also looks for opportunities to replicate the project for sale to other customers. Many companies struggle to transfer and share best practices. Making replication an integral part of the development project solves many of these difficulties.

- A rigorous approach to business planning in the form of the Growth Plan (see page 119)

MARKET PENETRATION CASE STUDY: SOFTWARE SALES

A software company identified education as a growth segment for its products. This company already had a presence in the education segment, but sales to this segment were low. A Six Sigma project was initiated to improve it.

A clear statement of the software product features, benefits, and value to the customer was developed (the Value Proposition). The value proposition captures the key aspects of the offering that are important to the customer and that drive customer buying behavior. To establish that education was a truly distinct segment with its own particular needs, all market segments were verified using hypothesis-testing methods and historical data.

The baseline performance of the value proposition, in terms of revenue and other performance characteristics, were measured. Sales were poor, market penetration was relatively low, and there were signs of low customer satisfaction.

The next step was to gain a thorough understanding of the education segment's particular needs. Sampling methods obtained a representative sample of schools (both existing and new customers) that provided focus groups.

Specific focus group questionnaires were developed that captured information about the product and competitors' offerings.

Analysis of the data generated by the questionnaires revealed several issues consistent across all schools, including shortcomings in the product features, price, and product training. In the case of the product training, schools commented that the students found the training material difficult to use and that they were not aware of the software's full functionality. There were clear value gaps between what schools wanted and what was being delivered.

The team brainstormed possible ways to improve the Value Proposition. Modifying the features of the software was costly and would have taken considerable time, so this was temporarily put aside. This left price and product training as the main gaps in value from the customer's perspective. Product financing and utilization of online eLearning courses were identified and validated with customers as significant potential improvements.

The new Value Proposition included financing and eLearning. It became the standard package for the education segment. Sales people found approaching customers much easier, and revenue began to improve. Results were verified by a statistically significant improvement in the baseline sales numbers captured in the Measure Phase.

REVENUE IMPROVEMENT CASE STUDY:
PACKING MATERIALS

A supplier of packing materials had noticed that one of its customers, a major retail chain, kept considerable amounts of inventory in centrally located warehouses and at numerous stores, and paid substantial sums of money to a logistics company for transportation. Client executives had the idea of helping customers reduce their inventory holdings and logistics costs by providing direct shipping to store locations. The team felt that the new service would help customers reduce their running costs and would easily justify an increase in the product price.

The packing material company had an effective logistics department that was experienced in making frequent deliveries of small quantities of packing material. The team decided that offering such value-added logistics services to retail customers was an extension to their current offerings (D²MAIC). A baseline Value Proposition, which detailed the proposed delivery approach and the benefits the customer would gain from the new offering, was developed.

The project objective was twofold, first to reduce the total inventory and logistics costs the customer was paying for its internal operations, and second to improve the margins for the supplier. The specifics of the new approach had to be developed and verified. To gain a better understanding of the current customer processes of storage and logistics, process mapping techniques were used.

The team worked with the customers to validate process maps and gain an understanding of the customers' total economic picture. Activities in the customer process were studied for unmet needs, costs, inventory holdings, and handling effort. These were quantified at each step (see Figure 7.20). The result was a thorough understanding of the customer's current processes and total economics.

The team then compared the customer's current processes and needs against the baseline Value Proposition. Gaps and shortcomings in the Value Proposition were identified and validated.

The team identified improvements that closed the gaps and developed detailed process maps of the new logistic processes. The Value Proposition was refined and put in terms of the (validated) total savings and performance improvements to the customers. The new Value Proposition was discussed with the customers, and agreement was gained to proceed with implementation. Several pilot runs with customers confirmed the viability of the new approach.

The final phase involved developing a "scale up" plan that would implement the improvements on a limited scale before converting fully to the new approach. Control measures and standard operating procedures were developed and put into place to ensure that the new method was sustainable.

CHAPTER 6

D²MADV—Growth through New Offerings and Solutions

Resources, to produce results, must be allocated to
opportunities rather than to problems.
—Peter Drucker[1]

Customers' behavior and requirements have changed radically in recent years. Today's customer is:

- Sophisticated and price sensitive

- Short of time and demands more convenience

- Aware of growing product parity among competing suppliers

- Less brand sensitive

- Demanding of high quality and service

- Less loyal to suppliers

This change has increased the pressure on firms to differentiate their offerings from the competition. Many companies that traditionally developed and sold stand-alone products are changing their strategies and are now creating high-value collaborative projects and "solutions" aimed at solving customer problems. This often entails developing offerings that combine elements of existing offerings and may even incorporate competitors' products.

This new approach changes the game profoundly. Instead of the traditional product-centric view, the focus is now on understanding customers' problems and finding ways to solve them profitably. This cuts across organizational boundaries and often involves collaborative efforts with customers and suppliers.

Developing customized solutions for customers requires a rigorous design and development process. Many organizations have turned to Design for Six Sigma (DFSS) to achieve this. Design for Six Sigma was created to enhance a vital competitive advantage: innovation. It is a managed approach to innovation, which leads to the development of high-quality products and services that customers value.

DFSS is used to design new products and services, and also major modifications of existing offerings. Recently, DFSS has been expanded to help companies diagnose and understand customer problems and to develop offerings to solve them. In all cases, businesses are looking to grow by finding ways to give customers more for less—and to develop new offerings that help customers.

Solutions typically start with a customer's business problem or opportunity. Suppliers and customers work together to understand the issue and develop offerings that enable the customer to capitalize on the opportunity. Success is often judged by improvements in customer metrics—not internal measures of performance or product revenues—and profit-sharing arrangements are not uncommon. Solution development involves collaborative efforts and often blurs the boundaries between customer and supplier by sharing resources and intellectual property. One well-known company found that several of their key customers—also Six Sigma companies—refused to discuss business issues and solutions unless Black Belts from both companies were present at meetings. For this firm, the use of Six Sigma tools is now a key factor in the sales process, both as a means to communicate and as a rigorous methodology for identifying opportunities and developing solutions.

This chapter discusses the traditional DFSS application and its more recent focus on solutions. From a technical perspective, both approaches are very similar and utilize many of the same tools, but the way the tools are applied is significantly different.

Careful business planning is required, particularly in the case of collaborative projects or profit-sharing arrangements. Furthermore, the emphasis is often on profiting by managing the entire life of the product, not just the sales transaction. Selling a product is not enough; it must be sustainable and deliver value to customers throughout its life.

D²MADV is a six-phase approach:

D²MADV Phases	
Discovery	Identify growth opportunities.
Define	Define the opportunity, goals, requirements and assumptions.
Measure	Gather customer needs; translate them to measurable solution requirements.
Analyze	Analyze requirements and develop basic solutions. Prioritize alternate solutions. Validate the value proposition.
Design	Develop detailed solution design and optimize.
Validate & Replicate	Implement solution, test and monitor performance, seek opportunities to replicate solution to other customers.

Figure 6.1   D²MADV Phases for New Offering and Solution Development

Typical D²MADV growth projects include:

- Developing profitable solutions to customer problems

- New product or service development

- Customizing existing offerings

- Major redesigns in existing offerings

- Developing joint or shared business processes

DEVELOPING SOLUTIONS AND NEW OFFERINGS

A Six Sigma for Growth project enters the Define Phase when it has been officially launched by the leadership team. The project has

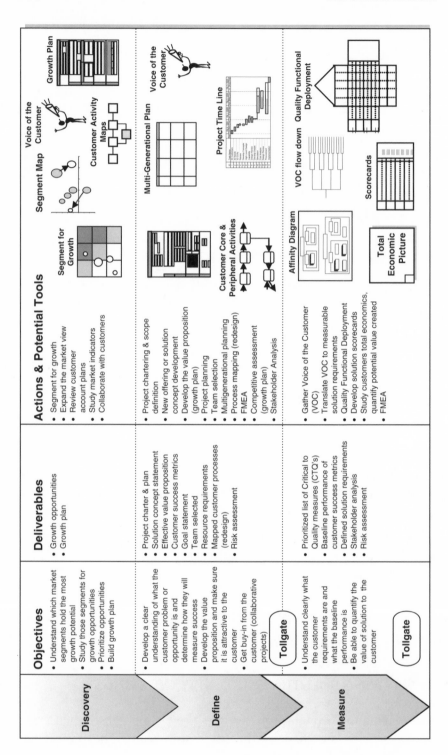

Objectives

Discovery
- Understand which market segments hold the most growth potential
- Study those segments for growth opportunities
- Prioritize opportunities
- Build growth plan

Define
- Develop a clear understanding of what the customer problem or opportunity is and determine how they will measure success
- Develop the value proposition and make sure it is attractive to the customer
- Get buy-in from the customer (collaborative projects)

Tollgate

Measure
- Understand clearly what the customer requirements are and what the baseline performance is
- Be able to quantify the value of solution to the customer

Tollgate

Deliverables

- Growth opportunities
- Growth plan

- Project charter & plan
- Solution concept statement
- Effective value proposition
- Customer success metrics
- Goal statement
- Team selected
- Resource requirements
- Mapped customer processes (redesign)
- Risk assessment

- Prioritized list of Critical to Quality measures (CTQ's)
- Baseline performance of customer success metrics
- Defined solution requirements
- Stakeholder analysis
- Risk assessment

Actions & Potential Tools

- Segment for growth
- Expand the market view
- Review customer account plans
- Study market indicators
- Collaborate with customers

- Project chartering & scope definition
- New offering or solution concept development
- Develop the value proposition (growth plan)
- Project planning
- Team selection
- Multigenerational planning
- Process mapping (redesign)
- FMEA
- Competitive assessment (growth plan)
- Stakeholder Analysis

- Gather Voice of the Customer (VOC)
- Translate VOC to measurable solution requirements
- Quality Functional Deployment
- Develop solution scorecards
- Study customers total economics, quantify potential value created
- FMEA

Segment Map

Voice of the Customer

Growth Plan

Customer Activity Maps

Voice of the Customer

Segment for Growth

Multi-Generational Plan

Project Time Line

Quality Functional Deployment

Customer Core & Peripheral Activities

Affinity Diagram

Total Economic Picture

VOC flow down

Scorecards

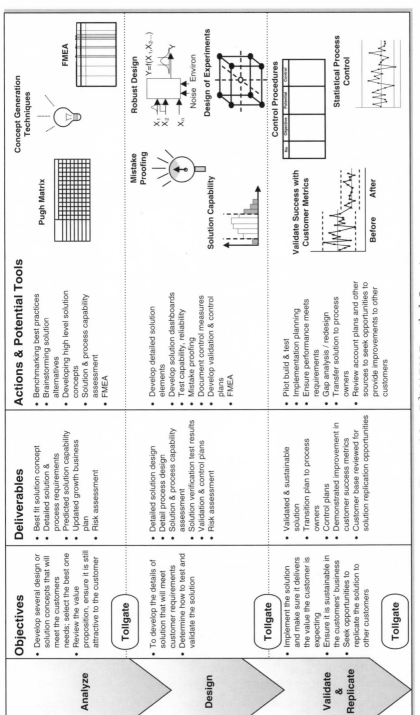

Figure 6.2 D²MADV Detailed Overview

been selected from a large number of opportunities identified in the Discovery Phase and is considered a serious growth opportunity for the organization as a whole.

A key task in the Define Phase is to validate the project selection rationale and to develop a detailed Growth Plan (see Target Step page 119). Profitably solving customer problems requires Six Sigma teams to become very familiar with the customers' issues and total economic picture.

Projects may be collaborative, requiring teams from both the supplier and the customer to agree on the project definition and the business rationale. Management teams from both organizations must work closely to articulate the measures of success and agree on specific goals. The aim is agreement on the scope of the project and a common understanding of what is to be improved, modified, or created.

Next, management teams decide on the appropriate allocation of resources for the project. The decision on resource allocation includes:

- Formally announcing the Executive Champion(s)

- Nominating a team leader

- Identifying team members, often from both organizations

Naturally, team selection is a crucial step, and members must be assessed carefully for the contributions they will bring.

Troubled and unsuccessful projects tend to develop problems at the Define Phase because the project's goals, scope, charter, and resources are not clearly articulated and agreed upon.

The essence of the Define Phase is to define the project clearly enough for all participants to understand it fully and to appreciate its scope. It is especially important in collaborative projects to define the measures of success. The measures should be clearly understood by all parties and serve as the final means of determining if the project has been successful.

In the Measure Phase, the focus is on identifying all direct and indirect customers, understanding their essential needs, and listing the critical-to-quality measures (CTQs).

Once there is a clear understanding of the scope of the project and the people involved, the stakeholder analysis should be updated.

This technique examines each person involved in the project and assesses whether they support, resist, or are neutral to the initiative (see page 211).

The key customer needs must be expressed in ways that are measurable. The goal of the design effort is to fulfil these needs as defined in the list of CTQs. Auxiliary methods of generating CTQs include benchmarking with competitors and creative internal development, which often uncover real customer needs that the customers themselves are unaware of. The final list of CTQs should be:

• Defined in detail

• Consistent in approach (all must be measurable)

• Ranked in order of priority

The design group then assesses related existing offerings and defines their performance levels in the same terms that are used in the CTQ list. A reality check must be performed, using Measurement System Analysis, to test the quality of the data.

Using a design scorecard, the group outlines the planned design development with the goal of a final offering that meets Six Sigma standards for defects—this can be complex, since many as-yet-undeveloped design elements may be needed to produce the offering.

The Analyze Phase begins by analyzing the CTQs by function. The design team works to produce a number of high-level designs that offer different functional solutions. The design options are carefully evaluated against a predetermined set of criteria. In general, this process cycles through a series of iterations as designers refine, alter and combine design options, reevaluate them, and repeat the process. This is an intrinsic feature of design as an activity. As designers develop their understanding of the nature of the project, they constantly adjust and improve in a necessary but apparently repetitive process.

Many tools are available to assess and evaluate the design options, including:

• Functional analysis

• Process capability

- Risk analysis

- Financial analysis

The design group must not lose sight of the performance goals, which are to meet or better the CTQ requirements and be economically feasible.

The growth business plan needs to be updated at each phase in the development process. At this point, estimates of the value the solution will bring to the customer should be reviewed again, in the light of new knowledge of the customer's process. The value proposition should be reviewed and agreed upon by the customer before any further development work.

Once the design process is complete, one of the high-level designs is selected and validated. The chosen design is analyzed to produce the best-fit design, establishing the specifications for more detailed design work in the Design Phase.

The objective of the Design Phase is to produce the optimum design that meets all requirements, including the needs of manufacturing and service.

Using Design of Experiments (DOEs), the high-level design selected in the Analyze Phase is tested to produce the optimum design in detail. A number of tools are used, both ones that assume linear relationships between the design parameters as well as nonlinear approaches, such as response surface methods. These experiments provide the information needed to focus on reducing tolerances, which improve quality and standardization.

The design group then compares the new design against existing manufacturing and service processes using tools such as:

- Reliability analysis

- Serviceability analysis

- Design for Manufacturability (DFM), Design for Assembly (DFA).

When this comparison is complete, the design is tested, using risk analysis tools, and the group makes final adjustments to fit with the planned production capabilities.

Finally, the design is verified using tools such as:

- Prototyping

- Pilot testing

- Simulation

and the results are reported in a formal review.

In the Validate and Replicate Phase, the first object is to make sure that the solution will meet the criteria for cost, quality, and reliability—when it is in full production and for its entire lifetime. Lifetime and service issues vary very widely, so the design group must take care to select the appropriate tools to explore any possible difficulties.

All the process control plans and other documents must now be compiled as a set of well-planned operation manuals. These should include clear definitions of tolerances and control limits. The manuals are transferred to the appropriate process managers, such as manufacturing.

The final step for the development team is to establish opportunities for replication by looking proactively for other potential customers for the new offering. Customized products and services are great for customers, but they can be very costly to develop. In focusing on developing customized solutions for customers, companies such as IBM have realized that the only way for such offerings to be profitable is to replicate them for other customers. The development team has first-hand knowledge and best practices, which facilitate customizing the solution for other customers and may be able to capture substantial new growth opportunities.

DESIGN FOR SIX SIGMA (DFSS)

DFSS has numerous advantages over traditional design methods. It:

- Reduces development lead times

- Ensures new offerings that meet or exceed customers' requirements

- Anticipates and mitigates problems before they occur

- Reduces the offering's total life cycle costs

- Minimizes design changes

- Improves a product's quality and reliability in the field

- Reduces costs of production

- Builds a strong improvement culture

DFSS is based on a concurrent development approach, in which design activities run in parallel to each other by using cross-functional teams comprised of members from many different functional groups, including design, R&D, sales, marketing, engineering, and manufacturing. This is a major enhancement of traditional design approaches, which are typically run in a series, moving through each functional department one at a time. A series approach tends to lengthen development times and increases the chance of mistakes and inefficiencies appearing.

Applying DFSS techniques directly to customer processes, as opposed to internal development projects, is in itself a considerable change. The scope is expanded to examine how the new developments can be optimized in the customer's environment and how they can work seamlessly with their current processes. In addition, it often requires a close collaboration between customer and supplier, and in some instances offerings may be priced based on the benefits generated for the customer. This new set of circumstances requires modifications to classical DFSS methods.

The development process begins at a high level, selecting a customer problem or opportunity (identified in the Discovery Phase) and then carefully analyzing their needs, both stated and implied. The same principle is applied to redesign—a new and improved offering that does not meet customer needs will, after all, be a failure.

BASIC DEVELOPMENT METHODOLOGY

There are a number of other DFSS approaches, including:

IDOV: Invent, Develop, Optimize, and Verify

DMEDI: Define, Measure, Explore, Develop, and Implement

DCCDI: Define, Customer, Concept, Design,
           and Implement

DCOV: Define, Characterize, Optimize, and
           Verify

Each of these approaches uses common tools and follows a similar development sequence (see Figure 6.3). The sequence starts by identifying the customers and gathering their requirements. The requirements are analyzed, prioritized, and translated into technical specifications. From this, design concepts are generated, and the capability of each design—its ability to meet customer requirements—is estimated. The design that is best able to meet customer requirements is selected and developed into a detailed design.

In addition to designing the product or service itself, the production process must also be designed to minimize costs and defects. The product, the process, and any related subsystems must be designed to meet Six Sigma quality levels.

The product then goes through validation steps to confirm that it is capable of meeting or exceeding customer requirements.

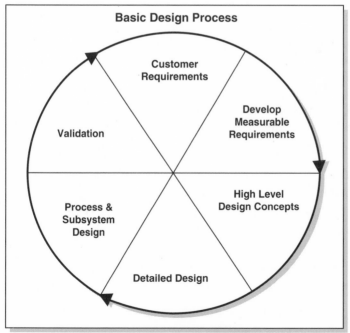

Figure 6.3   Typical Design Process

Creating Solutions with Design for Six Sigma

Some important modifications have been made to the traditional DFSS approach in order to drive business growth. These differences include:

- Project selection follows a rigorous approach—the Discovery Phase.

- The focus is directly on the ultimate customer and gaining a deep understanding of the customer's business and activities. Projects are directed at customers and are often collaborative.

- Success is measured using the customer's metrics, not the manufacturer's.

- Developed solutions may include your competitors' products.

- Customized offerings are developed, not stand-alone products. The offering may include several products and services.

- The customer's future needs and direction are essential elements. Future needs provide growth opportunities.

- The concept of identifying customers' core and peripheral activities and rigorously analyzing them for value-creating opportunities is introduced.

- The approach aims at understanding the customer's total economics and using it to assess the value added by the new offering.

- The approach incorporates marketing tools such as cluster analysis and conjoint analysis.

- The Validate and Replicate Phase is introduced. This seeks to ensure that the value is sustainable in the customer's environment and looks for opportunities to replicate the project to other customers. Many companies have struggled in taking improvements made in one area and copying them in other areas. Making efforts to find such replication opportunities part of the project—which must be completed before the project can be signed off—solves this problem.

- A rigorous approach to business planning takes the form of the Growth Plan (see page 119).

CASE STUDIES

Confusion sometimes arises over the term "solution," but there is no need to be overly rigid in our definition. Customized offers range from straightforward enhancements that are proposed and managed by the supplier, through varying degrees of collaboration. A joint initiative may develop a new offering rather than a solution, although a solution may only require minimal collaboration from the customer. It is customization that is the essence of the approach—no two projects will be exactly the same, because every customer has different needs.

The following two case studies illustrate this. In the first case, a supplier identified a customer's problem, arranged a collaborative project, and later was able to adapt the proven solution for other customers. In the second case, the customer sought a supplier that was capable of assuming the responsibility for managing a large part of a complex manufacturing process involving other contractors; Six Sigma methods enabled all parties to work together closely to meet a very demanding set of criteria.

IN PRACTICE: HELPING AIRLINES REDUCE INVENTORIES

A major airline carried many millions of dollars' worth of inventory in the form of replacement parts and spare aircraft engines. Survival in the airline business depends heavily on cash flow, and hence freeing up cash was a priority.

An improvement team at an aerospace component supplier saw this problem as an opportunity during joint Six Sigma training sessions and workshops. It was clear to the team that the time taken to repair or replace components was having a major impact on the airline's inventory levels.

The component supplier approached the airline and agreed on a joint Six Sigma initiative to work on the problem.

Airlines need to hold enough parts to minimize aircraft downtime. Stocks of parts that can be replaced or repaired quickly are kept low, but items that are difficult to obtain or repair must be held in sufficient quantities to prevent costly delays.

The costs of holding inventories had become so high that many airlines were willing to pay a premium for a very fast repair service.

From the supplier's perspective, it became evident that by reducing the time to repair parts, airlines would benefit and would naturally select it as a preferred supplier. The growth opportunity was clear: helping customers reduce their inventories would lead to a competitive advantage and, ultimately, increased revenues.

The joint Six Sigma team quickly realized that one reason for the delays was the way in which both companies processed their paperwork. It took up to two weeks from the point that the airline realized a part needed to be serviced to the issue of a purchase order for the repair. Another two weeks was needed for the supplier to prepare quotations for the repair and gain customer acceptance. A large number of parts spent one month in storage waiting for paperwork to be cleared.

A Design for Six Sigma (D^2MADV) approach was taken to effect a major change in the way the two companies worked together. The project started by defining the opportunity and benefits for both parties. A core and extended team of Black Belts and Green Belts from both organizations was assembled.

The team developed a multigenerational plan that addressed improvements to the way the companies handled paperwork. The first stage of the plan would reduce the airline's inventories significantly. This process would continue in subsequent stages until the airline had no component inventories, since they would be owned by the supplier. The supplier was able to handle inventories far more efficiently because its parts could be used by multiple airline customers.

Teams gathered the requirements for the first-generation improvement. This was done collaboratively through process mapping and observation, and by interviewing administrative staff in both companies. As is typical with transactional processes, the teams realized that procedures were not clearly defined; a considerable effort was made to understand how the paperwork was actually being generated.

Analysis of the documentation process requirements and subsequent brainstorming sessions generated several possible approaches to the problem. After careful consideration, the team selected the option with the greatest impact—to partially integrate the computer systems of the airline and the supplier. This would allow the airline to generate a component service request that would automatically appear in the supplier's system. The airline would rapidly receive a quotation and be able to approve it online. The ordering process would be reduced from one month to approximately four days.

Based on this high-level design, a value proposition was updated and agreed upon by both parties. Both firms would provide development resources and share in the investment in the computer systems.

Detailed designs of the new process were developed in the Design Phase. Test systems were developed to judge the effectiveness of the design, and solution verification plans were set up.

In the Validate Phase, the new system was tested and shown to be effective. The new system was piloted and progressively scaled up until it completely replaced the old purchase order and quotation methods. To ensure sustainability, control plans were established, including training the various groups involved and documenting the new procedures.

The solution built closer ties with the airline and was win-win. Subsequently, the supplier was awarded a major long-term contract. This established a major barrier against competitors.

When the implementation was complete, teams from the supplier took the Replicate step, and found ways to adapt the new process for other airlines. Several other airlines enthusiastically adopted the solution.

IN PRACTICE: SEMICONDUCTOR COMPONENTS

A major semiconductor manufacturer (the customer) was unable able to find a supplier that could meet the performance levels for a component used in a large percentage of the world's new cars.

Six Sigma quality levels are mandatory in automotive safety and security devices. Often, quality levels are much higher; critical components seldom fail in the lifetime of the vehicle. The issue was further complicated by a difficult assembly process, large production quantities, and strict inventory and logistics requirements. The customer did not have the resources to develop an in-house production capability.

A main supplier was needed that would not only deliver a product but also assume risk by guaranteeing quality and managing several aspects of the business. Assuming risk for a customer, entering into business partnerships, and helping them with several different aspects of the business are common themes in developing solutions.

The customer approached a supplier that had experience of solving such problems using Six Sigma methods. This supplier had found that more and more of its customers were expecting it not only to sell them products but also to provide other value-added services such as solving technical problems. In response, the firm had established a tailored solutions service as an integral part of its sales process.

Joint teams from the customer, main supplier, machine manufacturer, and raw material suppliers employed Six Sigma methods and worked concurrently to design a solution that included manufacturing processes, quality control measures and just in time logistics. As part of the solution, the main supplier would not only manufacture components and deliver them just in time to manufacturing lines, but it also guaranteed to ensure that production was capable in the statistical sense (well within specifications and stable) and that there would be zero defects.

In return, the customer awarded them 100% of the business and signed an open-ended 10-year supply agreement.

Design for Six Sigma methods were central to developing the solution. The customer's measures of success included the technical performance of the finished assembled unit (the customer's finished product), rather than the suppliers' subcomponent performance. From the customer's point of view, this was a key measure that could be easily related to its future sales performance. Aligning suppliers directly with this goal, and obtaining guarantees, gave it greater control of the project at a lower risk.

The joint design teams worked for several months to develop a solution. The collaborative efforts blurred the boundaries between the companies and included the sharing of technical resources, intellectual property, and equipment. Initial pilot runs were successfully completed, and production grew steadily.

As the main supplier became more familiar with the customer's business activities and total economics, other opportunities to add value emerged. Six Sigma teams studied the customer's processes and developed lists of opportunities to add value to the customer. These opportunities were reviewed by the supplier, and new value propositions were developed.

One such opportunity was to help the customer's research and development efforts by leveraging the supplier's in-house R&D capabilities. Optimizing R&D across both organizations would generate considerable savings for the customer, enabling it to concentrate on its core technologies and leave the development of many ancillary components to the supplier.

Embedding Six Sigma resources with customers is a very effective way to build closer ties and often reveals previously hidden growth opportunities. It is the hallmark of the customer-centric companies who are applying Six Sigma methods to drive business growth. In this case, both the customer and the supplier recognized that their collaboration had generated far more profit for both companies than had been anticipated at the outset of the initial project.

RETHINKING VOICE OF THE CUSTOMER (VOC)

Most companies assume that they have a good understanding of their customers' needs, but in many cases they fail to identify the true requirements. Two principal reasons for this are:

1. Customer requirements change rapidly, and

2. Many customers really don't know what their requirements actually are.

Although companies may use valid Voice of the Customer (VOC) methods to obtain information about customers, they often do not succeed in capturing a complete picture. For instance, traditional market research often generates mountains of data with no actionable insight. Conventional customer satisfaction surveys are important, but they tend to look at the past rather than the future. The majority of VOC techniques are discrete—for example, yearly satisfaction surveys, customer complaints and suggestions are unconnected events, and do not provide a continuous flow of information from customers. In addition, it is generally difficult to identify those needs that customers themselves do not recognize.

To get closer to their customers, companies need to expand the range of VOC techniques they use. A continuous flow of information in real time about customer needs and issues may sound unattainable, but it has become a reality for firms who have established unusually close relationships with their key customers, using the Six Sigma for Growth approach.

There are three broad categories of voice of the customer information:

Reactive Sources

These provide indicators that are usually after the fact, such as product returns and complaints. Typically, companies have large amounts of data in the form of customer complaints, product returns, web page hits. Reactive sources are a good starting point for a Six Sigma project, but such historical data should usually be validated using proactive or continuous sources of customer information.

Proactive Sources

These involve engaging with the customer proactively through methods such as focus groups and interviews. One excellent way of gathering information about needs and requirements is to observe how customers use a product. For example, Toyota sales people sit next to customers while they test drive their cars and carefully note their behavior, such as the way they adjust the seat, the items that attract their attention, and what they look for. At the end of the test

---

Voice of the Customer Sources

Proactive Sources
- Surveys
- Questionnaires
- Focus groups
- Interviews
- Observation
- Casual contacts
- Workshops, seminars

Reactive Sources
- Complaints
- Compliments
- Suggestions
- Product returns
- Experience
- Service calls
- Market research reports
- Web page hits
- Customer defections

Continuous Sources
- Embedded resources with the customer
- Collaborative projects
- Shared processes & Partnerships

Figure 6.4   Voice of the Customer Sources

drive, the sales person is required to file a report about the customer experience.

Continuous Sources

Wherever possible, organizations should strive to develop continuous sources of information from their key customers. Seeing the customer's business, their issues, and future direction through their eyes is the foundation of sustained growth.

As discussed earlier, companies such as GE and Honeywell are extending their Six Sigma programs to the sales and distribution channels and, in many cases, to the customers themselves. GE's At the Customer, For the Customer program favors embedding Six Sigma personnel with key customers, while Honeywell collaborates with customers at varying degrees of intensity according to the individual case.

Embedding is just one approach to gaining a continuous flow of VOC information. If it is not feasible or desirable to place Six Sigma resources directly with the customer, other forms of close collaboration may be equally effective in producing answers to such questions as:

- Can we map the entire customer value chain?

- How can we add value to it?

- Can we make it easier for the customer to buy our products?

- Can we help customers with other issues?

- Why do they choose a competitor's products over ours?

The goal of VOC must now be to become sophisticated about the customer's business, to know the issues and how the business really works. Through continuous direct contact with customers, we are able to identify solutions to their problems and unlock their enthusiasm, budgets, and loyalty.

The typical industrial customer has many buyers, decision makers, and sources of influence scattered throughout its organization. In recent years, sales teams have become increasingly sophisticated in their approach to these complex sales and go to great lengths to establish a constant flow of information in their efforts to close sales.

The sales function, however, cannot obtain a complete and accurate view of customer needs on its own; all functions must be involved. The goal is to piece the picture together from a very wide range of information to arrive at the issues that are central to the customer's present and future prosperity.

Perhaps the greatest challenge is to accurately identify those needs that the customer is unaware of or does not articulate. The customer may be organized into functional silos with poor interdepartmental communication. In such cases, it becomes the supplier's job to identify these silent needs, define them, and give them a voice. Two powerful tools for doing this are to map customers' core and peripheral activities and to analyze their total economic picture (see page 238–239).

Establishing shared processes or developing business partnerships with customers can be an excellent source of continuous feedback. When FedEx partnered with Intel to take over Intel's logistics, for example, the process resulted in significant gains for both organizations and gave FedEx a source of continuous feedback about their performance. Such partnerships are becoming increasingly common, and mark a significant change in the way business is conducted.

The notion of a continuous source of customer feedback is not new. Many Japanese companies insist on it. Toyo, for example, sends guest engineers to work at Komatsu for two days every two weeks to attend joint technical design meetings. Guest engineers are assigned for three years at a time.[2]

How better can a supplier understand a customer's new product development process than by being part of it? How better to understand how a customer uses a product or service than to use it with them? This practice blurs company boundaries and creates a business where organizations along the whole value chain work on issues together, sharing resources and information to improve the overall efficiency and value to the ultimate customers.

CHAPTER 7

Growth Tools and Methods

Six Sigma teams have a great number of tools and methods at their disposal, but it takes considerable experience to know which of them to apply in a specific case. Seasoned Six Sigma practitioners will be familiar with the exhaustive studies of Six Sigma tools such as graphical methods, statistical process control, measurement system analysis, and they will not be repeated here. This chapter examines the principal tools that are central to the Six Sigma for Growth approach and discusses their application from a growth perspective.

Six Sigma for Growth programs generally create a customized Green Belt curriculum. Customer-facing groups such as sales, marketing, service, and credit, typically attend one-week training courses and work on projects on a part-time basis. It is hoped that Six Sigma organizations will gain from this section by reviewing their existing approaches and integrating new tools into their existing Six Sigma program.

Market Indicator Analysis (MIA)

To achieve sustained growth, it is vital to identify growth opportunities continuously and consistently. Market Indicator Analysis is a powerful tool for uncovering such opportunities.

MIA is a brainstorming method that uses a list of market indicators or areas that signal changes and opportunities in the marketplace, building on the work of Alex Osborn, who pioneered brainstorming methods in the 1930s, and of the influential innovation guru, Peter Drucker, who developed a list of focus areas in 1985.[1]

Figure 7.1 shows some typical market indicators that build upon Drucker's original list. This is by no means exhaustive, and organizations should identify areas appropriate for their particular businesses.

Market Indicator Analysis: Focus Areas	
❖ Unexpected Successes	❖ High Growth Areas
❖ Unexpected Failures	❖ Converging Technologies
❖ Unexpected External Events	❖ Perception Changes
❖ Anomalies	❖ Demographic Changes
❖ Strengths & Weakness	❖ Declining Profits
❖ Market & Industry Changes	❖ New Knowledge

Figure 7.1   Market Indicator Analysis

UNEXPECTED SUCCESSES

Have any existing products and services been unexpectedly successful? What does this tell us about the customers?

Unfortunately, unexpected successes are often ignored or looked on as temporary aberrations. If studied carefully, they may generate excellent growth opportunities.

Typically, managers' discussions at sales performance reviews focus on problem areas where results have not hit their targets. If some minor product or service happens to be selling better than expected, few people care. Six Sigma practitioners can easily fall into this "if it is not broken, don't fix it" way of thinking if they only focus on identifying and fixing problems. Six Sigma's methodology is also ideally suited for improvement in areas that are already performing well and taking them to even higher levels of performance.

An unexpected success may well be a sign that your company is missing an important change in the market. Further investigation may reveal that the firm must drastically redefine its business and innovate. This can only happen if:

- you are alert to the possibility that unexpected successes can occur,

- you are aware that they may be very significant, and

- the business is organized to identify and respond to them.

It is a self-fulfilling prophecy to ignore the unexpected success as irrelevant. If you fail to exploit the new opportunities, this is a signal that a competitor will eventually move in and capture the market.

For many firms, it is comfortable to ignore the unexpected success if they do not fit into management's carefully laid plans for the future. Very often, reporting systems are structured in ways that prevent the unexpected success from being noticed by senior executives.

In the context of unexpected success, innovation does not mean diversification but *extending* the firm's existing activities by using its expertise. This does not necessarily mean product innovation—it may simply suggest changes to distribution channels or to back-up services.

Take an objective look at the unexpected successes your company has experienced and at those of your competitors and suppliers. They can generally be identified from any type of sales target that has been exceeded.

Questions to ask:

• Have any of our offerings been an unexpected success recently?

• Did this success occur in any particular region?

• Did the success occur in a particular market or segment?

• Have any of your customers or suppliers had unexpected successes recently?

• What are the reasons for the success?

• Are there any new customer prospects that are making strange enquiries or were not previously thought to be potential customers? Are they signaling that there is a new market out there?

• How can we exploit these successes to the maximum—in both the long and short term?

UNEXPECTED FAILURES

Have any existing products experienced unexpected failures? What does this tell us about the customers?

Almost by definition, unexpected failures are a rich source of growth potential because they imply unnoticed changes in the market. We define failures as "unexpected" when they have been well planned, researched, and executed, and have nevertheless flopped—in other words, where able and experienced people have done their best, but have made assumptions about the market that have proved to be invalid.

The opportunity for innovation after such a failure lies in detective work. Rather than simply analyzing the problem using preconceived notions, managers need to get out in the field and listen to the customers. It makes no difference whether it is your own company or one of your competitors who has suffered the failure; the clues for innovation are still out there to be discovered. Perhaps customers have changed their attitude, are splitting into different markets, or are being affected by developments in an apparently unrelated field. A thorough investigation can generate insights into how they have changed.

The classic example of unexpected failure is Ford Motor Company's introduction of the Edsel automobile in the late 1950s. Contrary to popular belief, the introduction of the Edsel was not an ill-conceived gamble. In fact, it was one of the most conscientiously researched mass-market products ever produced. The standard of quality was excellent, and Ford had taken immense pains to incorporate customer needs into its design. Faced with a completely unexpected failure of the Edsel to sell, Ford responded positively and tried to find out why.

Ford soon discovered that their categorization of the U.S. market into four socioeconomic groups was no longer valid. This notion had been established in the 1930s by its main competitor, General Motors, and had become an unchallenged assumption for the entire auto industry. The Edsel was planned as Ford's offering to the second-highest socioeconomic group, the "upper middle," but customers were now segmenting in different ways, choosing cars according to lifestyle rather than social class. Ford quickly decided to address these new customer attitudes with an innovation, the Thunderbird, which proved to be a huge success and completely restored the company's position as a major player.

Take an objective look at the unexpected failures your company has experienced, and at those of your competitors and suppliers. They need not be absolute failures—a disappointment in a specific market or locality may be very instructive.

Questions to ask:

- Have any of our offerings failed unexpectedly recently?

- Did this failure occur in any particular region?

- Did the failure occur in a particular market or segment?

- Have any of our customers or suppliers had unexpected failures recently?

- Have any of our competitors had unexpected failures recently?

- What were the true causes of the failure?

- What new offerings or approaches could we use to exploit our new understanding of these causes?

To discover the true causes of the failure, get out in the field and talk to the customers. Your company may have made incorrect assumptions about the causes of a failure, which have become the received wisdom internally—check if they match the reality.

Unexpected External Events

Shocks such as the September 11 attacks have wide ranging effects on many businesses; have unexpected events changed our customers?

Events outside an industry may have dramatic repercussions within it. In the early 1970s, the OPEC oil cartel suddenly put up the price of oil, sending Western economies into a tailspin. In 2003, a new disease, SARS, suddenly appeared in Asia, drastically affecting travel and tourism in the region, which was already reeling from the fallout from the equally unexpected September 11 terrorist attacks.

Since the attacks, the global demand for security services and products of all kinds has surged. There is reason to believe that this demand will not be short-lived. This represents a huge opportunity for businesses that are willing to adapt their existing expertise to enter these markets.

Devices such as remote thermal imaging cameras or MRI scanners emerge unexpectedly and are immediately adopted, making older products obsolete almost overnight.

Companies can use their existing expertise to search for ways to extend their own offerings when such events occur. The innovations should be based on existing knowledge to have a good chance of success.

Major changes in an industry may also be unexpected. Back in the 1960s, everybody "knew" that computers had to be physically massive and run by a priesthood of technicians wearing white coats.

When the first microcomputers came along in the 1970s, computer professionals dismissed them as toys for hobbyists. When it rapidly became clear that micros were going to be a hit, computer giant IBM woke up and designed the PC, using its market power to establish it as the standard hardware for the industry—the perfect response to a completely unexpected challenge.

Unexpected events don't really come out of nowhere. Before SARS, there were other new untreatable epidemics, and doctors have warned for years that there are likely to be more in the future. The OPEC price hike was a shock, but it is said that industry insiders had discussed the possibility of such an event earlier. September 11 was a dramatic outrage, yet fundamentalist terrorist attacks have occurred for decades. The mainframe computer priesthood was arrogant in the 1960s, and many young computer enthusiasts were frustrated at their limited access to hardware. In other words, the event itself may be unexpected, but there is usually, if not always, knowledge available that this *type* of event could possibly occur.

Trying to forecast unexpected events precisely is probably futile, but any organization can improve its readiness to respond to a given category of events. Your company may have developed and rejected projects in the past that suddenly become feasible. Rejected proposals may be a rich source of well-developed plans that can be adapted to the new situation.

Questions to ask:

- What unexpected events have occurred recently? These might be political, economic, technological, industrial, medical, or social issues.

- Do we have any projects that are on the back burner or that have been rejected that might be revived?

- What offerings do we have that could be extended or adapted to exploit the unexpected event?

ANOMALIES

Are there any problems or structural flaws in the industry that we could use to develop business?

Sometimes, there is a glaring flaw in an industry or public service, some anomaly so obvious that everybody knows it is there: an industrial process that is intrinsically inefficient, for instance; an essentially uneconomic activity that everyone undertakes anyway; a class of products that plainly doesn't satisfy customers' needs; heavy industrywide investment in areas that create more inefficiency, not less.

Although everybody is aware of the anomaly, it is not at all clear if it can ever be fixed, and the industry still trundles on in spite of it. People know about the problem but have given up on finding a solution. This, of course, suggests that there are good opportunities for innovation.

The innovators are likely to be people within the industry who have a full understanding of how it works, but they may well not be the dominant players, who are likely to have deeply held, but incorrect, assumptions that they are unwilling to abandon. The innovation is likely to be simple and will be ignored by the major players until it has captured a large share of the market.

Questions to ask:

- Are there any basic flaws in our industry? Is there any basic activity that is clearly inefficient?

- Why has it not been fixed? Could it be fixed? Could we work in partnership with other organizations to fix it?

- Could we devolve some responsibilities onto our customers or suppliers to produce efficiency gains for all parties? For instance, could we make ordering more efficient by giving customers access to our inventory information?

- Do we have expertise that we could lend to our customers or suppliers?

- Do they have expertise that they could lend to us?

STRENGTHS AND WEAKNESSES

Six Sigma has always been concerned with improving processes to provide customers with higher quality. Such continuous improvement efforts are now often expected by customers and are required at entry level in many industries.

Six Sigma needs to be applied to an organization's strengths and weaknesses. Many Six Sigma companies focus exclusively on problems and often fail to recognize opportunities that come from building on strengths.
Ask:

- What do we do well? If we build on these strengths, will we add value to our customers and make profits?

- What do we do poorly? Are there any weaknesses in our products and services that could be removed to profitably add value to our customers?

An organization's processes must be scrutinized continuously for the value they create. Weak processes should be strengthened, and activities that do not add value should be eliminated. Processes that are performing well should also be studied for opportunities to enhance their strengths further.

It is one of the central premises of the current outsourcing trend that process strengths can provide opportunities to add further value to customers. Organizations with superior processes can offer them as services to their customers. Leveraging process strengths to add value offers significant growth opportunities. For example, Johnson Controls, a major automotive interior supplier, delivered added value to Chrysler by providing car seat research and development services.

CASE STUDY: JOHNSON CONTROLS

Johnson Controls (JCI) was a late-comer to the automotive industry, only entering the market in 1985, at a time when car sales overall were falling. JCI was only a medium-sized supplier, and margins were low. JCI's main customers were the Big Three auto manufacturers, whose processes were massively inefficient. The Big Three were making efforts to streamline, and JCI decided to try to help them proactively. JCI was a major supplier of the new Japanese auto plants in the United States and was well placed to study the superior efficiency of the Japanese supply and manufacturing methods. Soon, American manufacturers were coming to JCI because of their leadership in lean manufacturing and just-in-time techniques.

JCI only made the foam and metal frames of car seats—the rest of the components came from other manufacturers. The company decided to become a manufacturer of complete seats, and acquired a number of companies to give itself this capacity. This transformation enabled JCI to apply its efficient manufacturing methods to capture the margin on complete seats, not just some of the components.

A new opportunity to add value then emerged: designing seats.

Manufacturers who would have been unwilling in better days to out-source any part of automobile design were now willing to listen—and JCI decided to focus on one major customer, Chrysler. JCI sent a team to study Chrysler's processes in detail and changed the tone of their relationship from an adversarial one to one of partnership, jointly defining the product criteria with its customer. The seat design was a success, adding value to both firms, and other manufacturers were soon approaching JCI for design work.

Questions to ask:

- What are our company's processes that add value to the customer?

- Where are the blockages and weaknesses?

- What are the strengths of our processes?

- How do our processes compare with our competitors'?

- Do our customers or suppliers have weaknesses that we can help with?

- Do our customers or suppliers have strengths that we can leverage?

- Can we leverage our process strengths to improve upon any of our customers' processes?

- Are there weaknesses in the interaction between the processes of customers/suppliers and our own? How could we fix these?

- Product/process strengths—what are we good at? Are there ways to enhance our strengths further in order to add value to customers?

- Competition—is the competition providing better products and services? How can we beat them?

- Customer issues and economics—can we develop offerings that help our customers reduce their costs and improve their business? What are their issues and pain points?

MARKET AND INDUSTRY CHANGES

Have there been changes in the industry? Are our market segments fragmenting or shifting? What does this tell us about our customers?

Industries and markets frequently change. Wide-ranging deregulation in healthcare, telecommunications, and utilities, for example, can present turmoil and threats for some, but opportunities for others. The explosion in Internet applications is changing industries in radical ways. Once expensive international telephone calls can now be made online for free. This has created enormous challenges for the telecommunications industries and opportunities for Internet service providers.

Another example of market changes can be seen in the recent popularity of low carbohydrate diets. In a relatively short period, large numbers of consumers have changed their dietary habits and moved from low-fat to low-carbohydrate. This has severely affected makers of cereals, bread, pasta, and a host of other products. At the same time, it has presented opportunities for those companies willing to promote low-carbohydrate products.

Analyzing structural changes in the marketplace can reveal previously nonexistent growth opportunities.

Questions to ask:

- Are there any structural changes occurring among your customers and their businesses?

- Are there any structural changes occurring among your suppliers and their businesses?

- Are there any structural changes occurring among your competitors and their businesses?

- Are these changes occurring in any particular area?

- Are specific market segments being affected?

- How can we exploit such changes?

HIGH-GROWTH AREAS

High growth leads to major structural change in an industry. Can we fore-see and prepare for such changes?

If an industry or part of an industry is growing very fast, it is highly likely that major structural changes are imminent. The methods and assumptions of the market leaders are likely to lag behind the changing reality.

Within a few years, rapid growth can demolish industry structures that seem very stable and have lasted for many decades—telecommunications is an obvious recent example.

Once again, the successful innovations will be simple. Outsiders are able to perceive the coming changes and can enter the market with a new product, service, or business model. By contrast, insiders will tend to view the changes as a threat and will react defensively, leaving the innovators several years to establish themselves.

"High growth" is a relative term; it is "high" in comparison with the country's GDP growth, population growth, or the average growth across the entire industry or sector. Look for areas where there are few players, and search for high growth in your customers' and suppliers' markets too.

Questions to ask:

- Which parts of your business are growing at an above-average rate?

- Which parts of your suppliers' and your customers' businesses are growing at an above-average rate?

- Are competitors' businesses growing at an above-average rate?

- Are there any high-growth areas in related businesses?

- Of these high-growth areas, which ones have the weakest competition?

CONVERGING TECHNOLOGIES

Opportunities can occur when two or more technologies start to merge. These technologies are often previously unrelated and come together in unexpected ways. A recent example is the convergence of telecommunications, computing, and photography in the form of smart phones and mobile phones with computers and cameras built in.

Often, these technologies are not growth candidates on their own, but when taken together, they offer great opportunities. There are countless examples of technologies converging, and there are likely to be many more in the future.

Questions to ask:

- What technologies in your business have been merging?

- Are any of your technologies being merged with outside technologies?

- Are there opportunities to converge technologies?

- Are there opportunities in your suppliers' and customers' technologies?

- Are your competitors leveraging merged technologies?

PERCEPTION CHANGES

How are customers' perceptions of your offerings changing? How can we convert these into new opportunities?

Many people's perceptions of sports shoes have changed recently. Not so long ago, sports shoe markers such as Nike made shoes targeted at specific sports such as basketball or running. Now, however, consumers see these shoes as prestigious fashion items. Quick to capitalize on this change in perceptions, sportswear manufacturers are launching new shoes targeting the fashion conscious. In some instances, sportswear manufacturers have teamed up with well-established fashion houses to create highly priced sports shoes for this new market segment.

Unlike the other market indicators, perceptions can often be influenced through clever advertising and PR. If successful, this may generate much better returns than investing in improving the offering itself. Your product may already be superior to a market leader—changing customers' perception can be the key to improving market share.

Perception changes and attempts to influence them can bounce back on you, as politicians are constantly discovering. Business is vulnerable too. Nestle, for example, has suffered for years from a vocal campaign against the sale of powdered baby milk in developing countries, despite the fact that it is on record as saying that it would like to get out of this low-profit market entirely but feels that it would be socially irresponsible to do so.

Your company needs to be alert and to scan the horizon constantly for signs of changes in perception. If it can respond quickly and appropriately, perception changes can generate lucrative innovations.

Questions to ask:

- How are my customers' perceptions of our offerings and our company changing?

- Are the lifestyles and values of my customers changing?

- What intangible reasons have customers been developing in support of our offerings?

- Is the image of my main customer base changing? (e.g., are they aging?)

- Are there any new customer groups who are buying our offerings for a new reason? Can we build on this?

DEMOGRAPHIC CHANGES

Are changing demographics likely to affect market demand?

In countries that produce reliable statistics, demography is a relatively exact science. Although most organizations choose to ignore the long-term implications of demographic data, it is possible to make good predictions. Most developed countries, for example, have aging populations, and it is possible to predict in broad terms how this is likely to affect existing pension systems, immigration policies, housing, medical care, and so on.

Entrepreneurial managers have many opportunities to exploit these trends because they tend to be ignored by large organizations until such changes are actually happening. Demographic changes have very long lead times, so it is possible to foresee the impact of a major shift decades before it occurs.

The key measurements are age distributions because people's needs, attitudes, values, and disposable income vary so much at the different stages of life. In many countries, substantial immigration is also a major factor, bringing new market segments as second and third generation immigrant families begin to exercise their power as consumers.

After studying the numbers, go out into the field to study and listen to your customers.

Questions to ask:

• What are the demographic trends over the next few decades?

• How might these affect demand for your offerings?

• Could these changes create new markets you can enter?

• What government regulatory action do you anticipate in response to these changes? What is the likely time lag between the changes affecting your markets and the regulatory response? There is likely to be a gap of several years at least.

This kind of forecasting requires true objectivity, a high degree of numeracy, and a flair for interpretation. Not everyone can do it well. For instance, there were many spurious extrapolations during the recent internet and telecommunications booms that were at best naïve and at worst deliberately selected to "prove" preexisting assumptions. Have your forecasts checked for logical errors by statisticians, and remember that this kind of forecasting is about probability, not certainty.

DECLINING PROFITS

Can we see any changes in the market that might lead to declining profits?

Declining profits may signal fundamental shifts in the marketplace. In the past, large companies often viewed growth in market share as being closely correlated to profit growth. As many markets have matured, this link has become increasingly tenuous. Once-great industries such as autos, airlines, and integrated steel mills have been in trouble for years, and large unprofitable areas have appeared in parts of the value chain across many sectors.

In food retailing, power has shifted to the major retailers, who are squeezing their suppliers and undermining their brands. In consumer electronics, particularly computers, distributor margins are often wafer-thin. In the fast-growing IT sector, companies have to reinvent their offerings constantly to stay profitable in markets that never stop changing. The "correct" business model does not stay profitable for long because international deregulation (the prime driver of globalization) continues to reduce barriers to entry and destabilizes long-held business strategies. In this environment, strategies, such as investing more heavily in fixed assets or seeking market domination at all costs, may simply accelerate the decline in profits.

The simple answer is to get out of areas where profits are declining—but this may be short-sighted. By reinventing the design of the business, which may entail becoming more customer-centric, it is often possible to achieve sustained profit growth in fields that competitors regard as unpromising. The classic example is Coca-Cola, which had financed its original growth in the 1890s by selling off U.S. bottling franchises in perpetuity, a legacy which had become a problem by the 1980s:

CASE STUDY: REINVENTING COCA COLA

At the beginning of the 1980s, Coca-Cola was essentially a manufacturer of syrup that was bottled and distributed in the United States (then the major market) by independent entities that were blocking the more obvious avenues for growth. In the grocery store segment, Coke was losing market share to Pepsi, and, in any case, the entire grocery segment was becoming increasingly unprofitable. Coke was a powerful old brand that seemed to be settling down for a long old age of declining profits. But by completely changing its entire business design, Coca-Cola achieved an increase of its stock market capitalization by a multiple of more than 30 times by the end of the 1990s.

Coca-Cola had to stay in the low-margin grocery segment because it sought brand ubiquity, which is what its customers wanted—in other words, to be able to get a Coke anywhere, anytime. Price was less important: customers were perfectly happy to pay far more for a Coke at a vending machine or a "fountain" (restaurant) than at their local supermarket.

To maximize profits, Coca-Cola had to gain control of as much of the value chain as possible so that it could manage it efficiently. During the 1980s and 1990s, the company undertook a massive program of acquisitions of bottlers, brokering sales to cooperative independent owners where it was not possible to acquire a firm itself.

It then spun off a holding company, Coca-Cola Enterprises, which owned the bottlers, but retained a controlling stake—this removed the capital-intensive, low-profit bottling business from Coca-Cola's accounts while keeping the bottling element of the value chain in line with the firm's overall strategy.

With the U.S. market now under control and increasingly profitable, Coca-Cola turned its attention to the international market where it could set up and control the value chain from a low base. By the late 1990s, the international market was generating 80% of Coke's profits, dwarfing U.S. business and giving the brand a massive global lead over its rivals.

Coca-Cola may have a long and unique history, but many other large firms have equally awkward areas of declining profit that demand business redesign.

Questions to ask:

- Where are the areas of low profit in my company's markets?

- Do those customers have needs that we are ignoring?

- What changes could I make to serve those customers better?

- What changes could I make to generate higher profits in those—or new—areas?

- What changes could I make to gain control of those markets?

- How could we gain a continuous flow of information about our customers' needs and how they are changing?

New Knowledge

The term "new knowledge" refers to inventions, new discoveries, innovations, and the like. Such new knowledge will, over time, lead to opportunities for new offerings. In some instances, such new knowledge can take decades to be commercialized into profitable products. In other instances, no such commercially viable applications for new knowledge are found. Only a small portion of the patents that have been lodged have resulted in marketable products.

Often, such new knowledge or inventions take large amounts of research, time, and resources to develop. It does present significant barriers to overcome and perhaps is the most difficult of the market indicators to search. Nevertheless, new knowledge presents the most significant of the areas for those able to develop and commercialize it.

Questions to ask:

- What new knowledge and discoveries are applicable to your business?

- What new inventions or patents are relevant to your business?

- Can we commercialize any new knowledge?

Project Charter and Growth Plan

The project charter and growth plan are key documents in the Six Sigma for Growth initiative and are referred to throughout the project. In the case of collaborative projects with customers, these documents become even more important as a means to clearly communicate the expectations and responsibilities of the project.

The project charter is the basis of all Six Sigma projects. It provides:

- An overview of the project

- The business and financial justification

- The scope and resource requirements

- The project goals and deliverables

- Timelines and milestones

- Any assumptions

Review and acceptance of the project charter by the sponsoring management signals the official start of a project. In the case of collaborative growth projects, the project charter acts as a shared document that both parties develop. It clearly describes, from the outset, what the project will achieve for both parties. Both parties sign the charter, acknowledging the importance of the project and their support of it.

The growth plan is needed to ensure that the project has a sound business logic. It looks at the initiative from several perspectives:

- *Customer's Perspective.* How does the customer view the proposed offering? Ideally, this section is completed with the help of the customer.

- *Business Perspective.* This includes sales and marketing plans and detailed financial justification for the project. Such information is typically for internal reference only, unless investments are made by the collaborating parties.

- *Internal Perspective.* This looks at the organizational capabilities to develop and deliver the offering to customers. Projects often fail because the organization was not capable in the first place. Careful consideration of internal capabilities and resource requirements are important in order to ensure a project's success.

- *Competitive Perspective.* This outlines who the competitors are and how they will likely respond to the new offering. Many projects forget to consider the competition and are surprised when competitors launch counter-initiatives. Such risk should be anticipated and wherever possible mitigated.

Both the project charter and growth plan are "living documents" and should be updated and be reviewed at each tollgate. The following are example templates for the project charter and growth plan. As mentioned in the Target step (See page 119) each organization needs to develop formats which are most appropriate. Particularly in the case of the growth plan, organizational requirements and polices must be adhered to.

Project Charter

Project Title	

Project Leader(s)		Project Reference	

Project Champions	Customer	Internal

Mentor	

Justification

Business Case	Details business case and justification for the project. Includes details of benefits for customers as well in case of collaborative projects.
Opportunity Statement	Specific description of the opportunity
Goals	What the project will achieve

Metrics

Metric(s) Baseline	Customer	Internal
Metric(s) Goal	Customer	Internal
Implementation Cost	Customer	Internal
Total Benefits	Customer	Internal

Timeline

	Planned	Actual
Start Date		
Define		
Measure		
Analyze		
Improve/ Design		
Control/ Validate		

Scope

Project Scope:

The offerings or processes involved

Team

Team Members

Customer	Customer
Internal	Internal

Signatures

		Date				Date
Champions	Customer	_____	Product / Process Owners	Customer	_____
	Internal	_____		Internal	_____
Mentor		_____			

Figure 7.2 Project Charter Template

Growth Plan

Project Title	

Project Overview	Executive summary of opportunity	Project Ref.	

Key Customers	Which segments or customers is the offering for?

Customer Perspective

Value Proposition	Give details of the value proposition. What will this do for the customer? What are the specific features of the proposition?

Performance Measures	How will the customers judge and measure success?

Compliance	Any health, safety, or government requirements ?	Risk Assessment	Are there risks for the customer?

Business Perspective

Sales and Marketing | Financials

Market Assessment	Nature and size of target segments	Return on Investment	ROI

Marketing Mix	Price, Product, Promotion, Place (attach details)	Profit Analysis	How does the offering make a profit?

Internal Perspective

Capability	Do we have the resources, skills and people to deliver this offering?

Organizational Alignment	Does the offering fit with existing business operations?

Risk	Has a thorough risk assessment been completed?

Competitors Perspective

Competitors' Positions	Competitor	Market	Products	Objectives	Position

Competitors' Reactions	How will major competitors react to the new offerings?

Figure 7.3   Growth Plan template

Leading Growth Teams

Programs such as General Electric's At the Customer, For the Customer (ACFC) demand very talented Black Belts who are able to work in the customer's business and interact with several different management layers. Some business units within GE only allow certified BBs, with several successfully completed projects under their belts, to work on customer projects. Such collaborative projects require skillful leadership more akin to the talents of a good consultant than to those of a traditional Black Belt.

An important feature in most improvement projects is that they are handled by a cross-functional team. For interorganizational development projects the team includes members from both organizations and from various functional groups. Having a cross-functional or organizational structure allows members to interrelate with each other from an early stage, enabling them to make recommendations and help set realistic targets. A team normally consists of:

- Customers and/or suppliers

- Black Belts

- Process owners

- Design engineers

- Manufacturing engineers

- Sales and Marketing Personnel

- Purchasing

- Finance

Teams are typically organized into a small group of core members that are typically full-time, as well as an extended noncore group that works on projects on a part-time basis. Noncore members join and leave the development team, depending on the specific skills needed and during different phases of the development process.

Working with customers requires excellent leadership skills. Black Belts need to be coached on how to work in their customers' environment and to lead teams comprised of members outside their organization and authority. The following two are particularly important skills that need to be mastered:

• Project Management

• Team Management

PROJECT MANAGEMENT

The importance of good project management skills cannot be emphasized enough. Six Sigma projects often fail because of poor project management. Simple steps, such as developing project timelines, identifying project milestones, and scheduling team and tollgate reviews help projects enormously.

Most Six Sigma practitioners are aware of such tools and of their importance. Despite this, it is not uncommon to find projects without even the most basic project timelines. To avoid this, some organizations insist that dates for phase gate reviews and reviews with project champions be fixed at the beginning of the project. This, from the outset, sets the expectations of the project and gives improvement teams clear deadlines to work toward.

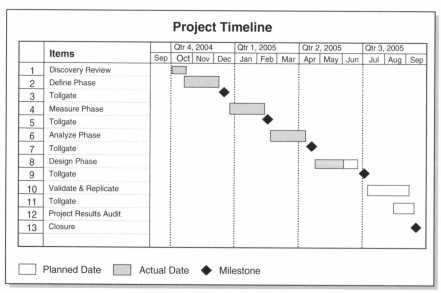

Figure 7.4   Gantt Chart

Every project should have a well-defined project plan that includes:

• Objectives

• Resources

• Timelines and milestones

Gantt Charts, developed by Henry Gantt at the turn of the century, are an excellent tool that capture project activities as well as planned and actual project schedules (Figure 7.4).

In the case of new offering development or collaborative projects with customers, tools such as Gantt Charts are essential. They help ensure that teams from both organizations are working smoothly together and that each understands what they must achieve and by when.

TEAM MANAGEMENT

Understanding how to run team meetings and to keep people motivated and committed is crucial. Team leaders need to be well versed in such skills, and understanding typical team dynamics is a good way to start.

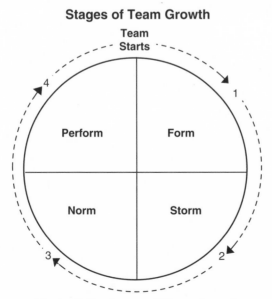

Figure 7.5   Stages of Team Growth

Team dynamics tend to go through predictable phases during a project. The duration and intensity of the phases vary from team to team, but it is important to recognize that these phases are normal and to adapt behaviors accordingly.

Form Phase. When the team is forming, members get to know each other and cautiously explore boundaries and acceptable behaviors. The stage marks the transition from individuals to member status and tests the leader's ability to guide the team. Forming typically includes:

- Team members feel excited and optimistic

- Members have only a tentative attachment to the team

- Members have pride in being selected

- There is fear and anxiety about the project ahead

Storm Phase. This can be one of the most difficult phases. The team usually becomes fully aware of the project requirements and what is expected from them. They become anxious and unsettled about the task they have set out to achieve. Members typically argue about what actions the team should take. They tend to rely solely on their experience and resist efforts to collaborate with other members. Storming typically includes:

- Arguments

- Defensiveness and the formation of competing groups

- Questioning the project itself and its goals

- Disunity, tension, and jealousy

Norm Phase. During this phase team members learn to reconcile their differences and start to work collaboratively. They accept the team ground rules, embrace their roles, and respect other team members. The norm phase typically includes:

- Team cohesion, collaboration, and a spirit of common goals

- Acceptance of being a team member

- Feelings of relief as the team finally starts to work together

Perform Phase. Team members have now settled their differences and begin performing. Members are energetic and enthusiastic about solving problems and implementing changes. This is the team at its most productive. Teams in the perform phase typically exhibit:

• Positive energy and enthusiasm

• Understanding of each others' strengths and weaknesses

• Satisfaction with the team and its progress

• Attachment to the team

Knowing that every team goes through these phases—form, storm, norm, and perform—relieves much fear and tension that team leaders have about their role. Team leaders should realize that such phases are normal, regardless of the team's ultimate success or failure.

Thought Process Map

Thought Process Mapping is an invaluable tool in managing complex projects. There are numerous versions of this technique, which is sometimes referred to as "Thought Mapping" or "Thought Management."

Simply put, a Thought Process Map is a diagrammatic representation of your current thinking about a particular situation or project. Since it represents your thinking process, successful application relies on identifying the format and symbols that are most meaningful to the individual; not all thought process maps are the same.

Typical items in a thought process map include:

• A flow chart representation of a logical thought sequence

• Questions and answers

• Reminders about things to do

• Tools or techniques that are used or needed

• Any decisions that were made

These maps are very much living documents and are updated frequently. They contain ideas or questions and demonstrate the logical flow of the individual's thinking. Given complex situations, referring to the thought process map allows you to quickly retrace your previous thinking and reminds you of any pending actions. A thought process map is similar to a diary, in that it helps remind you of your thoughts and issues.

Thought process mapping was an important part in planning this book. Figure 3.5 on page 69 is an example of the thought process map that was used. It quickly conveys the approach outlined in the book, making it easier for reviewers to grasp the approach and verify the logic behind it. Similarly, for Six Sigma projects a thought process map should be a central document that is used by teams to verify their logic and explain their approaches to others.

Risk Analysis Using FMEA

Risk mitigation is an important part of Six Sigma. Each stage in the improvement or development process should be assessed in terms of risk. Failure Mode Effects Analysis (FMEA) is a widely used tool and is useful in identifying risk areas.

Setting customer's expectations through the promise of mutual gains and then failing to deliver on them can turn a happy customer into an angry one. FMEAs are conducted throughout all phases of the Six Sigma project. Each project review session or tollgate should include a risk management discussion based on a FMEA.

All risks should be studied carefully to identify a list of mitigating actions. These actions must be agreed upon and implemented by the relevant parties.

FMEA was developed in the aerospace industry, where the prevention of failures is critical. During the 1970s, consumer product manufacturers who were vulnerable to product liability litigation, such as auto manufacturers, adopted FMEA to increase the safety of their offerings. In the mid-1990s FMEA was formally incorporated into QS-9000 quality standard for auto suppliers. FMEA has been extended from failure prevention into improving customer satisfaction by reducing customer complaints, and is now widely used in many industries.

FMEAs are constructed as follows (see Figure 7.6):

1. List the items or function under consideration. These items can vary significantly, depending on the issue at hand. Business decisions, specific product features, and product designs can all be analyzed. FMEA offers a flexibility that makes it very useful for anticipating and mitigating risk in a wide variety of circumstances.

2. List all possible product and process failures and their consequences. This describes how the item or function could possibly fail. This list is usually generated through team brainstorming sessions.

3. List the potential failure effects. This describes the effect of the potential failure. Consider what the customer would experience and the ramifications of the failure.

4. Rate the severity of each of these potential failure modes. Severity is ranked from 1 to 10—from least to most severe.

5. List the potential causes of the failure. This is a comprehensive list of all the root causes of the failure. Resolution of these root causes would directly affect the failure mode.

6. For each item, analyze the likelihood of the failure occurring. Ranking is done from 1 to 10 where 1 is unlikely and 10 is very likely.

7. List the current controls that are in place that can prevent the failure mode from occurring. Control methods include methods such as Statistical Process Control, Mistake Proofing.

8. Detection ratings assess the probability of detecting the potential cause or potential failure mode. Ranking is done from 1 to 10 where 1 is almost certain the failure will be detected and 10 is absolutely uncertain it will be detected.

9. The Risk Priority Number (RPN) is then calculated by multiplying the severity, occurrence and detection ratings together (RPN $= S \times O \times D$).

10. The corrective actions column describes the actions taken to mitigate the failure mode.

11. Based on the mitigation actions, a revised RPN is calculated.

Failure Mode Effects Analysis

| Item / Function | Potential Failure Mode | Severity | | Occurrence | | Detection | | | RPN = S x O x D | |
		Potential Effects of Failure	S	Potential Causes	O	Current Controls	D	RPN	Revised RPN	Corrective Action
Hotel guest checks in	Doesn't receive messages at check in	Guest is dissatisfied	5	Clerk forgetful	2	None	10	100	6	Computer prompt

Mitigate risk of strategies, business decisions, products, designs, and customer engagements

Severity: 1 – 10 (low to high) **Occurrence:** 1 – 10 (unlikely to most likely) **Detection:** 1 – 10 (very detectable to least detectable)
RPN: Risk Priority Number

Figure 7.6 FMEA Template

The results of these steps become the objectives for further analysis. Input from all parties should be welcomed, and a culture of devil's advocacy encouraged.

Failure prevention is a trade-off between costs and benefits. Too much prevention can be too costly and may have very negative effects on customer satisfaction.

Stakeholder Analysis

Almost all Six Sigma initiatives encounter resistance from some company employees (stakeholders) involved. Based on experience, any group of 10 people tends to have two that will be supportive of an agenda, one or two who are against and the rest neutral. Effective change lies in working with people who are supportive, addressing the issues of those against change, and providing direction to those who are neutral. Extending the Six Sigma initiative to customers and suppliers can complicate things, and careful planning is required. It is important to realize that such resistance is quite natural, and can be effectively resolved by using a combination of well-tried methods of change management.

The first step is to identify and analyze the key stakeholders in terms of their attitude toward the initiative and to Six Sigma in general. The key stakeholders are, in this context, those individuals who are in a position to influence the behavior of other stakeholders involved in the Six Sigma initiative. For example, if a sales representative has the ability to sway other colleagues through status or power of personality, he or she would be considered a key stakeholder regardless of the official job title or position in the sales force hierarchy.

Having identified the key stakeholders, one can then rank them by the degree of influence they have and assess their individual attitudes toward the initiative. The ranking gives the priority in which their particular case should be addressed. Typically, individuals can be assigned to one of five possible degrees of cooperativeness:

Strongly for   proactively makes the initiative
                  happen and advocates it

Slightly for	completes assigned tasks without resistance
Neutral	understands Six Sigma but is indifferent (passively complies with the initiative)
Slightly against	openly does not comply
Strongly against	campaigns against the Six Sigma initiative

A stakeholder analysis table might look like the following, indicating each stakeholder's present attitude and target attitude: (see Figure 7.7).

Not all key stakeholders need to be "strongly for" the initiative; the aim is to obtain sufficient cooperation at an appropriate level to complete the initiative successfully.

Resistance commonly arises for four different reasons:

1. Territoriality

2. Internal politics

3. Skill deficit

4. Personal problems

Stakeholder Analysis Table

Key Constituent Group	Stakeholder	Priority	Strongly for	Slightly for	Neutral	Slightly against	Strongly against
Production Head	Customer	5	△◄--○				
Marketing Manager	Company	3	△◄-----○				
Salesperson 1	Customer	1	○-----------►△				
Distribution Head	Customer	2				△◄----○	
VP Human Resources		5	△◄---------------------○				

○ Current Stance   △ Target   **Priority:** 1 to 5, Low to High

Figure 7.7   Stakeholder Analysis

Territoriality. Individuals may perceive a Six Sigma initiative as somehow encroaching on their personal area of control, and the stakeholder may fear a loss of ownership. Often this can be successfully resolved by inviting the stakeholder to own that part of the initiative impinging on his or her territory and to take the lead in implementing early successes. If stakeholders can see that it is possible to participate in the leadership and find ways of using Six Sigma to improve their own area of business, they can make a valuable contribution and often become strongly for the project.

Internal Politics. Individuals may see the initiative as a direct threat to their career path or even the survival of their role. They may indeed be correct. Six Sigma's drive for efficiency may force a firm to drastically reduce the size of a department or even to eliminate it altogether. The major goal here should be to prevent individuals who are "strongly against" from recruiting others to their cause. This can be done by:

• When their fears are justified, openly admitting this to resistors

• Gaining support from others who will benefit from the changes

• Publicizing the tangible benefits being generated by the initiative as they occur

In many cases, stakeholders will perceive the direction in which the political wind is blowing and will become more cooperative. As a last resort, an individual's employment may have to be terminated.

Skill Deficit. It is very common for stakeholders to feel threatened by Six Sigma's rigor and, especially, the statistics involved. They may fear that they will be unable to perform the new tasks that are expected of them and may be poorly informed about the nature and purpose of Six Sigma methodologies. Well-directed, nonthreatening training is highly effective. As individuals begin to understand Six Sigma and to perceive that they can, in fact, make a useful contribution and perform well, their attitudes become much more favorable.

Personal Problems. Stakeholders who have serious trouble at home may be in no mood for major change at work. They may be suffering from high stress levels with no one to share their problems, and may appear neutral to the Six Sigma initiative. The initial challenge is to correctly identify the true cause of the problem, either by informal private conversations or by discreetly speaking to close colleagues. A diplomatic and empathetic approach is best, and a combination of patience and an emphasis on the personal benefits the stakeholder will gain by cooperating more fully may yield results over time. The workload can be reduced and the individual given time to stabilize his or her private life. Such toleration will be appreciated.

In summary, the key points in managing key stakeholder resistance are:

- Resistance to change is normal and must be anticipated and analyzed

- The resistance usually arises from some fear of loss

- Correctly identify the root cause of resistance in individuals and use appropriate strategies to win them over

- Recognize that not everyone will become a Six Sigma cheerleader—sufficient cooperation in line with the individual's role is all that is needed

Value Strengths and Weaknesses Analysis

It is a fundamental concept in Six Sigma to compare what the customer needs with what we are giving them. It may seem obvious that a value proposition should be fundamentally geared toward customer needs, but the problem is that customer needs are constantly changing, and what was once an effective value proposition can quickly become obsolete. Customer needs change and competitors develop new offerings; to remain effective, organizations must continually assess customer needs and the degree to which they are fulfilled.

An organization may wish to target a new market segment that shows potential for growth. Such segments may have their own particular needs and so the value proposition must be modified and further "needs/gets" comparisons conducted to reveal gaps in value or opportunities to further enhance the value created.

Figure 7.8 illustrates Value Strengths and Weaknesses Analysis, a useful tool that can be used by growth teams to identify improvement opportunities. The matrix is developed in the following steps:

1. Characteristics of the value proposition are listed in the uppermost cell. The value proposition description (see Target step page 123) details the offering's features, benefits, price, and quality. Each aspect is noted on the top of the matrix.

2. The customer needs are listed. These needs are gathered by working with customers and using multiple voice of the customer techniques such as focus groups, surveys, and questionnaires. The results are entered on the left-hand side of the matrix. As noted in Kano analysis (page 152), needs should be grouped into:

   a. Spoken requirements

   b. Unspoken desires

   c. Assumed requirements

3. Each customer need is rated based on the importance to the customer. Such ratings help the team prioritize customer requirements later on. A typical rating scheme is as follows:

   1—Not important

   2—Low importance

   3—Moderately important

   4—Important

   5—Very important

4. Next, the features of the value proposition are compared with customer needs. This comparison—done in the center of the matrix—typically uses the same numbering scheme as point (3). This portion of the matrix shows which needs are completely met or not met at all.

   These comparisons should reveal any gaps in value. Needs that are not being addressed by any characteristic of the value proposition (denoted by a circle) are shown.

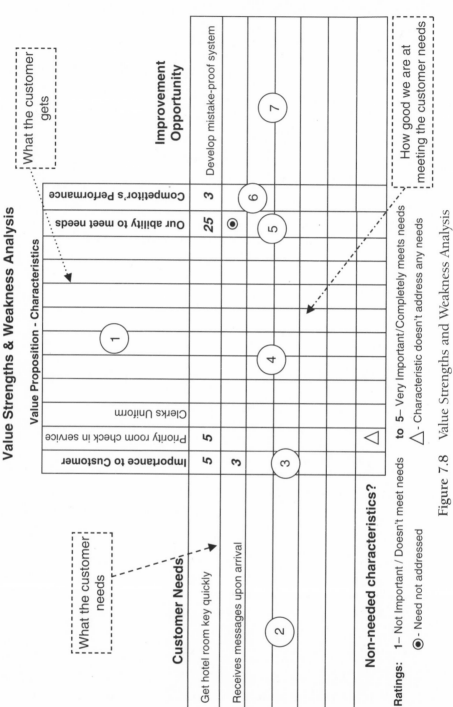

Figure 7.8   Value Strengths and Weakness Analysis

Any aspects of the value proposition that do not serve any customer needs (denoted by a triangle) are also highlighted.

5. Multiplying the importance to the customer (3) and the ability to meet that need (4) gives an overall rating of the ability to meet the customers' needs. Higher numbers indicate a greater ability to meet specific needs. Sorting this column in descending order leads to a prioritized list of needs.

6. Customers are also asked to rate competitors' performance in meeting specific needs. Such comparisons can include several competitors.

7. The next step is to identify improvement opportunities. These are typically one of the following:

   a. Develop improvements to meet a specific customer need

   b. Develop improvements that remove unnecessary value proposition characteristics (things that may increase costs but do not add value)

   c. Develop improvements that target the competition and outperform the competition on specific customer needs

Value Comparison Curves

It is important to understand how products and services compare to the competitors' offerings. After identifying the key offering characteristics (value drivers), it can be very useful to construct a value curve. The data for such analysis comes from a variety of sources, including current, lost, and potential customers. In many instances, companies will engage third parties such as consultants or market research firms to conduct independent research.

Key value drivers are identified, gaps in value are closed, and strengths—the areas where you are already providing superior value—are studied for ways to enhance them further.

Competitors may be offering products and services of superior value, so it is also necessary to understand how your value propositions compare to those of the competition. Conversely, the competition may be doing a poor job of fulfilling the customer's needs, giving you opportunities to gain market share.

The value comparison curve is a graphical depiction of the different elements in a value proposition. It compares value propositions and highlights strengths and weaknesses relative to the competition.

This helps identify areas in which the competition is outperforming and encourages closing value "gaps" (areas where we fail to meet customer expectations) and building on strengths and differentiating offerings further.

In Figure 7.9, for example, delivery is poor compared with the competition. Teams can study this factor in greater depth and develop improvements. Likewise, finance is a distinct advantage against the competition. By further enhancing finance, the organization may be able to differentiate itself further from the competition and perhaps gain business share.

This comparison of value drivers also allows teams to effectively apply other techniques such as conjoint analysis. Various value propositions may be constructed—in the above example, a proposition

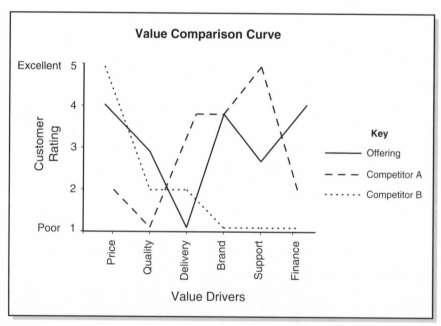

Figure 7.9   Value Comparison Curve

with improved delivery and financing options is needed—and makes it possible to gauge customer reaction to such propositions.

Value curve analysis asks four basic questions:

1. What elements can be reduced from industry norms?

2. What elements can be removed completely?

3. What new elements can be added to create an entirely new offering?

4. What elements can be elevated far above industry standards?

In addition to the value characteristics for specific offerings, value curves can be extended to include customer peripheral activities and purchases. Identify the total solution that the customers need when buying a product; for example, someone buying an airline ticket must also pay for travel to the airport, parking, travel from the airport of arrival to the final destination, gifts to bring to their hosts, and so on. Many experienced travelers avoid cheap airfares from out-of-the-way airports because these ancillary costs add up to more than a regular ticket from a major airport.

Ask:

• What does your customer have to do before, during, and after purchasing your product? Can you include any of this in a new offering?

Broaden your view of the competition to include all the possible substitutes your customers could choose instead of your offering. For instance, a consumer not only has a choice between different brands of soft drinks but also could decide to drink alcohol instead, or tap water, or any kind of beverage, or conceivably may even choose to eat fruit or smoke rather than drink anything at all. Examine all the potential substitutes for elements that could be incorporated into an innovation.

Multigenerational Plan

Multigenerational Plans (MGPs) are techniques for breaking down a massive development project into a consecutive sequence of steps or generations. This helps teams scope and manage the development process. There should be a minimum of three generations in an MGP. A frequently-used example of an MGP is the U.S. Space Program of the 1960s, for which NASA planned three generations of spacecraft design:

Mercury	tested weightless human flight
Gemini	tested maneuvering one or more vehicles in space and the capacity for astronauts to operate outside the spacecraft
Apollo	the program to reach the moon

The grand vision of the Space Program required a massive mobilization of resources and had to be easy for outsiders such as politicians to understand at a high level. The three generations of the MGP provided three clear visions that fell naturally into a sequence that anyone could grasp at once.

Breaking down large projects into smaller more manageable steps makes working on collaborative projects less risky. To encourage both organizations to work together effectively, it is often best to make the first generation of the project fairly easy to achieve. Success in the early stages builds team confidence and keeps the momentum going.

Each generation (subplan) of an MGP should contain:

• A clear vision, explicitly stating the long-term aim of the plan. For business, this implies a well-researched projection of how customers, customer needs, and competing businesses are likely to evolve in the future.

• The distinctive features of the generation, such as special technologies and specific applications.

• The process and methods—how existing knowledge and capacity can be used to achieve the long-term goal—and a statement of what new technology platforms must be developed.

Paper airline tickets to etickets - MGP

	Generation 1	Generation 2	Generation 3
Vision	**'old style' tickets** ○ Provide customers with internet-based flight & seating information	**paper tickets** ○ Give customers freedom to reserve tickets online	**etickets** ○ Buy airline tickets on the internet anywhere, anytime
Features	○ Check flight schedules & seating availability online ○ Purchase tickets from travel agent ○ Present ticket and passport at airport check in	○ Make reservations tickets online ○ Pick up tickets at travel agent ○ Paper printout of ticket & passport needed for airport check in	○ No physical ticket ○ Check in requires only a passport at airport ○ Order tickets online
Process & Methods	○ Airline website links to internal database to show flightseat availability	○ Secure online reservation system	○ Secure online reservation & payment system

Figure 7.10   Multigenerational Plan

To illustrate how an MGP is drawn up, consider an airline that wishes to move away from the regular tickets toward paperless "etickets." First, tentatively outline the visions for each generation:

- *Generation 1.* Allow customers to check flight schedules and seating availability online. This first step requires integration of the airline's internal reservation and ticketing database with a public domain website. Customers are able to use the web site to plan trips and learn about any promotional offerings.

- *Generation 2.* Allow customers to reserve tickets online. This provides customers with ability to select flights and reserve seats at any time. Tickets are collected from a local travel agent who prints new paper tickets.

- *Generation 3.* No more paper tickets. Customers can see flight and seating availability and buy tickets online 24 hours a day, 7 days a week. The system generates etickets, removing the need for presenting paper tickets at the airline check-in counter. All that is required is the customer's passport.

Normally, the first generation of an MGP is the easiest to describe because it is the most immediate. The team can nominate one individual to draw up a high-level vision-features-platforms chart, concentrating initially on the vision section, for group discussion.

By developing the MGP, teams are able to take complex long-term development projects and break them down into manageable sub-projects. Typically, after developing an MGP, teams decide what items are "in-and-out-of scope" for the first generation by:

- Brainstorming possible facets of the plan

- Creating a circle on a flipchart or display board to indicate the boundaries of the development team's scope

- Placing the brainstormed facets of the plan in or outside the circle, thereby indicating which facets are within their scope

Having clearly defined the scope of the first generation of the development effort teams can then focus on the specifics.

Quality Functional Deployment

Quality Functional Deployment (QFD) or the "house of quality" is a technique for structured product planning and development. It enables a development team to specify clearly the customers' wants and needs, and then evaluate each proposed offering or solution systematically in terms of its impact on meeting those needs.

QFD was developed in the 1960s by two Japanese professors and was first adopted by Mitsubishi Heavy Industries in the early 1970s and then by Toyota in 1977. In 1984, it was being researched by Xerox and Ford Motor Company and was soon adopted by them and many other companies looking to enhance their efforts to understand the customer's view. The method is now used extensively and is standard in most Design for Six Sigma projects.

QFD involves constructing one or more matrices or tables. The first of these displays the customers' wants and needs (the Voice of the Customer) along the left hand side of the table. The development team provides its technical response to meeting those needs along the top of the table. The QFD matrices consist of several subtables joined together by interrelated information (See figure 7.15).

CUSTOMER WANTS AND NEEDS MATRIX

The whole point of QFD is that it pays close attention to the voice of the customer. Data is gathered through various VOC techniques including market research methods. Customer wants and needs data is then entered into the table as a structured list of customer requirements. These primary requirements are further expanded to secondary and sometimes tertiary requirements. Importance ratings based on VOC methods are included to help prioritize requirements.

In the conventional design approach, engineering, marketing and product development teams tend to imagine what the customers want. It may be true that the teams have knowledge of the customers' requirements, but they may also have prejudices and inaccurate opinions. QFD sidesteps this by ensuring that customers are asked what they want and their answers are recorded, in their own words.

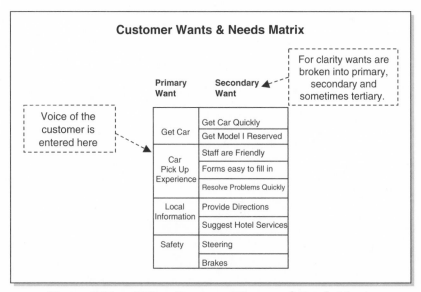

Figure 7.11   QFD—Customer Wants and Needs Matrix

There are numerous techniques for gathering the Voice of the Customer. Teams must plan such activities very carefully so as to avoid the "garbage in—garbage out" effect. If data entered into this matrix do not truly reflect what is important to the customer, efforts will be wasted.

PLANNING MATRIX

The Planning Matrix (see Figure 7.12) helps teams understand how customers rate performance and allows them to prioritize aspects of the offering. It is a systematic method for comparing the capacity of an offering to meet customer needs with that of competing offerings.

Competitive information is gathered from multiple sources including voice of the customer and market research.

The rating scale is typically 1–5 or from poor to excellent respectively.

Additional columns indicating goals, improvement ratios and sales capability estimates are sometimes added.

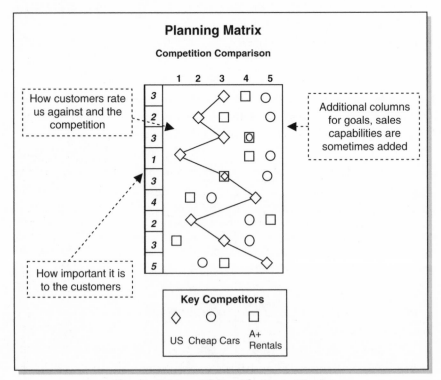

Figure 7.12   QFD—Planning Matrix

TECHNICAL RESPONSE MATRIX

This section is a high-level technical description of the product or service the team plans to develop. This matrix translates the Voice of the Customer to the Voice of the Developer. The team uses its internal technical language to describe the offering. This language is used to develop a technical response to customer requirements and lists them along the top of the matrix. Each customer want and need is then systematically assessed for specific measurement requirements.

QFD practitioners sometimes describe the customer requirements and technical response as a "Whats/Hows" relationship. The customer wants/needs matrix captures what is desired, and the technical response matrix captures how the developers will respond to the "Whats."

RELATIONSHIPS MATRIX

The Relationships Matrix is a mapping between the Voice of the Customer and the technical response, or Voice of the Designer. This section contains the development team's judgments of the strength of the relationship between each element of their technical response and each customer want and need.

Relationships of strong, medium, weak, and none, or numerical weights of 9, 3, 1, and 0 respectively, indicate how the technical response relates to the customer requirements.

Estimating the technical responses impact on customer wants allows the design team to prioritize elements in the technical response. These ratings are entered into the priorities row at the bottom of the Relationships Matrix.

TECHNICAL CORRELATION MATRIX

The top of the QFD—the "roof" of the house of quality—contains the team's assessment of the interrelationships between elements of the technical responses.

Design for Six Sigma is a concurrent design initiative, involving teams from multiple functions and sometimes multiple organizations. Teams working on different portions of the design effort must

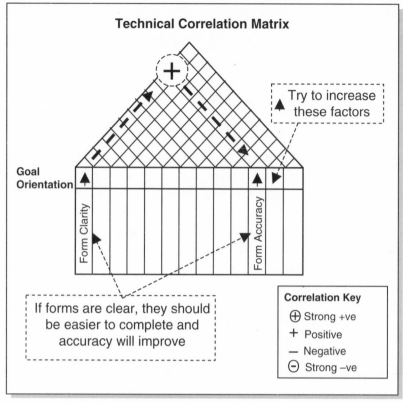

Figure 7.13   QFD—Technical Correlation Matrix

understand how their efforts correlate to other teams' efforts. The Correlation Matrix highlights which areas require close collaboration and which do not.

Four symbols are typically used to represent the strength of any relationships which are either strong positive, positive, negative, or strong negative.

The goal orientation section is constructed by asking the following questions:

- If we reduce this element ($\downarrow$), will it help us achieve what the customer wants?

- If we increase this element ($\uparrow$), will it help us achieve what the customer wants?

- If we meet the target (⊙), will it help us achieve what the customer wants?

TECHNICAL MATRIX

This section (see Figure 7.14) contains three types of information:

1. The computed ranking and ordering of the technical response

2. Comparative information on the competitors technical performance

3. Technical performance targets

Competitive benchmarks are rated 1 for poor to 5 for excellent.

No organization would commence developing a new product or service without a firm grasp of what the competition is offering. The competitive benchmarking section of this matrix looks at how characteristics compare to the competition. Instead of benchmarking all characteristics—a costly and time-consuming exercise—the prioritization of technical responses allows teams to focus in key areas.

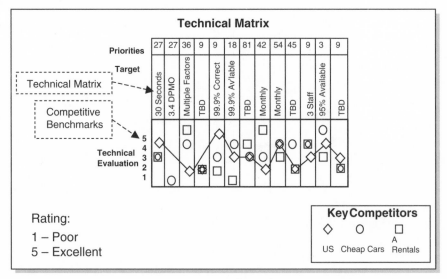

Figure 7.14   Technical Matrix

Quality Functional Deployment

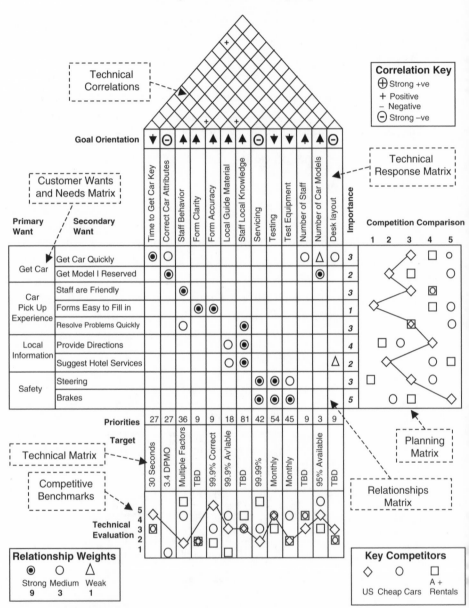

Figure 7.15   Complete Quality Functional Deployment

QFD FLOW DOWN—PRODUCT

The quality of an offering is inextricably tied to the quality of the process that delivers it. We must consider both. In solution selling, we must ensure that the solution we develop is sustainable in the customer's environment and that it will consistently meet customer requirements. Several QFD matrices can be created to develop a very detailed understanding of the variables that must be controlled to ensure that customer requirements are met.

Developing several levels of QFD requires considerable time and effort. In the case of solution selling—where performance and profits depend on sustaining solutions in the customer's environment—such efforts can be invaluable. Needless to say, the initiative needs to be carefully managed to avoid errors and unproductive efforts.

QFD Tips

QFD is a powerful design tool that is still, nearly half a century after its invention, the preferred approach to new product development. The technique has been adapted and integrated into many sophisticated design software packages.

The technique is exacting and can lead to several problems if not carefully conducted. To help avoid these, some key points are listed below.

1. Wherever possible, customer wants and needs, gathered from VOC methods, should be very specific. This helps enormously in the construction of an effective QFD.

2. QFD is a cross-functional team effort. It helps to broaden each team member's view of what the new offering requires. Properly conducted, it prevents difficulties and uncomfortable truths from being ignored—whether they are customer needs or technical factors—and puts the onus on designers to solve the right problems and optimize all elements of the design. Every assumption and preconception is challenged, and since the document is "public," it provides the opportunity for any participant to challenge specific weaknesses.

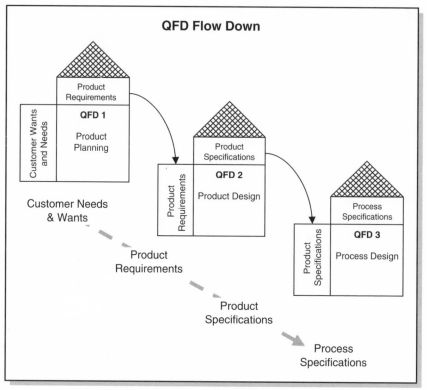

Figure 7.16   QFD Flow Down to Subsystems

3. VOC techniques such as surveys must be conducted carefully to prevent bias in the customer response data.

4. QFD development typically takes a lot of time and resources. To reduce the effort, teams generally focus on only a handful of high-priority parameters in the QFD.

5. Developing an effective QFD is an iterative process and takes many repetitions to achieve meaningful results.

6. QFD matrices also serve as a high-level record of the product plan that can be revisited at any stage of development, and when related or later generations of the offering are initiated.

7. Search for patterns visible in the QFD matrix. Empty rows in the Relationships matrix indicate customer needs that are not being met. Empty columns in this matrix can indicate the presence of requirements that may not be needed.

Conjoint Analysis

Conjoint analysis is a well-established market research tool introduced in the late 1970s and has become commonplace in many Six Sigma training programs that have been customized for sales and marketing. It has been applied successfully to a wide range of marketing challenges, including:

- Segmentation

- Pricing

- Distribution

- Promotion and advertising

- Product design and

- Strategic issues

The technique is a form of experimental design that measures how purchasers make trade-offs when choosing a product or service. It considers key product attributes and estimates how much each attribute is valued on the basis of the choices purchasers make from a range of product concepts that are varied in systematic ways. The respondents' value systems are inferred from their behaviors as reflected in their choices. The technique makes two main assumptions:

1. The total value of a product is based on the sum of the individual "utilities" they assign to product features and benefits

2. Purchasers prefer and are more likely to buy a product that they perceive has a high overall utility.

As with any design of experiment, conjoint analysis looks to optimize the resources expended. This is achieved through an experimental design that identifies—from the purchaser's perspective—the main value-creating attributes in the fewest tests possible. Good experimental practice is to verify the results with a series of more focused experiments and common sense. Where products are highly dependent on their brand or image, such as cigarettes and jeans, accurate verification of the results is crucial.

THE APPROACH

Conjoint analysis breaks a product or service down into relevant "attributes" that may be of value to the customer. For example, the relevant attributes of a pizza might be: crust, pepperoni, and price.

These attributes are then tabulated against the values they can adopt, known as "levels" (Figure 7.17). These attribute levels will affect the consumer evaluations and should be selected carefully. For example, if you price the pizza at $7.00, $7.15, and $7.30, price will be relatively unimportant. On the other hand, if you price it at $7.00, $14.00 and $21.00, price will become an important factor. As a general guideline, levels should be selected so that the ranges are somewhat greater than those found in the marketplace. Selecting attributes that are not too far beyond marketplace levels ensures that the study is believable.

A very large number of characteristics can be generated by varying the levels with the attributes, so usually respondents are only given a limited selection.

There are two general approaches to constructing the conjoint analysis: *two-factor evaluation* and *multiple-factor evaluation*.

In two-factor evaluation the respondents evaluate two attributes at a time until all possible pairs of attributes have been evaluated. This approach requires respondents to complete the matrices illustrated in Figure 7.18.

The advantage of this approach is that it is easier for respondents to make judgments. The relative disadvantage is that it requires more evaluations than the multifactor approach and evaluations may not be as realistic.

Pizza Attributes and Levels			
Attributes		Levels	
Crust	Thin	Thick	Deep Dish
Pepperoni	Small	Medium	Large
Price	$6.95	$8.95	$10.95

Figure 7.17   Conjoint Analysis—Pizza Attributes and Levels

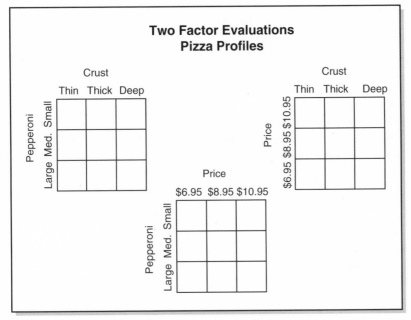

Figure 7.18   Two-Factor Evaluations

Multiple-factor evaluations utilizing full or complete profiles for all the attributes are more commonly used. In evaluating various pizzas, for example, respondents may be asked to rate each pizza's attribute combination such as large pepperoni, deep dish, $10.95. This is a full-factorial approach. In the case of three attributes with three levels, each respondent is required to respond to $3 \times 3 \times 3 = 27$ profiles. It is not always necessary to evaluate all possible cases and the number of profiles can be greatly reduced by using fractional factorial designs.

Figure 7.19 shows a factional factorial design with 9 profiles.

At this stage, the research data provide information on which attributes are more important to respondents, and which levels within each attribute are preferred.

The data in conjoint studies can be metric or nonmetric. In the case of nonmetric data, the respondents are typically asked to provide rank-order evaluations. These rankings involve the relative evaluations of attribute levels. In the metric form, respondents provide ratings (rather than rankings) such as a 9 point Likert scale (1—not preferred, 9—greatly preferred).

Multiple Factor Evaluations – Fractional Factorial				
Pizza Profiles				
Profile Number	Pepperoni	Crust	Price	Preference Rating
1	Small	Thin	$ 6.95	9
2	Small	Thick	$ 8.95	8
3	Small	Deep Dish	$ 10.95	4
4	Medium	Thin	$ 8.95	5
5	Medium	Thick	$ 10.95	6
6	Medium	Deep Dish	$ 6.95	3
7	Large	Thin	$ 10.95	5
8	Large	Thick	$ 6.95	7
9	Large	Deep Dish	$ 8.95	6

Ratings (1-9):

1 – Not Preferred
9 – Greatly Preferred

Figure 7.19   Multiple Factor Evaluations—Fractional Factorial

The results of the questionnaires are then analyzed statistically in various ways to measure respondents' relative strength of preference for each level or each attribute. There are several different analysis procedures, the simplest of which is regression using dummy variables.

The analysis offers answers to questions such as:

• Which attributes are more important?

• How important are specific levels within each attribute?

• Are there any critical barriers/transitions between levels?

• Are there groups of respondents with similar preferences?

This information can be used for segmentation.

It is important to remember that conjoint analysis, like any experimental design, makes a number of assumptions and has some limitations. First, it assumes that the important attributes of a product can be identified. Furthermore, it assumes that consumers choose alternative products based on these attributes and make trade-offs. As noted earlier, in situations where image or brand name is important this may not always apply.

Another limitation is that data collection may be complex, particularly if there are a large number of attributes. Careful planning is required to ensure that the data collected are unbiased and that appropriate experimental designs are used to minimize data collection and maximize the accuracy of the information gathered.

SEGMENTATION

Conjoint analysis is effective in identifying market segments and provides information that can be used to design appropriate marketing messages.

To continue with the pizza example, it might emerge that there are two clearly distinct segments:

- a "thin crust" segment preferring a lot of pepperoni and not much cheese (a segment that likes "New York–style" pizzas)

- a "deep dish" segment that likes a deep dish crust, medium pepperoni, and a lot of cheese (a segment that likes "Chicago–style" pizzas)

The relative size of these segments can be estimated and market gaps identified. In many studies, it is often possible to identify price-conscious, quality-conscious, and "designer" segments, for example, and further research can be conducted to explore these.

Product Design

Conjoint analysis is useful in product design to establish the customers' attitudes toward proposed modifications, the trade-offs involved, and the optimal design. It can be used both for incremental product improvements and to explore the potential for new product concepts.

This research can be extended to simulate the competitive effects of introducing new or improved product lines, which may have important effects on strategy. For example, suppose that it is found that a new product will be eagerly adopted by the market, but that it will take market share exclusively from the market leader, who is in a position to take strongly undesirable retaliatory actions. In this case, it might be appropriate to choose a design that will take market share from weaker competitors.

Pricing

Price should almost always be included as an attribute in conjoint analysis, because if it is omitted respondents may make private assumptions about price that the study does not identify.

Where pricing is extremely sensitive—for example, in Fast Moving Consumer Goods (FMCG)—conjoint analysis can be used to help:

- Forecast brand demand at different price levels
- Establish price elasticity in different scenarios
- Model price war scenarios
- Develop pricing strategies
- Set sales goals

It is particularly useful when applied to new products, where statistical tests that rely on historical data cannot be used.

Promotion and Distribution

Although conjoint analysis is less frequently used in promotion and distribution, there is strong evidence that it can be highly effective.

For example, in FMCG distribution it is often difficult to gauge the reactions of individual retailers to marketing "push" strategies initiated by the manufacturers. In this industry, the secular trend is for larger retailers to steadily gain the upper hand over all but the manufacturers of brand leaders. This presents serious problems in designing effective promotions.

Conjoint analysis can be used to understand retailers' responses better. For example, it can help to establish:

- Which combination of promotional techniques are more acceptable (e.g., coupons, corporate advertising, in-store "gondolas," and premium payments)

- The optimal combination for profit

- The implications for the sales function and the risks involved

The technique can also be used to generate useful data on shopper behavior in individual shopping centers and malls, where forecasting overall expenditure levels is proving to be a very challenging problem.

Mapping Customer Core and Peripheral Activities

Product-centric companies tend to forget the customer the moment the product leaves their warehouse and is shipped to the customer. Customer-centric companies recognize that this is the starting point for the customers who use the product, support and maintain it, and ultimately dispose of it. There are typically many associated activities that a customer engages in both with the product and around the product. These are often referred to as core and peripheral activities.

Carefully studying the customer's core and peripheral activities can often reveal opportunities to profitably add value to customers. Each aspect of the customer's business should be studied for pain points, which are unmet needs and therefore opportunities to add value.

Mapping the customers' core and peripheral activities is an excellent way to gain an understanding of the customers' business and their total economics. It helps sales, marketing, and service people gain a thorough understanding of the customers' business.

Expanding the field of vision by mapping core and peripheral activities is also an excellent means of quantifying the customers "total value equation." Key metrics at each activity are documented. Capturing such information also allows sales people to quantify the benefits of any new offerings in terms of the customer's total economics. Customers then become aware of the total benefits to them of any new offerings, as opposed to the unit sales price of the offering.

Customer value stream maps will form the basis on many of the subsequent tools. Customer activities should be scrutinized for:

- Opportunities to profitably add value
- Costs

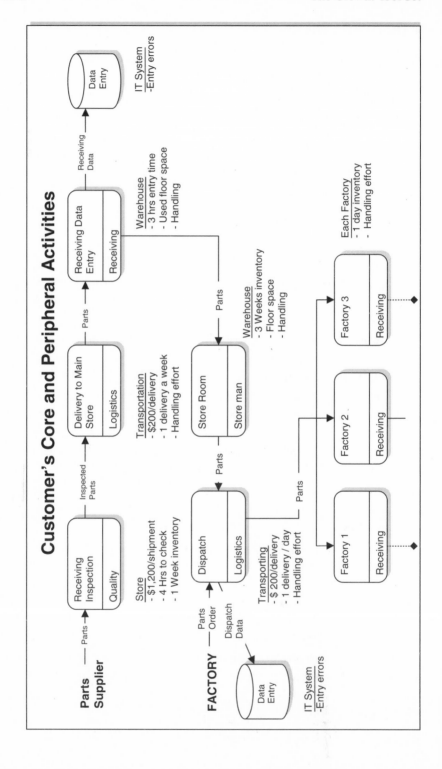

Customer's Core and Peripheral Activities

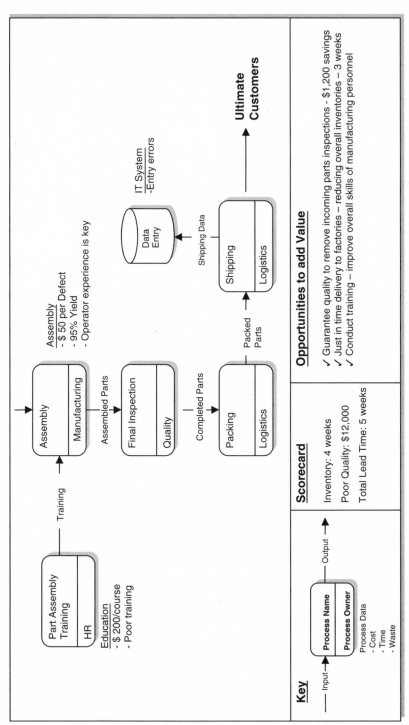

Figure 7.20   Customer Core and Peripheral Activities

- Time

- Key performance metrics

- Customer satisfiers

- Customer dissatisfiers

- Non-value-added activities

- Unmet needs

Figure 7.20 is an example of a parts supplier mapping their customer's core and peripheral activities. Maps include a scorecard that tallies key performance metrics and highlights specific opportunities to add value.

Opportunity Identification Matrix

Once customer core and peripheral activities have been mapped, they can be studied for opportunities to add value. Some opportunities may be obvious and can be entered directly onto the activity map. Others might require more careful analysis. A central premise of this book is that sustained growth comes from understanding what the customer requirements are today and making efforts to anticipate their future needs. The opportunity identification matrix (Figure 7.21) is a useful tool to aid such analysis. It builds upon core and peripheral process maps by transposing each activity onto a matrix and then systematically studies them for ways to add value and future scenarios.

The matrix is developed in the following manner:

1. Each activity identified in the customer's process—using the customer core and peripheral activity map—is transposed into the first column of the matrix.

2. Key measures for that activity are entered into the second column. Wherever possible, the metrics that the customer uses should be utilized.

3. Baseline performance for each key measure is calculated. Rough-cut estimates are fine initially and will be validated if specific opportunities are identified.

Opportunity Identification Matrix

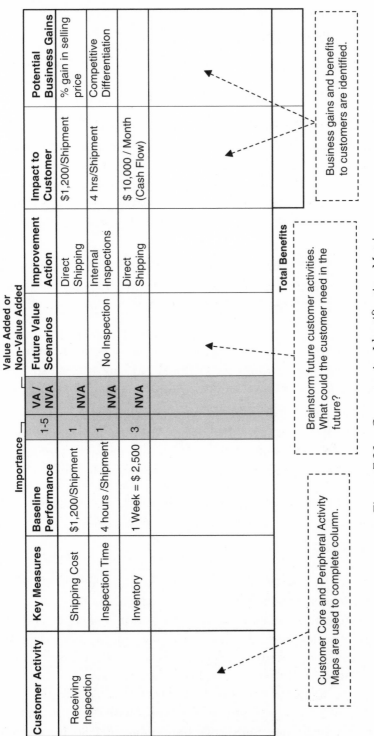

Customer Activity	Key Measures	Baseline Performance	Importance 1-5	VA / NVA	Future Value Scenarios	Improvement Action	Impact to Customer	Potential Business Gains
Receiving Inspection	Shipping Cost	$1,200/Shipment	1	NVA		Direct Shipping	$1,200/Shipment	% gain in selling price
	Inspection Time	4 hours /Shipment	1	NVA	No Inspection	Internal Inspections	4 hrs/Shipment	Competitive Differentiation
	Inventory	1 Week = $ 2,500	3	NVA		Direct Shipping	$ 10,000 / Month (Cash Flow)	
						Total Benefits		

Value Added or Non-Value Added

Customer Core and Peripheral Activity Maps are used to complete column.

Brainstorm future customer activities. What could the customer need in the future?

Business gains and benefits to customers are identified.

Figure 7.21   Opportunity Identification Matrix

4. Rating the importance of each activity from 1 to 5 (not important to very important) can help prioritize efforts later.

5. Each activity is scrutinized for the value it creates and identified as Value Added (VA) or Non-Value-Added (NVA). Wherever possible non-value-added activities should be removed.

6. Growth requires active efforts to anticipate what customer needs will be in the future. In the Future Value Scenarios column, teams brainstorm what the future requirements for the customer activity may be. Will the customer still engage in the activity in the future? Will the activity change? Looking at scenarios for future requirements can reveal opportunities to create new value adding offerings.

7. Teams then brainstorm improvement actions for each customer activity. Based on the understanding of the current customer activity as well as some possible future scenarios, teams then look for improvement actions.

8. The impact of the improvement action is then quantified. The impact of possible improvements should always be expressed in terms that are relevant to the customer—using their metrics.

9. Wherever possible, opportunities to profitably add value to the customer are sought. This means the benefits should exist for both parties. Impact in terms of gains to the customer and potential business gains are identified in the last column.

Customer Work-Outs

During the course of the project opportunities for quick wins may become evident. Such opportunities usually do not require a full Six Sigma project, possibly requiring many months of effort, and can be solved in a matter of days with a much simpler approach. Rapid problem-solving methodologies such as Root Cause Corrective Action (RCCA), Kaizen events, and Work-Outs are now a common part of Six Sigma programs and can yield significant benefits.

Regularly scheduled improvement events with customers should be part of any customer-centric organization's agenda. Such collaborative efforts help resolve problems between organizations, build ties, and show a true commitment to continuous improvement.

The Work-Out methodology was originally developed by General Electric as a way of reducing unnecessary bureaucratic activity (hence the name "Work-Out," meaning "get the irrelevant work out of the business"). It is a very effective means of dealing with a wide variety of problems and opportunities where they are relatively obvious, and it cuts out the time needed to implement a more rigorous traditional Six Sigma approach.

The first step in rapid problem solving is to bring together members from various functional groups or different organizations and hold a meeting to elicit a constructive dialogue between participants. The team works to understand the cause of the problem, using simple improvement tools such as Fishbone diagrams, and then generates recommendations for action that the sponsoring manager who ideally immediately approves where possible. The approved actions are then distributed to "owners" who undertake to ensure that they are implemented. In many instances, particularly in kaizen-like events, the solution implementation must be carried out immediately.

The rapid problem-solving approach is particularly useful in getting disparate functions to communicate their needs better to one another—a prime source of efficiency improvements. The power of such events can be even greater when instead of different internal functional groups, the event is held with customers. General Electric for instance, as part of their At the Customer, For the Customer (ACFC) program regularly holds Work-Outs with customers. Generally, it seeks to obtain quickly the low-hanging fruit of efficiency gains that can be readily defined and fixed to produce tangible results within a few months. Goals are set at the beginning of the meeting by the sponsor, and are carefully defined. Typical examples of goals are:

- How do we cut the time to issue purchase orders by 40% within 90 days?

- How do we improve our profitability in Market Segment X within 6 months?

- How do we cut customer complaints by 90% within 100 days?

- How do we speed up the time it takes to produce proposals for clients within 1 month from now?

The criteria for selecting a clearly defined goal are that it must:

- stretch the participants by challenging them to find a strong solution that is more than just a series of incremental improvements

- produce a measurable result that adds significant value

- be, in the sponsor's opinion, achievable

- be, in the sponsor's opinion, realistic

- be related to a specific timeframe

As well as the sponsoring manager, rapid problem solving requires an experienced practitioner who designs the program, a number of facilitators to run the improvement sessions, team leaders who guide cross-functional teams of participants, and the participants themselves, described as "team members."

Participants should be carefully selected for their potential value to the project. Typically, they are chosen for their particular expertise or their ability to implement anticipated proposals. Where appropriate, customers or end-users may be invited, as well as well-regarded cynics who may possibly be converted to become enthusiastic supporters.

Before the Work-Out, the session is carefully prepared by a design team working under the direction of the sponsor and the Work-Out consultant. Team leaders are selected and given preliminary assignments, and teams are provided with information packs to help them get ready for the session.

A rapid problem-solving event typically lasts between one and three days but can be extended for longer if appropriate. It comprises of five key steps, which can be elaborated upon and added to if necessary:

1. The introduction sets an enthusiastic tone and gives the background to the problem and sets the defined goal. A warm-up session follows, involving behavioral games to illustrate sources of difficulty.

2. The participants split up into teams to generate high-level ideas on how to meet the goal.

3. All the participants meet again to assess, select, and prioritize the ideas for further development. Overlapping and duplication of ideas are resolved during the selection process.

4. Teams then work on the selected ideas to produce well-defined recommendations with named "owners," measurement criteria, and risk analysis.

5. A meeting is held with all participants in attendance. The teams present their recommendations publicly to the sponsor for an on-the-spot, yes-or-no decision. Other senior managers may be in attendance as observers and are encouraged to make supportive contributions. A key role for senior managers, including the sponsor, is to voluntarily assume responsibility for the risks associated with the approved recommendations for action.

Coming at the end of the problem-solving sessions, the meeting is intended to generate positive group energies and enthusiasm for the approved action plans. The task then is to implement these plans successfully. The sponsor must confirm the roles of recommendation owners and give them the authority to implement them speedily, which may involve a temporary reassignment of their normal duties. Implementation teams are set up, some of whose members may not have been participants. Implementation team members are selected for their capacity to be effective, both from personal orientation and job description.

After a week or two, the energy generated from the event will tend to ebb away as problems are encountered. The sponsor must meet with the owners and assist them in advancing their projects, helping to clarify goals where necessary. Using a structured action plan, periodic review dates are set to ensure progress. The final review should assess whether the goals have been achieved, and the results can then be communicated to all participants and the company at large.

Project Reviews (Tollgates)

The review process of tollgates, sometimes referred to as "phase gates," is a formal review of each phase and is a stopping point within the improvement or development project. Reviews are held at the completion of each phase of the D^2MAIC or D^2MADV process. Tollgate reviews are held with the team, champion, and Master Black Belt, and key stakeholders in the project, which in the case of collaborative projects will include customer stakeholders.

These reviews are particularly important because they are opportunities to do several things:

1. Assess the deliverables from the tools and practices that were conducted during the previous phase

2. Make a thorough review of the project plan

3. Ensure that the steps in the D^2MAIC or D^2MADV methodology are adhered to

4. Assess the risks associated with the project

5. Provide a forum to discuss problem and barriers

Tollgate reviews should focus on preventive measures to keep flaws and mistakes from occurring in the next phase. As such, risk analysis tools such as FMEA are typically required at each stage.

In new product development, solution development or projects aimed at modifying the value proposition of an offering, more rigor is required in business planning. For these projects, it is best to include reviews of the team's Growth Plan in the tollgate process.

Gates are also used to develop work-around plans to keep things moving forward after difficulties have been identified. A well-run review process is proactive and takes into account that things will go wrong. It enables the team to deal with these inevitabilities. For complex projects, it is foolish to expect anything other than a series of unexpected problems. Approximately 25% of the time spent in the phase gate review should be looking at the work completed in the previous phase and 75% looking forward to the next stage.

The project is allowed to continue if it has passed the gate criteria with no major problems. If minor issues arise, work-around strategies are put into place, and the project is allowed to continue. If major problems emerge or the risk associated with the project is deemed too high, the project is halted.

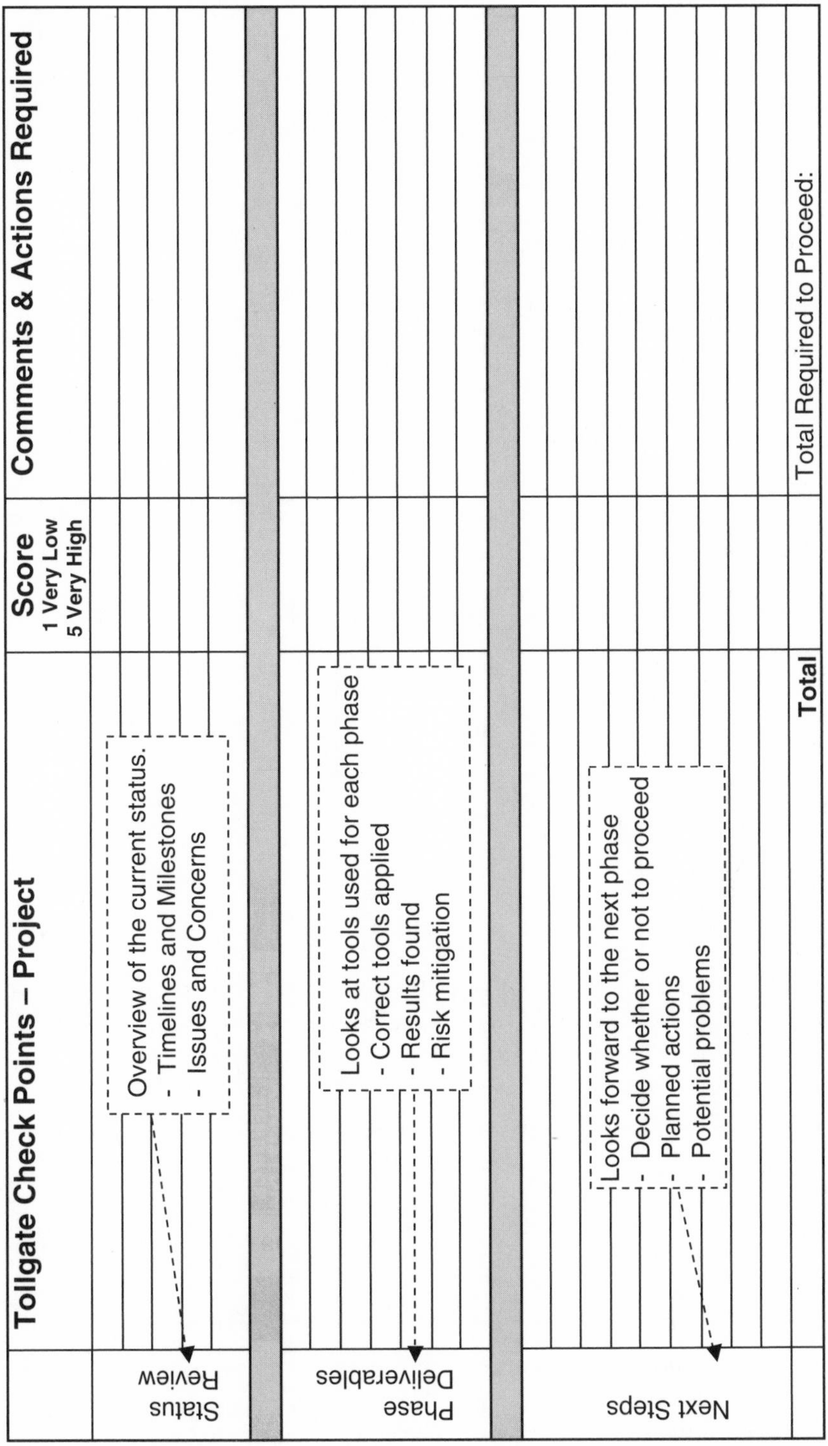

Figure 7.22 Tollgate Review Template – Project Plan

Tollgate Check Points – Growth Plan	Score 1 Very Low 5 Very High	Comments & Actions Required
Customer Perspective		
Business Perspective		
Internal Perspective		
Competitor Perspective		
Total		Total Required to Proceed:

Review the Growth Plan

- Develop standard review template
- Review each perceptive
- Validate assumptions
- Review resources required
- Review specifics of the plan
- Assess risk
- Decide whether or not to proceed with the project

Figure 7.23 Tollgate Review Template – Growth Plan

Dashboards are often used to assess each project's tollgate scores. Every organization needs to develop appropriate tollgate review questions and policies at the outset. Questions and review points should be specific to each phase. Questions to ask include:

D²MAIC or D²MADV Review Questions

- What is the opportunity?

- Who are the targeted customers?

- What impact will this project have on the customer?

- What are the most important customer needs for this product or service and how was priority determined?

- Are there S.M.A.R.T. goals for this project? What are they?

- Are the problems and need for a solution recognized by the customer?

- What is the status of the stakeholder action plan? What are the issues raised? What is the plan for addressing those concerns?

- Should this product or service continue to the next phase?

- Has a Project Plan been developed?

- Has the team defined how they will work together?

- Have Kano dimensions of needs been considered? Are there opportunities to delight the customer with this product or service?

- What is the status of your stakeholder action plan? What issues have you resolved since the last tollgate? What issues are still at play? Have any new concerns surfaced this phase?

- Have failure modes and their effects been identified?

- What problems occurred?

- How were these resolved?

- Have customer account plans been reviewed to seek opportunities to replicate this project for other customers?

Growth Plan Review Questions

- How does this project link to our overall business strategy?

- Has customer segmentation been considered?

- Have preliminary costs/benefits been quantified into a business case?

- If appropriate, how does the competition or other world class organization perform in meeting important customer needs?

- Has design funding been allocated to the project?

- Have appropriate resources been committed to the project?

- If appropriate, how does the competition perform relative to the CTQs?

Appendix

Six Sigma Readiness Assessment

ASSESSMENT AREA	TOTAL POINTS	MINIMUM REQUIRED POINTS
1. Process Management	0	0
2. Customers & Commitment	0	0
3. Employee Focus	0	0
4. Improvement Approach	0	0
5. Accountability & Incentives	0	0
6. Measures & Data	0	0
7. Collaboration & Resources	0	0
TOTALS	0	0

Before the assessment, minimum point scores for each area should be determined, depending on the size and scope of the engagement. This list should be expanded to suit the needs of the particular business and legal requirements.

Rating Scale:
1—Poor
2—A small extent
3—Moderate
4—A large extent
5—Excellent

	1. PROCESS MANAGEMENT	Score 1—5	Comments
1	Do they know how their customers view their product or service?		
2	Do they have clearly defined cross-functional business processes?		
3	Are processes designed based on customer/ market requirements?		
4	Are key process measurements identified?		
5	Are customer specifications used to gauge process capability (i.e. Cpk) and manage processes?		
6	How good or bad is the current capability?		
7	Is it clear who the process owners are?		
8	Are there improvement goals for processes?		
9	Is a control system in place to document, maintain, and approve process changes?		
10	Are improvement efforts prioritized based on impact to key processes?		
11	Do they know the sources of variability in the processes?		
12	Are processes benchmarked against the competition?		
13	Are the processes driven by business strategies?		
	POINT TOTAL:	0	

	2. CUSTOMERS & COMMITMENT	Score 1—5	Comments
1	Are there clearly defined internal and external customers?		
2	Are performance metrics identified and tracked on internal and external customer specifications?		
3	Are customer performance measures used to drive improvements?		
4	Is there an organization-wide feedback system?		
5	Are customer requests defined and understood by different levels of the organization?		
6	Is there a formal program to document, analyze and respond to internal/external customer complaints?		
7	Are there clear time scales applied to change programs?		
8	Is leadership actively participating in the change initiative?		
9	Is a system in place to initiate and lead improvement projects with appropriate goals, methods, and resources?		
10	Is management willing to allocate the full-time resources necessary to build and sustain the change?		
11	Is there a top down-bottom up approach to developing common goals and values?		
	POINT TOTAL:	0	

	3. EMPLOYEE FOCUS	Score 1—5	Comments
1	Does management solicit and accept feedback from employees?		
2	Is management active in removing barriers that hamper employee-driven improvements?		
3	Is market information, quality data, productivity, and financial information made clear to employees?		
4	Are there communication plans to ensure that employees understand customers' expectations and business issues?		
5	Are employees trained on new improvement methods and tools?		
6	Is there a willingness to develop skills through feedback and coaching?		
7	Are employees able to articulate the organization's approach to improvement?		
8	Is teamwork recognized and rewarded?		
9	Are there succession plans for team members after project completion?		
10	Is there an active training program?		
11	Is training effectiveness studied and improved upon?		
	POINT TOTAL:	0	

	4. IMPROVEMENT APPROACH	Score 1—5	Comments
1	How effective are the current improvement programs (if any)?		
2	Is there a clear and compelling need to change?		
3	Is there a mission and vision statement that is understood and practiced by all employees?		
4	Are quality issues analyzed for root cause elimination/reduction?		
5	Are there detailed change plans in place?		
6	Are there regular small-group improvement activities?		
7	Does management have a preventative approach to process improvement?		
8	Is there a universal quality assurance program?		
9	Are improvement efforts driven by Leadership?		
10	Are improvement efforts aligned to organizational goals?		
11	Does the reporting structure emphasize targets and goals?		
12	Are benefits from improvements tracked?		
13	Are improvement teams encouraged to continuously learn and apply knowledge to the organization?		
	POINT TOTAL:	0	

	5. ACCOUNTABILITY & INCENTIVES	Score 1—5	Comments
1	Do employees understand the criteria for acceptable and unacceptable work?		
2	Is inappropriate behavior disciplined?		
3	Is appropriate behavior rewarded?		
4	Are employees' responsibility and authority clearly stated?		
5	Do employees have clear goals for which they are rewarded, based on performance and on achieving these goals?		
6	Are team and individual awards commonplace?		
	POINT TOTAL: 0		

	6. MEASURES & DATA	Score 1—5	Comments
1	Is there a reliable data-gathering system for key processes and activities?		
2	Is data on customer loyalty and retention rates available?		
3	Is the effectiveness of improvements verified with data?		
4	Are measurement systems evaluated?		
5	Is there a system to ensure that invalid and/or obsolete measures are removed?		
6	Are there clear methods to calculate the costs associated with poor quality?		
7	Are decisions data-driven?		
8	Are statistical tools used to analyze problems?		
	POINT TOTAL:	0	

	7. COLLABORATION & RESOURCES	Score 1—5	Comments
1	Is there a shared vision between organizations of the importance of joint initiatives?		
2	Is there a willingness to discuss internal metrics and other sensitive information?		
3	Is leadership committed to collaborative projects?		
4	Do joint projects have clear returns for both parties?		
5	Has a joint steering committee with regular project review sessions been established?		
6	Have executive sponsors from both organizations been appointed?		
7	Have key stakeholders been identified and brought on board upfront for improvement efforts?		
8	Are there full-time improvement teams?		
9	Are teams well defined in terms of roles and responsibilities?		
10	Do teams have management support for their improvement efforts?		
11	Are there adequate resources available to improvement teams?		
12	Are team recommendations followed through by process owners?		
13	Is there a management structure in place to monitor and review improvements?		
14	Is there a system in place to promote improvement activities?		
	POINT TOTAL:	0	

References

INTRODUCTION

[1] Breyfogle, Forrest W., III, Cupello, M. James, and Meadows, Becki (2001), *Managing Six Sigma: A Practical Guide to Understanding, Assessing, and Implementing the Strategy That Yields Bottom-Line Success* (John Wiley & Sons, Inc.), p. 221.

CHAPTER 1

[1] Deming, W. Edwards (1994), *The New Economics for Industry, Government, Education* (MIT Center for Advanced Engineering Study), p. 10.
[2] Flaherty, Michael, *Six Sigma is no longer enough*. Reuters, May 15, 2004 (New York).
[3] Robert, M. (1995), *Product Innovation Strategy Pure and Simple: How Winning Companies Outpace Their Competitors* (McGraw-Hill, Inc.), p. 2.
[4] Deming, W. Edwards (1986), *Out of the Crisis*. MIT Center for Advanced Engineering Study, p. 18.
[5] Ibid., p. 5.
[6] Deming, W. Edwards (1994), *The New Economics for Industry, Government, Education* (MIT Center for Advanced Engineering Study), p. 10.
[7] Ibid., p. 2.
[8] IQPC Asian Six Sigma Summit May 2004.

CHAPTER 2

[1] Slater, Robert (1999), *Jack Welch's Battle Plan for Corporate Revolution: The GE Way Fieldbook* (The McGraw-Hill Companies), p. 109.
[2] Breyfogle, Forest W., III, Cupello M. James, and Meadows Becki (2001), *Managing Six Sigma: A Practical Guide to Understanding, Assessing, and Implementing the Strategy That Yields Bottom-Line Success* (John Wiley & Sons, Inc.), p. 71.
[3] Deming, W. Edwards (1994), *The New Economics for Industry, Government, Education* (MIT Center for Advanced Engineering Study), p. 226.
[4] Hirano, Hiroyuki (1990), *JIT Implementation Manual: The Complete Guide to Just-In-Time Manufacturing* (Productivity Press), p. 181.

[5] Deming, W. Edwards (1986), *Out of the Crisis* (MIT Center for Advanced Engineering Study), p. 135.

CHAPTER 3

[1] Deming, W. Edwards (1994), *The New Economics for Industry, Government, Education* (MIT Center for Advanced Engineering Study), p. 97.

CHAPTER 4

[1] Deming, W. Edwards (1986), *Out of the Crisis* (MIT Center for Advanced Engineering Study), p. 5.

CHAPTER 5

[1] Scholtes, Peter R. (1998), *The Leader's Handbook: A Guide to Inspiring Your People and Managing the Daily Workflow* (The McGraw-Hill Companies), p. 67.
[2] Deming, W. Edwards (1994), *The New Economics for Industry, Government, Education* (MIT Center for Advanced Engineering Study), p. 132.
[3] Ibid., p. 8.
[4] Naumann, Earl and Hoisington, Steven H. (2001), *Customer Centered Six Sigma. Linking Customers, Process Improvement, and Financial Results* (American Society for Quality). p. 25.
[5] Deming, W. Edwards (1994), *The New Economics for Industry, Government, Education* (MIT Center for Advanced Engineering Study), p. 8.

CHAPTER 6

[1] Robert, M. (1995), *Product Innovation Strategy Pure and Simple. How Winning Companies Outpace Their Competitors* (McGraw-Hill, Inc.), p. 40.
[2] Cooper, R. and Slagmulder, R. (1999), *Supply Chain Development for the Lean Enterprise: Interorganizational Cost Management* (Productivity Inc.), p. 102.

CHAPTER 7

[1] Drucker, Peter F. (1985), *Innovation and Entrepreneurship* (Harper & Row Publishers Inc.), p. 35.

Tables of Figures

261

CHAPTER 4

CHAPTER 5

CHAPTER 6

CHAPTER 7

Bibliography

Akao, Yoji (1991). *Hoshin Kanri: Policy Deployment For Successful TQM*. Productivity Press, Inc.

Altshuller, Genrich (2000). *The Innovation Algorithm: TRIZ, Systematic Innovation and Technical Creativity*. Technical Innovation Center, Inc.

Ammerman, Max (1998). *The Root Cause Analysis Handbook: A Simplified Approach to Identifying, Correcting, and Reporting Workplace Errors*. Productivity Press.

Born, Gary (1994). *Process Management to Quality Improvement: The Way to Design, Document and Re-engineer Business Systems*. John Wiley & Sons.

Breyfogle, Forrest W., III, and M. James Cupello (1999). *Implementing Six Sigma: Smarter Solutions Using Statistical Methods*. John Wiley & Sons, Inc.

———, M. James Cupello, and Becki Meadows (2001). *Managing Six Sigma: A Practical Guide to Understanding, Assessing, and Implementing the Strategy That Yields Bottom-Line Success*. John Wiley & Sons, Inc.

Brown, Mark Graham (1996). *Keeping Score: Using the Right Metrics to Drive World-Class Performance*. Quality Resources.

——— (1996). *Keeping Score: Using the Right Metrics toDrive World-Class Performance*, Productivity Press.

——— (2000). *Winning Score: How to Design and Implement Organizational Scorecards*, Productivity Press.

Brue, Greg (2002). *Six Sigma for Managers*. The McGraw-Hill Companies.

——— (2003). *Design for Six Sigma*. The McGraw-Hill Companies.

Chowdury, Subir (2002). *Design for Six Sigma: The Revolutionary Process for Achieving Extraordinary Profits*, Prentice Hall.

Churchill, Gilbert A., Jr., and Dawn Iacobucci (2004). *Marketing Research: Methodological Foundations*. Eighth Edition. South-Western Thomson Learning.

Cohen, Lou (1995). *Quality Functional Deployment: How to Make QFD Work for You*. Addison-Wesley Publishing Company.

Cooper, R., and R. Slagmulder (1997). *Target Costing and Value Engineering*. Productivity Inc.

Cooper, R., and R. Slagmulder (1999). *Supply Chain Development for the Lean Enterprise: Interorganizational Cost Management*. Productivity Inc.

Creveling, C. M., J.M. Slutsky, and D. Antis, Jr. (2003). *Design for Six Sigma in Technology and Product Development*. Prentice Hall PTR.

Daly, John L. (2002) *Pricing for Profitability: Activity-Based Pricing for Competitive Advantage*. John Wiley & Sons.

De Feo, Joseph A., and William W. Barnard (2004). *Juran Institute's Six Sigma Breakthrough and Beyond: Quality Performance Breakthrough Methods*. The McGraw-Hill Companies.

Deming, W. Edwards (1986). *Out of the Crisis*. MIT Center for Advanced Engineering Study.

——— (1994). *The New Economics for Industry, Government, Education*, MIT Center for Advanced Engineering Study.

Drucker, F. Peter (1985). *Innovation and Entrepreneurship*, Harper & Row Publishers Inc.

Eades, Keith M. (2003). *The New Solution Selling: The Revolutionary Sales Process That is Changing the Way People Sell*. The McGraw-Hill Companies.

Eckes, George (2001). *Making Six Sigma Last: Managing the Balance Between Cultural and Technical Change*, John Wiley & Sons.

——— (2001). *The Six Sigma Revolution: How General Electric and Others Turned Process into Profits*. John Wiley & Sons.

Goldratt, Eliyahu M. (1994). *It's Not Luck*. The North River Press.

Gupta, Praveen (2004). *Six Sigma Business Scorecard: Creating a Comprehensive Corporate Performance Measurement System*. The McGraw-Hill Companies.

Harvard Business Review on The Innovation Enterprise (2003). Harvard Business School Press.

Henderson, B. A., and L. J. Larco (2000). *Lean Transformation: How to Change Your Business into a Lean Enterprise*. The Oaklea Press.

Hirano, Hiroyuki (1990). *JIT Implementation Manual: The Complete Guide to Just-In-Time Manufacturing*. Productivity Press.

Jonash, Ronald S., and Tom Sommerlatte (1999). *The Innovation Premium*. Arthur D. Little, Inc. Perseus Books.

Kaplan, Robert S. and David P. Norton (2004). *Strategy Maps: Converting Intangible Assets into Tangible Outcomes*. Harvard Business School Press.

Kobayashi, Iwao (1994). *20 Keys to Work Place Improvement*. Rev. Ed. Productivity Press.

Kotler, Philip (1999). *Kotler on Marketing: How to Create, Win and Dominate Markets*. The Free Press.

Maskell, Brian H. (1996). *Making the Numbers Count: The Accountant as Change Agent on the World Class Team*. Productivity Press.

McBurney, Donald H. (2001). *Research Methods*. Fifth Ed. Wadsworth Thomson Learning.

Merli, Giorgio (1991). *Co-markership: The New Supply Strategy for Manufacturers*. Productivity Press.

———— (1993). *Breakthrough Management: How to Convert Priority Objectives into Results*. John Wiley & Sons, Inc.

National Science Foundation (1989), *Science and Engineering Indicators 1998*. National Science Board.

Naumann, Earl, and Steven H. Hoisington (2001). *Customer Centered Six Sigma: Linking Customers, Process Improvement, and Financial Results*. American Society for Quality.

Ohno, Taiichi (1988). *Toyota Production System: Beyond Large-Scale Production*. Productivity Inc.

Pande, Peter S., Robert P. Neuman, and Roland R. Cavanagh (2000). *The Six Sigma Way: How GE, Motorola, and Other Top Companies Are Honing Their Performance*. The McGraw-Hill Companies.

Pyzdek, Thomas (2003). The *Six Sigma Handbook: The Complete Guide for Green Belts, Black Belts, and Managers at All Levels*. Rev. and Expanded Ed. The McGraw-Hill Companies.

Rackham, Neil (1989). *Major Account Sales Strategy*. The McGraw-Hill Companies.

———— (1998), *Rethinking the Sales Force: Redefining Selling to Create and Capture Customer Value*. The McGraw-Hill Companies.

————, Lawrence Friedman, and Richard Ruff (1995). *Getting Partnering Right: How Market Leaders Are Creating Long-Term Competitive Advantage*. The McGraw-Hill Companies.

Robert, M. (1995). *Product Innovation Strategy Pure and Simple: How Winning Companies Outpace Their Competitors*. McGraw-Hill, Inc.

Scherkenbach, William W. (1982). *The Deming Route to Quality and Productivity: Road Maps and Road Blocks*. Mercury Business Books.

Scholtes, Peter R. (1998). *The Leader's Handbook: A Guide to Inspiring Your People and Managing the Daily Workflow*. The McGraw-Hill Companies .

————, Brian L. Joiner, and Barbara J. Streibel (1996). *The Team Handbook*. Second Ed. Joiner Associates Incorporated.

Shewhart, W. A. (1931). *Economic Control of Quality of Manufactured Product.* Van Nostrand.

Slater, Robert (1999), *Jack Welch's Battle Plan for Corporate Revolution: The GE Way Fieldbook.* The McGraw-Hill Companies.

Slywotzky, Adrian J., and David J. Morrison (2001). *The Profit Zone: How Strategic Business Design Will Lead You to Tomorrow's Profits.* Three Rivers Press.

———— and Richard Wise, with Karl Weber (2003). *How to Grow When Markets Don't.* Warner Books Inc.

Slywotzky, Adrian J., David J. Morrison, Ted Moser, Kevin A. Mundt, and James A. Quella (1999), *Profit Patterns: 30 Ways to Anticipate and Profit from Strategic Forces Reshaping Your Business,* John Wiley & Sons.

Ulrich, Dave, Steve Kerr, and Ron Ashkenas (2002). *The GE Work-Out: How to Implement GE's Revolutionary Method for Busting Bureaucracy and Attacking Organizational Problems—Fast!* The McGraw-Hill Companies.

Walton, Mary (1986). *The Deming Management Method.* Perigee Books.

Webb, John R. (2002). *Understanding and Designing Market Research.* Thomson Learning.

Womack, James P., and Daniel T. Jones (1996). *Lean Thinking. Banish Waste and Create Wealth in Your Corporation.* Simon & Schuster.

Yang, Kai, and Basem El-Haik (2003). *Design for Six Sigma: A Road Map for Product Development.* The McGraw-Hill Companies.

Index

269